Future of Distance Learning
Designing Interactivity

Future of Distance Learning
Designing Interactivity

V. K. Jagannath

AUTHORSPRESS

Worldwide Circulation through Authorspress Global Network
First Published 2003
by Authorspress

E-35/103, Jawahar Park
Laxmi Nagar, Delhi-110 092

e-mail: authorspress@yahoo.com
quantum_soul@mantramail.com

Typeset in NewCenturySchlbk by Chitra Computers

Future of Distance Learning: Designing Interactivity
ISBN 81-7273-128-0

Printed in India at Tarun Offset, Delhi.

Preface

'Distance learning' can be defined as 'the transmission of education or instructional programming to geographically dispersed individuals or groups'. It has been in existence since the nineteenth century in the form of correspondence courses. The current rush to implement distance learning programmes by colleges and universities is occurring for three major reasons: the convergence of communication and computing technologies, the need for information age workers to acquire new skills without interrupting their working lives for extended periods of time, and the need to reduce the cost of education.

Distance learning in higher education evolved to provide access to education where otherwise it might not have been available, due to such constraints as geography, time, job and family responsibilities, or finances. Over the years, traditional distance education programmes have provided opportunities for learning for people in large. Distance learning programmes have also provided options for individuals who desire to combine work and learning experiences, for those individuals who decided to return to school later in life and also for those who are physically handicapped.

The global environment has changed remarkably with respect to the application of Information and Communication Technologies (ICTs) at all levels of education. Distance education technologies are expanding at an extremely rapid rate. Too often, instructional designers and curriculum developers have become enamoured of the latest technologies without dealing with the underlying issues of learner characteristics and needs, the influence of media upon the instructional process, equity of access to interactive delivery systems, and the new roles of teacher, site facilitator, and student in the distance learning process. Today, most educational institutions are developing or planning to develop web-based course delivery capability. A significant number of government, institutional, corporate and private websites have emerged to chronicle the burgeoning numbers of virtual education initiatives.

Even though it is technology that is opening the doors to so many new distance learning models, the use of technology in distance education should remain transparent and user friendly, allowing the instructor and students to concentrate on the processes of teaching and learning. The trend is accelerating for distance learning programmes to use a broad mix of techniques, methodologies, and media.

The book is meant to provide a foundation from which educators throughout the world will view distance learning as an appropriate approach for meeting the ever-expanding needs of students. It examines the fundamental concepts of distance learning, the basic technologies that are now available, planning and design strategies for implementing distance learning programmes. It is designed for administrators, managers, teachers, distance learning coordinators, chief information officers, and media specialists, who are involved in initiating and interacting distance learning.

Editor

Contents

1

Trends in Distance Learning

Distance education is far from new, having roots extending to nineteenth-century correspondence courses. In recent years, new digital technologies have fostered a rapid expansion as well as a change in profile. Many more distance education courses are being offered than ever before, and the number is growing exponentially. The technologies used in distance education, the populations served, the institutions offering distance education programmes, and the partnerships that have emerged among providers differ in nature and scale from earlier models.

Different terminology is often used in discussing distance education, most notably the additional terms "distance learning," "distributed learning" and "distributed education." Some use these terms interchangeably; others use different terms to refer to different activities. There is general consensus on the most fundamental definition: "distance education is a form of education in which students are separated from their instructors by time and/or space". This characteristic is central to all variants of the field. Despite the lack of standard definitions, the term "distance education" appears to focus most clearly on the delivery of instruction with a teacher active in determining pace and content, as opposed to unstructured learning from resource materials.

The earliest form of distance learning took place through correspondence courses in Europe. This was the accepted norm until the middle of 20th century, when instructional radio and television became popular. According to Margaret Cambre, in the late 1950s and early 1960s, television production technology was largely confined to studios and live broadcasts, in which master teachers conducted widely-broadcast classes. Unfortunately, teachers who were expert in the subject matter were not necessarily the best and most captivating television talent, nor was the dull "talking head" medium the best production method for holding the interest of the audience.

In the early 1970s, the emphasis turned from bringing master teachers into the classroom to taking children out of the classroom into the outside world. This had the negative effect of relegating television to the position of enrichment, which was not perceived as really related to school work. This trend was reversed later in the 1970s, as professionally designed and produced television series introduced students to new subject matter that was not being currently taught, yet was considered to be an important complement to the classroom curriculum.

In the 1980s, the pendulum swung back to the basics. The most recent trend has been one of multiculturalism, humanities, and world affairs. As increasingly sophisticated interactive communications technologies became available, however, they were adopted by distance educators. Currently, the most popular media are computer-based communication including electronic mail (e-mail), Bulletin Board Systems (BBSs), and internet; telephone-based audio-conferencing; and video-conferencing with 1- or 2-way video and 2-way audio via broadcast, cable, telephone, fiber optics, satellite, microwave, closed-circuit or low power television. Audiographic teleconferencing using slow scan or compressed video and FAX is a low-cost solution for transmitting visuals as well as audio.

Each region has developed its own form of distance education in accordance with local resources, target audience, and philosophy of the organisations which provide the instruction. Many institutions, both public and private, offer university courses for self-motivated individuals through independent study programmes. Students work on their own, with supplied course materials, print-based media and postal communication, some form of teleconferencing and/or electronic networking, and learner support from tutors and mentors via telephone or e-mail.

It should be noted that distance education is not necessarily separate and distinct from on-campus education. An individual course may contain both classroom and distance education components. Some online courses require brief periods of on-campus instruction, for example, while many classroom courses use digital technology as a tool for directed research, delivery of resource materials, or communication between teachers and students.

Distance education courses available today are geared towards all levels of students, from kindergartners through retirees. They take advantage of a wide range of technologies to enrich and expand the distance education experience. Such programmes have also become increasingly integrated into educational institutions as a whole. In connection with their distance education activities, institutions are drawing upon their library resources, promulgating copyright policies, and participating in accreditation processes.

Today, distance education is utilised at every level of the educational spectrum. The most extensive use as a substitute for the classroom experience is in higher education. Elementary and secondary school students are using computers in increasing numbers. Computer use in elementary and secondary education, however, does not generally involve distance education in the sense described above, in which the course as a whole is delivered remotely. Education in this area tends to focus on software packages designed to be used as an adjunct to classroom instruction. These could include computer programmes in basic reading or math that the student can use at home, or in class projects that involve using computers as research or learning aids. At the higher levels of secondary education, distance education activities are more extensive. Distance education programmes are providing high-school students with the opportunity to take classes not otherwise available to them, such as advanced placement or college equivalency courses, through remote means. The field of post-secondary distance education is growing most rapidly. Courses are available in community colleges and universities, at the post-graduate level, for professional development and training, and for continuing education.

Distance education courses use digital technology extensively for varied purposes and in varied ways. The addition of digital technologies to the distance education palette has produced new models of learning, resulting in a richer and more interactive class environment. In the first part of the twentieth century, radio was a favoured medium for distance education. Telecourses produced by educators and distributed by the public broadcasting services have had a large audience since the 1950s. Such telecourses and video are still widely used, and are expanding their services in both the analogue and digital environment. The 1990s have seen the advent of computer networks and multimedia technologies as a powerful new addition to the tools of distance education. These technologies have experienced by far the greatest rate of growth in distance education in the last several years.

Today, distance education programmes use combinations of available technologies in varied ways. These may involve one or more of the following: e-mail among teachers and students, class chat rooms, links to resources on the World Wide Web, incorporation of preexisting content in the course of instruction, and the delivery of supplementary materials in electronic form. The use of older technologies, like videoconferencing, is also prevalent, particularly by rural schools. Even in distance education courses delivered entirely through digital media, however, students continue to use textbooks. The determination of which technologies are to be used in a distance education course is generally based on the intended audience for the course, and the availability and cost of the technology. Older working students, for example, may require fewer multimedia bells and whistles than the average college student, and programmes prepared for them may focus more on unvarnished text. Rural students or students in other countries may have less access to sophisticated equipment with advanced capabilities.

Many educators try to incorporate interactive elements into their distance education classes, but in the past they were limited by the technologies available to them. The traditional model for distance education has been the one-way transmission of instruction from teacher to remote students, with interaction between the instructor and the student, or between the students themselves, often limited to phone lines or correspondence. The addition of digital technologies enables more teacher-to-student and student-to-student interaction. E-mail and chat rooms, for example, allow continuous collegial discourse among students separated by distance.

As a result of the new technologies, distance education programmes are offering a more interactive experience that more closely parallels face-to-face teaching in effect creating a virtual classroom. The new technologies have also made distance education courses more convenient and better suited to the needs of different students.

Historically, distance education programmes have been divided into two categories, synchronous and asynchronous. Examples of the former are programmes delivered by broadcast and closed circuit technologies, which are set in real time, allowing the student to participate from a distance, but imposing scheduling constraints. Traditional asynchronous programmes are exemplified by correspondence and videotape courses. They allow for a time lapse between the delivery of material by an instructor and its reception by a student, but do not involve live elements. With the advent of interoperable digital media, distance education has increasingly incorporated both synchronous and asynchronous tools into the same course, providing students with the benefits of both. Asynchronous technologies, such as e-mail, threaded discussion and self-paced testing, are often used in conjunction with synchronous elements such as chat rooms and streaming audio. The same material may be delivered by both synchronous and asynchronous methods.

In the course of providing distance education programmes, institutions draw on their library resources in several ways. Often, they rely on librarians in negotiating and obtaining licenses, since librarians tend to have experience in this area. Libraries also provide facilities and support staff for making online courses available to students, assist in preparing materials in digital form, and advise on copyright law. Frequently, distance educators provide access to selected library resources in digital form for their classes. These selected resources may be designated as electronic reserves, or e-reserves, similar in concept to the use of reserve materials for on campus classes, which the instructor sets aside for outside reading to supplement primary course materials.

Educational institutions are making significant efforts to adopt and implement appropriate policies on the copyright issues involved in distance education. These efforts include promulgating written policies, conducting training for faculty and staff, and educating students about copyright law. As distance education programmes become increasingly incorporated into mainstream curricula, the issue of accreditation has become a focus of attention. Essential to the continued success of distance education courses is public acceptance of such courses as comparable in quality to classroom instruction. This is an important issue both for students, who must choose among available programmes, and for educators who must assess the knowledge imparted by those programmes.

Formal accreditation has traditionally provided that assurance of quality. Many distance education programmes offered by nonprofit public and private universities are formally accredited by the same bodies that provide accreditation to those institutions for traditional courses and programmes. For-profit universities have also recently begun to receive accreditation by these bodies. Some have raised questions about the standards for accreditation in this context, on the ground that distance education courses have unique characteristics that require specialised evaluation. Regional accrediting bodies, for example, will have to find new ways to evaluate distance education programmes with dispersed components such as administrative offices located far from academic headquarters. Some distance education programmes may involve stand alone courses offered through collaboration among multiple institutions, rather than by a single already-accredited institution.

Distance education provides the advantage of convenience and flexibility. With digital technologies enabling courses to reach and appeal to wider audiences, interest in distance education is growing. Distance education owes much of its explosive growth over the last decades to its responsiveness to the needs of an older, non-traditional student population. The average distance education student is thirty-four, employed full-time and has previous college experience. Many students drawn to distance education at higher education levels are professionals whose jobs prevent them from attending classes on a campus. This is a fact that institutions offering distance education courses have recognised. Retirees often take advantage of distance education opportunities as well. Greater disposable income and/or greater leisure may lead older students to take courses for life-enhancing reasons, rather than for academic or professional advancement.

Although many distance education programmes are offered by established public and private colleges and universities, the traditional model of nonprofit K-12 and post-secondary education is no longer as predominant. Distance education courses are offered today by both nonprofit and for-profit entities, on both a nonprofit and for-profit basis, and through varieties of partnerships involving both educational institutions and corporations.

The providers of distance education courses and components of courses cover a broad spectrum. There are providers at the K-12 level, among community colleges, among public and private universities, in continuing education, and among educational publishers. There are also providers who are solely engaged in the provision of distance education courses, sometimes called virtual universities. With greater technological capabilities available and increasing technological sophistication among educators, the number of institutions offering digital distance education has correspondingly increased.

Once a primarily nonprofit activity, distance education is now perceived as a potentially lucrative market. Nonprofit institutions continue to offer nonprofit courses, but new for-profit educational institutions have entered the field, while some nonprofit institutions have begun to engage in distance education activities for profit. The predominant model remains nonprofit. Schools at all levels continue to produce distance education offerings on a nonprofit basis. The tuition paid for a distance education course at these institutions is typically no different than that charged for an on campus course, although additional fees may be charged to cover technology costs. For-profit entities play an increasing role in distance education. There are a number of educational institutions, with the University of Phoenix (UOP) the most well-known example. As the largest for-profit based university in US, the UOP online campus enrolls about 9,000 students.

Corporate entities, such as commercial publishers, are also entering this market directly as providers of full-service distance education curricula. A hybrid category is comprised of nonprofit educational institutions that are launching for-profit distance education projects. New York University, for example, is planning to create a wholly-owned, for-profit subsidiary to offer online courses apart from those offered by the university itself. The courses will be marketed to corporations, colleges and universities, and individual students.

As the result of the growth of distance education, two distinct varieties of partnership have emerged—one between nonprofit and commercial entities, and the other among educational institutions. In recognition of the value of the educational market, and the need for courses tailored to accommodate busy schedules and business training needs, corporations have partnered with universities to design, produce and transmit distance education courses. One major benefit of these arrangements is that educational institutions have the costs of expensive distance education technologies defrayed by their corporate partners, while the corporate partners acquire an invaluable laboratory for application of their technology in educational environments, and often gain access to the latest research of leading academics as reflected in their curriculum. Educational institutions, recognising the potential of sharing resources and expertise in this expanding field, are collaborating with each other to create programmes that span state lines and university systems. These partnerships can provide a mechanism for different institutions to offer classes through a unified distribution system, or for institutions new to the field of distance education to access an infrastructure through which to offer online courses.

DISTANCE EDUCATION THEORIES

The theoretical basis on which instructional models is based affects not only the way in which information is communicated to the student, but also the way in which the student makes sense and constructs new knowledge from the information which is presented.

Currently, there are two opposing views which impact instructional design: symbol-processing and situated cognition. Until recently, the dominant view has been the traditional, information processing approach, based on the concept of a computer performing formal operations on symbols. The key concept is that the teacher can transmit a fixed body of information to students via an external representation. She represents an abstract idea as a concrete image and then presents the image to the learner via a medium. The learner, in turn, perceives, decodes, and stores it. W. Horton, modifies this approach by adding two additional factors: the student's context (environment, current situation, other sensory input) and mind (memories, associations, emotions, inference and reasoning, curiosity and interest) to the representation. The learner then develops his own image and uses it to construct new knowledge, in context, based on his own prior knowledge and abilities.

The alternative approach is based on constructivist principles, in which a learner actively constructs an internal representation of knowledge by interacting with the material to be learned. This is the basis for both situated cognition and problem-based learning. According to this viewpoint, both social and physical interaction enter into both the definition of a problem and the construction of its solution. Neither the information to be learned, nor its symbolic description, is specified outside the process of inquiry and the conclusions that emerge from that process. Prawat and Floden state that, to implement constructivism in a lesson, one must shift one's focus away from the traditional transmission model to one which is much more complex, interactive, and evolving.

Though these two theories are totally different in nature, effective designers usually start with empirical knowledge: objects, events, and practices which mirror the everyday environment of their designated learners. Then, with a firm theoretical grounding, they develop a presentation which enables learners to construct appropriate new knowledge by interacting with the instruction. To quote the AI researcher, Herbert A. Simon, "Human beings are at their best when they interact with the real world and draw lessons from the bumps and bruises they get".

Schlosser and Anderson refer to Desmond Keegan's theory of distance education, in which the distance learning system must artificially recreate the teaching-learning interaction and re-integrate it back into the instructional process. This is the basis of their Iowa Model: to offer to the distance learner an experience as much like traditional, face-to-face instruction, via intact classrooms and live, two-way audio-visual interaction. In contrast, the Norwegian Model has a long tradition of combining mediated distance teaching with local face-to-face teaching.

Hilary Perraton defines the role of the distance teacher. When, through the most effective choice of media, she meets the distance students face-to-face, she now becomes a facilitator of learning, rather than a communicator of a fixed body of information. The learning process proceeds as knowledge building among teacher and students.

Distance education systems now involve a high degree of interactivity between teacher and student, even in rural and isolated communities separated by perhaps thousands of miles. The Office of Technology Assessment stresses the importance of interactivity: distance learning allows students to hear and perhaps see teachers, as well as allowing teachers to react to their students' comments and questions. Moreover, virtual learning communities can be formed, in which students and researchers throughout the world who are part of the same class or study group can contact one another at any time of the day or night to share observations, information, and expertise with one another.

DESIGNING EFFECTIVE EDUCATION SYSTEMS

Traditionally, we think of distance learners as adults. Whole institutions of higher learning, such as the United Kingdom's Open University, Vancouver's Open Learning Agency, Norway's NKS and NKI Distance Education organisations, Florida's Nova University, and a host of others, have been dedicated to providing distance education at the post-secondary level for decades. The University of South Africa (UNISA), in Praetoria, serving both black and white students, has had a successful distance learning programme for decades. The

Televised Japanese Language Programme, developed at North Carolina State University, provides instruction in Japanese to ten colleges and universities in five Southeastern states. The adult learner tradition is now changing as new programmes, such as the US. Federal government's Star Schools Programme, come into existence to serve the K-12 student population.

At the elementary and middle school levels, distance learning usually takes the form of curriculum enrichment modules and ongoing telecommunications projects. Some examples of current projects are: De Orilla a Orilla, National Geographic Kids Network, Biomes Exchange Project, Earth Lab, Ask Professor Math, and AskAScientist. Other modules are television-based, with the teacher as facilitator. Students work in collaborative groups, using manipulatives and hands-on activities in a distance learning environment.

At the secondary level, locally or federally funded distance education addresses the needs of small rural school districts or underserved urban school districts. Some secondary school students may enrol in courses to meet graduation requirements which their own districts are unable to offer; some take advanced placement, foreign language, or vocational classes; others may be homebound or disabled. In many instances, talented or gifted high school students have been selected to attend distance classes because of their high academic ability and capacity for handling independent work. This makes classroom management easier, but it may disenfranchise students who lack discipline or time management skills. The resulting inequity of access then becomes a policy problem, not a technology problem.

Although technology is an integral part of distance education, any successful programme must focus on the instructional needs of the students, rather than on the technology itself. It is essential to consider their ages, cultural and socioeconomic backgrounds, interests and experiences, educational levels, and familiarity with distance education methods and delivery systems. Students usually adapt more quickly than their teachers to new technology. On the other hand, teachers who have begun to feel comfortable with the equipment don't mind having their students teach them new tips and tricks. The most important factor for successful distance learning is a caring, concerned teacher who is confident, experienced, at ease with the equipment, uses the media creatively, and maintains a high level of interactivity with the students.

B. Willis describes the instructional development process for distance education, consisting of the customary stages of design, development, evaluation, and revision. In designing effective distance instruction, one must consider not only the goals, needs, and characteristics of teachers and students, but also content requirements and technical constraints. If unusual delivery systems are required, they must be made accessible to all participants. Revision based on feedback from instructors, content specialists, and learners is an ongoing process. Provisions must be made for continually updating courses which depend on volatile information, to keep the subject matter current and relevant.

Successful distance education systems involve interactivity between teacher and students, between students and the learning environment, and among students themselves, as well as active learning in the classroom. Though students felt that the accessibility of distance learning courses far outweighs the lack of dialogue, there is still a considerable lack of dialogue in telecourses when compared to face-to-face classes.

G. Millbank studied the effectiveness of a mix of audio plus video in corporate training. When he introduced real-time interactivity, the retention rate of the trainees was raised from about 20 per cent (using ordinary classroom methods) to about 75 per cent. A key element in Porter's New Directions in Distance Learning (NDDL) project is the enhancement of independent learning materials through the use of interactive communications technologies and teacher mediation. He projects a completion/success rate of around 60 per cent over the life span of the pilot project.

Interactivity takes many forms; it is not just limited to audio and video, nor solely to teacher-student interactions. It represents the connectivity the students feel with the distance teacher, the local teachers, aides, and facilitators, and their peers. The quality and integrity of the educational process depends upon sustained, two-way communication.

Without connectivity, distance learning degenerates into the old correspondence course model of independent study. The student becomes autonomous and isolated, procrastinates, and eventually drops out. Effective distance education should not be an independent and isolated form of learning; it should approach Keegan's ideal of an authentic learning experience.

As active participants in the learning process, students affect the manner in which they deal with the material to be learned. Learners must have a sense of ownership of the learning goals. They must be both willing and able to receive instructional messages. The mental effort which a learner will invest in a learning task depends on his own perception of two factors:

i) the relevance of both the medium and the message which it contains

ii) his ability to make something meaningful out of the material presented.

Television proved to be mentally less demanding than printed text when comparable content was employed. By giving students some expectations about the purpose of their viewing, he was able to influence the effort that students invested in processing the content of television instruction.

Instructional television can motivate and captivate students, and stimulate an interest in the learning process. However, there are unintended side effects of educational television in particular as well as edutainment in general. Reliance on exciting visuals may distort the curriculum by focusing students' attention on the entertaining and provocative features of the presentation rather than encouraging thoughtful analysis of their underlying meaning.

If complex issues are presented in short units, through powerful images which may occur in any order, the end result may be oversimplification and superficiality. Students must learn to discriminate between "junk" information and quality information, to judge its reliability or bias, to identify distortions and sensationalism, to distinguish facts from persuasion, and to understand how the technology itself shapes the information it carries.

Ben Shneiderman cautions all instructional designers to begin with an understanding of their intended users, and to recognise them as individuals whose outlook is different from the designer's own. W. Horton states the golden rule for designers of instructional visuals: "communicate unto others as they would communicate unto themselves" . In other words, if you want the learner to construct an idea which is similar to yours, then use an image for your presentation which will trigger a similar idea in the learner's mind, in the context of the learning environment and the learner's prior experiences.

No two learners will form the same idea, nor is it likely that their idea will be the same as that of the designer. How can this problem be solved? The key to good instructional design lies in the image presented. To quote Marshall McLuhan, "the medium is the message". W. Horton notes that it is up to the designer to

i) use advance organisers to create an appropriate context for instruction

ii) select effective images, using appropriate objects with relevant attributes, that will convey the same idea to the user as they did to the designer.

LEARNING STRATEGIES

Teachers need training in instructional message design, strategies for delivering instruction on-camera, methods of diversifying types of presentation, selecting various mixes of student-teacher activities and interactions, choosing situations and examples which are relevant to their students, and assessing the level of learning by distant students. They also need plenty of guided, hands-on practice developing and delivering courseware using audio, full-motion video, graphics, and text, in front of a live audience, yet still in a non-threatening situation.

Strategies such as using fewer overheads and more moving video, interspersing "talking heads" with videos of sites, using hands-on experiments, incorporating text and graphic art, and other guidelines for effective video production are also valuable. Site facilitators, too, benefit from training programmes which emphasise hands-on practice with the equipment they are expected to use. Those who had participated in structured training programmes felt comfortable using the equipment, were able to engage their students in the learning process, and had mastered classroom management in a high-tech classroom.

Foreign language instruction presents special instructional challenges, not only because of the lack of immediate 2-way interaction that characterises many distance education programmes, but also because of the loss of visual detail in videoconferences due to signal compression—especially detailed lip movements. This can be overcome by providing students with oral practice and feedback through telephone conversations with the instructor, and by instructional strategies that encourage frequent student-teacher and teacher-student dialogue.

Effective distance learning requires extensive preparation, as well as adapting traditional teaching strategies to a new learning environment which often lacks visual cues. Porter speaks of the triad consisting of the student, the teacher, and the site facilitator, all of whom must function as a team. Students must quickly become aware of and comfortable with new patterns of communication, learn to manage their time, and take responsibility for their own learning. Teachers must enable students to establish contact with them, as well as interact among themselves. Site facilitators can act as the on-site "eyes" and "ears" of the teacher, stimulating interaction when distant students are hesitant to ask questions or participate in discussions.

B. Willis describes the strategies which are effective in distance learning: namely, developing appropriate methods of feedback and reinforcement, optimising content and pace, adapting to different student learning styles, using case studies and examples which are relevant to the target audience, being concise, supplementing courseware with print information, and personalising instruction.

The variety of available media, too, presents a formidable research problem. One cannot compare print-based independent study courses, electronic projects on the Internet, classroom BBS postings, audioconferences, and live, two-way interactive television, and expect that these comparisons will be valid. To add to this dilemma, media selection is often a question of media assignment. Teachers and site facilitators need training in those technologies which they are expected to use.

More experimental studies are needed in the area of media selection, where researchers can compare the effectiveness of different technologies which deliver similar content to similar audiences. It would be useful to analyse the content of a learning module, the goals of the students, teacher, and the school itself, implement some different technologies, and determine what factors influence successful delivery.

Inquiry teaching promotes an environment that tolerates ambiguity and encourages students' questions. In their studies of classrooms using the "Voyage of the Mimi" multimedia programme, the US Office of Technology Assessment (OTA) researchers observed that teachers tended to ask the majority of the questions, rewarded students for guessing correctly, and required continual help in maintaining a classroom climate that emphasised reasoning rather than right answers. Only those teachers who had experience in inquiry-based instruction used the materials in open-ended ways. They found that it was important not only to provide training in the scientific concepts covered in the materials, but also to give participating teachers rich and varied suggestions for classroom activities.

Progressive teachers who are early adapters of technology can become change agents for their peers. They can support other teachers by planning ahead as a group, and by working with the learning modules and equipment before using them in the classroom. Facilitators can try out learning modules as videotapes, building in interactivity as it suits the learning styles of their particular students, and then integrate real-time satellite programmes into their schedule later on.

Technology providers, too, are available to answer questions from new users. The Satellite Educational Resource Consortium (SERC), for example, provides a contact person who visits the site, answers telephone calls, or provides printed support material. Studio teachers are available between sessions to reply to FAX messages or telephone calls. The process of adapting new learning resources to the classroom, such as instructional television and videoconferencing, is not immediately transparent.

Administrators cannot expect teachers to feel comfortable with the technology, to use it effectively, and to maintain it as well, without giving them extra resources and time. Instructors need access to data links and E-mail, as well as video links. They need to download and upload resources and lesson plans, consult with other teachers, and try out new learning modules.

Many important issues stem from the characteristics of distance learners, whose aims and goals may be quite different from those of traditional students. Distance education systems were originally developed at the post-secondary level, and are only recently being used at the K-12 level.

Adult learners have a wide variety of reasons for pursuing learning at a distance: constraints of time, distance, and finances, the opportunity to take courses or hear outside speakers who would otherwise be unavailable, and the ability to come in contact with other students from different social, cultural, economic, and experiential backgrounds. As a result, they gain not only new knowledge but also new social skills, including the ability to communicate and collaborate with widely dispersed colleagues and peers whom they may never have seen.

Another important variable in learning effectiveness is the preference of the student for a particular mode of learning, i.e., cooperative, competitive, or individualised. Many current distance education projects incorporate cooperative learning, collaborative projects, and interactivity within groups of students as well as between sites.

Knowledge-building is accomplished through student-initiated interactions and reflections, in real-time in class, and in delayed-time using an electronic bulletin board system (BBS). R.A. Pea's distributed multimedia learning environments involve a dialectical opposition between the symbol-processing and constructivist viewpoints, to enable students to construct and transform knowledge through progressive discourse.

Effective learning, however, requires both knowledge of learner styles and advance preparation on the part of the teacher or site facilitator. Teachers and site facilitators are better able to make curriculum decisions to suit the preferences of their students, such as grouping certain students productively for project work, or assigning particular students to individual research projects, if they can determine the prevalent learning modes within their own classrooms. Site facilitators have the advantage of eye-to-eye contact and personal contact with students in their classrooms, whereas studio teachers must often rely on televised images, telephone conversations, or electronic messaging for feedback on student preferences.

If a teacher recognises the existence of these alternate learning styles, and if he attempts to make a match between these modes and the content to be learned, then he can develop a local instructional theory. As with most distance learning situations, a localised theory has a greater prospect of success than a general instructional theory intended to function satisfactorily in variety of settings, with a variety of practitioners.

With greater autonomy, student characteristics such as active listening and the ability to work independently in the absence of a live instructor become crucial for success. In a study Bernt and Bugbee, examined two types of study strategies used by distance students: primary, cognitive strategies, such as active listening, and secondary, affective strategies, such as ability to work independently of the instructor. They found that students who passed their courses differed significantly in primary strategies from those who failed: in testwiseness, concentration, and time management skills. They found little difference among them in secondary strategies: active learning, diligence, and positive attitude.

Instructors tend to blame the high dropout rate among post-secondary students on poor time management and procrastination. However, in a study of the effectiveness of university-level audioconference courses in Alaska, B. Sponder found that climate, geography, the efficiency of the postal system, the university support network, telecommunications facilities, students—hearing problems, and other factors also come into play. Miscommunication between students and teachers, and lack of course relevance to students, may also have negative repercussions.

Teacher mediation increases the completion rate for distance education courses. Neither can we assume that all students have sharpened their primary study skills to the same extent, nor that a positive attitude will make the difference between success and failure. Students need support and direction to enable them to make the transition from traditional classroom environments to self-directed learning—particularly tools to help them monitor their progress and obtain timely feedback on their activities.

There are many ways of facilitating learner support. Studio teachers may visit the distant site, or students may take a trip to the studio. Audio and video teleconferences or interactive chats with mentors and other students are two real-time alternatives to site visitation, office hours or telephone calls. Interaction and support may also take place by delayed time. Students may e-mail or FAX questions to their instructors or fellow students, or post them on electronic BBSs.

Teachers and peers, in turn, may respond at their convenience. Frequent teacher-student interaction enables the teachers to get to know the students better than if their only contact were via a televised image from a distant classroom. Students, too, need guidance in putting information together, reaching their tutors, completing and submitting assignments, and charting their progress.

Teachers also need support when they are learning about new technology, regardless of their level of classroom experience. As they begin their hands-on training with new technologies, some feel intimidated by the equipment, even in a non-threatening environment. At this point, they need to be able to communicate with other teachers who have gone through this process themselves, and who are competent to advise them and serve as role models.

For example, the University of South Florida has set up a mentoring system and an online discussion for participants in the telecommunications course. Athabasca University assigns ten students to one mentor in the Master of Distance Education programme.

The University of Wisconsin uses audioconference seminars to link instructors together. The University of British Columbia uses teleconferences with other students and tutors, as well as a telephone tutoring system. Georgia College has an electronic BBS with online resources, electronic conferencing, and a Teacher Clearinghouse for contacting other teachers interested in telecommunications.

OPERATIONAL ISSUES

Operational issues of distance learning involve planning, administration, management, and economics, all of which are crucial for a successful distance education programme. In particular, we must consider the roles of the teacher-facilitator-student triad, training of teachers and staff, implementation and adoption of new technology, and policy issues such as facilities, cost, and scheduling.

Teacher-facilitator-student triad: Distance learning teachers are not in direct classroom contact with their students. Communication is mediated not only by the technology, but also by a host of team partners which may include editors, designers, producers, technicians, media specialists, local tutors, aides, site facilitators, and service providers. Since many people must collaborate to produce and disseminate quality distance educational programming, the need to plan and coordinate staff activity is essential. In particular, we must define the roles of two key people: the teacher and the site facilitator.

The teacher: Distance learning teacher, or studio teacher, is the common thread throughout the distance learning process. She must be certified for the appropriate grade level, knowledgeable in her subject area, and trained in effective distance education strategies. She is responsible for knowing the subject matter, preparing lesson plans and producing an instructional module or course, selecting support materials, delivering the instruction effectively on-camera, determining the degree of student interaction, and selecting the form of distance evaluation or assessment. A studio teacher must be better organised than an ordinary classroom teacher. Additionally, she must be at ease with the equipment, and not let the technology get in the way of her presentation. This requires ongoing training in the form of regular observation of a master teacher, training in the use of carefully selected print, audio, graphics, and video materials, hands-on hardware training, and the chance to network with other teachers and facilitators on course progress. For example, the Iowa Department of Education requires a teacher, who is appropriately licensed and endorsed for the educational level and content being taught, to receive training regarding effective practices which enhance learning by telecommunications.

Today, few teachers have had sufficient training or field experience to enable them either to be effective distant teachers or to use technology successfully in their classrooms. Proper training would help distance learning teachers to change their method of teaching and give more attention to advanced preparation, student interaction, visual materials, activities for independent study, and follow-up activities. Schlosser and Anderson identify the new skills which teachers must learn as they assume the role of distance educators:

i) understanding the nature and philosophy of distance education
ii) identifying learner characteristics at distant sites
iii) designing and developing interactive courseware to suit each new technology
iv) adapting teaching strategies to deliver instruction at a distance
v) organising instructional resources in a format suitable for independent study
vi) training and practice in the use of telecommunications systems
vii) becoming involved in organisation, collaborative planning, and decision-making
viii) evaluating student achievement, attitudes, and perceptions at distant sites
ix) dealing with copyright issues.

The site facilitator: Responsibilities of the site facilitator are to motivate and encourage the remote site students, keep up their enthusiasm, and maintain discipline in the classroom. He is also responsible for smooth running of equipment, helping students with interaction, handing out, collecting, and grading papers, guiding collaborative groups who are working with manipulatives, answering questions when necessary, and assisting the studio teacher when asked. The site facilitator also carries out the assessment procedure defined by the teacher, via print, portfolios, online communications, or FAX.

Site facilitators have an average of four classes, are mid-career staff rather than beginning teachers, are anxious about using new technology, and are selected by their principals because of their subject background, availability, and general teaching ability, rather than volunteering to be assigned as facilitators. Talab and Newhouse identified a number of concerns about instructional design and classroom management which were voiced by site facilitators, including:

i) facilitating vs. traditional teaching
ii) preparation
iii) timing and scheduling
iv) classroom logistics other responsibilities.

Classroom management, like technology expertise, is not a skill that is mastered once and for all by instructors in high-tech classrooms. They progress through a three-stage model of survival, mastery, and impact. It may take them at least two years to change their focus from being anxious about themselves, their new physical environment, equipment malfunctions, and student misbehaviour, to anticipating problems and developing alternate strategies, exploring software more aggressively, sharing ideas more freely, increasing student motivation and interest, and using technology to their advantage.

As classroom contexts change, so do classroom management issues. Educational change takes time, a great deal of support, and peer networking and guidance. In general, teachers tend to focus on the increased workload and drawbacks associated with an innovation before the benefits of change emerge and the innovation takes hold. Since their activities are closely related to those of the teacher, facilitators need similar training. However, some site facilitators perceive themselves as end users, rather than designers, of distance instruction, so they feel that they require less emphasis on instructional systems design.

Typical comments of site facilitators about the teaching/ learning experience are that they have benefited from:

i) hands-on training and practice with assigned equipment
ii) a technical support team who can install, troubleshoot, and maintain classroom equipment and outside resources
iii) their own experiences anticipating equipment problems and working around them
iv) site visitation by studio teachers.

Technology adoption: Maintaining appropriate equipments, training teachers and facilitators to use it effectively, are necessary conditions, but are not sufficient in themselves to assure a school district of an excellent distance education programme. There are other factors involved, many of which are affective rather than cognitive, such as user-friendliness and the ability to implement learner support.

School organisation has been traditionally hierarchical and bureaucratic, whereas new technologies challenge this model. Many teachers are slow to incorporate new technologies into their classrooms because they are now seen as workers, rather than as instructional leaders or motivating forces within their classrooms. On the other hand, the technological innovations that have been adopted by teachers are those which solved problems that the teachers themselves identified as important, regardless of outside change agents, the school administration, or the opinions of non-teachers.

Successful technological innovations must take into consideration the social and political climate of the school, and must also reinforce the authority of the teacher, rather than undermine it. There are many powerful examples of creative teachers using computers and other learning technologies to enhance and enrich their teaching. A widely accepted technology is most often defined by a single characteristic: it makes a task rewarding for the user, where the "user" includes the student first, and the faculty second. If it does not make performance of a task rewarding, there is little motivation to accept the technology. Conversely, if it simplifies or expedites accomplishment of a goal, the probability of acceptance is high. Teachers and facilitators adopt technology innovations in a hierarchy of needs, with the most basic needs generally being fulfilled before the higher ones. From basic needs to higher level ones, these are:

i) time and accessibility
ii) dependability
iii) ownership and authority
iv) control
v) integration.

Site facilitators who believe in their own abilities to design instruction using satellite technology, and who are willing and able to continue in their role as teaching partners, have successfully incorporated technology into their classrooms. These site facilitators:

i) are committed to the concept of equality of education that satellite-based education provides
ii) see opportunities for professional advancement through learning new skills and networking
iii) seem revitalised by the observation of a master teacher and exceptional instructional design

iv) realise that the programme will not work without their participation

v) receive training in satellite-based instruction, either live or on tape, professional troubleshooting, and programme feedback.

This success is based upon a match between the identified needs of the facilitators and the resources which are available to them:

i) they are given time and accessible equipment

ii) they are given assistance with equipment operation and troubleshooting

iii) they take part in training and programme planning, and they control the grading, classroom management, and classroom activities

iv) they influence the programme through feedback

v) they see the need for technology integration in order to take part in the programme.

Management and policy issues: Distance education changes the learning relationship from the common, centralised school model to a more decentralised, flexible model. It also reverses social dynamics by bringing school to students, rather than students to school. This leads to a host of new issues for administrators to debate, including:

i) the impact of electronic education on tenured teaching

ii) balancing the budget with potentially low-cost electronic learning options

iii) redefining what it means to have a teacher present in the classroom

iv) revising teacher certification requirements to accommodate those teachers who electronically cross service area boundaries.

Each school has its own aims, goals, and objectives, both stated and unstated. Each school also has its own culture, urban or rural, as well as its own perceived value of student learning. There are personnel issues, with clerical, technical, and educational support staff forming a vital link between teacher and student. Many facets of the project must be considered, especially linking student needs within the particular school district with current and projected technology resources.

As opportunities arise, so do problems which must be dealt with. New policy issues must be addressed, as well. Items for further consideration include:

i) new forms of assessment and evaluation, including means to insure that the student's work is original and authentic
ii) a set of nationally accepted institutional accreditation standards to insure the quality of distance education
iii) a nationally accepted set of teacher certification standards which meet a minimum criterion, including training in distance education theory, methods, and strategies
iv) the need for cooperation among business, government, and education sectors
v) technology training and accessibility for all, not just for progressive students and teachers.

Team personnel: A distance education delivery team requires well-trained individuals in addition to teachers, site facilitators, and administrators. Old roles are redefined, and new roles emerge. The principal or district administrator handles logistics, acquires equipment, and provides training and support. Some school districts have funds for a media specialist or technology coordinator. Certain technologies, like microwave videoconferencing, require a technician to run specialised equipment in a control room. Technical support staff install, maintain, and upgrade equipment. Clerical personnel process requests for equipment acquisition and repair, as well as reproduction and distribution of course material. Technologically astute students often assist teachers with new hardware and software and serve as peer tutors for slower students.

A development team should include subject matter experts, instructional designers, writers and editors, audio and video production staff, and curriculum developers. It is important to identify these "people resources", and assign appropriate tasks, responsibilities, and timelines, so that quality control can be maintained. Moreover, it is important that learning modules be delivered on time to mesh with both the school schedule and that of the service provider.

One indicator of the need for distance learning teams to cooperate is the continuously rising costs of production. According to Margaret Cambre, local productions in 1962 cost about $165 per 15-minute programme. Today, the estimate for high-quality instructional television programmes is approximately $3000 per minute. Implementation of distance education is resource-intensive. Sufficient money and time must be allocated to deliver whatever courseware was promised. Schlosser and Anderson note that because funds come from the district, not from individual schools, distance education enterprises need to show a high degree of fiscal accountability.

Although prices for technology are declining, taxpayers, school boards, and state legislatures, as well as both government and non-government funding agencies, expect to get the most for their funds. If money is short, then there are two options: either downsize the project or extend the time frame. Many proposals are written without regard for the time it takes to resolve development and delivery problems. People also require resources and time to build an effective team, to start and maintain the instructional development project, to develop a plan for formative evaluation, and to obtain a commitment on compensation issues.

Once developed, the programme schedule may not fit in with the school schedule. Programmes may be too long, too short, or broadcast at the wrong time, resulting in a loss of real-time interactivity. One may always videotape the programme and show it later. However, it is important to realise that interactivity costs a lot more than a videotape. The cost/benefit of technology can vary significantly with the specific characteristics of schools and students. A successful programme in one location may be less successful elsewhere.

While technology often improves educational quality, it is not necessarily cost-efficient. Citing a report by Danish researcher Hans Siggard Jensen of the Copenhagen Business School, Jerry Pournelle comments that teacher productivity can be raised only if the instructors behave as if they are in a virtual classroom, rather than deal with point-to-point or one-on-one communication situations. Though videoconferencing is effective, many classrooms lack access to dedicated telephone lines and modems, much less several thousand dollars worth of software and proprietary hardware.

TECHNOLOGIES IN DISTANCE EDUCATION

Technologies played an important role in the evolution of distance education. In the past decade, digital technologies have transformed the way distance education is accomplished, as well as affecting its potential impact on markets for copyrighted works. The relevant technologies can be broken down into three major categories, with some overlap:

i) technologies that facilitate licensing;
ii) technologies that deliver the content of the course; and
iii) technologies that protect the delivered content.

One area of technology that facilitates licensing is the ability to attach licensing-related information to a work in a digital format. This information can be linked to or embedded in the work, and accessed by the user. In some instances the user will need special software to read information imperceptibly embedded in the work, and in others he can click on an external link to the information. Information so accessed can identify the copyright owner, point the user to the appropriate licensing site, or list licensing terms and conditions. Also useful are online rights and permissions services that can support a range of license and delivery functions, although not all services offer all functions.

Electronic licensing and electronic delivery are separable, independent activities, and either or both can be accomplished by the same online service. Such services can provide central access to a large group of materials, standardised licensing terms that can be customised according to the content provider, and a quick turnaround time for requests. Several different online rights and permissions services are currently in use or development.

The online permissions process itself allows a high degree of specialisation. Menus for these online requests can divide users into different categories and subject them to different licensing terms, including grants of permission without a fee. For example, an educational requester could be asked to specify whether the proposed use is for a classroom, seminar, or dissertation. Users could be asked to identify themselves as non-profit or for-profit, accredited or non-accredited, or any other characteristics that are significant to the copyright owner. The user could also respond to standard queries on the method of delivery, the size of the class, or the security of the website.

Any information relevant to the decision whether to license and how much to charge can be obtained, and this information can be used to generate an automatic response based on preestablished agreements between the service and the copyright owner, or to query the copyright owner directly for permission. In addition to processing licensing requests, some services may also accept payment for the license and deliver the content to the user digitally.

Depending on the particular service, the material could be delivered with whatever technological protections the copyright owner specifies already attached. As well as enabling licensing and delivery to take place online, technology can also facilitate access to licensors by the direct linking of works in a digital form to rights and permissions databases. This may be done with a link, such as an icon, at the end of text or an image, that a user may click on to go straight to an online licensing database. An important development in licensing for digital uses is the convergence of permissions systems with other systems designed to identify and protect material. In the analog world, licensing tends to be a discrete transaction, separate from how the user gains.

Distance education today is delivered via both analog and digital technologies, including diverse combinations of telephone connections, telecourses, video conferences and computer transmissions. Because our mandate is to consider issues relating to the use of digital technologies, particularly the need for an exemption "for distance education through digital networks," we focus here on the use of digital network technology. Other types of digital technologies may also be used to deliver distance education, such as digital television broadcasts or videoconferencing. These are examples of traditional media being used to carry digital, instead of analog, information. Telecourses and video conferences incorporate different degrees of interactivity, and may involve one-way video with two-way audio, or two-way video and two-way audio.

At the highest level of interactivity, videoconferencing allows instructors and students to see and speak to each other in real time as if they were in a classroom together. These types of digital technologies function much like their analog counterparts, but are usually capable of carrying more information more efficiently. It is important to note that even non-networked transmissions, whether digital or analog, may incorporate elements of digital network technology. For example, telecourses or video conferences are often transmitted in conjunction with a computer connection between the students and the instructor, allowing simultaneous online interaction.

Computer is the most versatile of distance education instruments, since it can incorporate or perform the same function as a television or telephone, as well as providing more interactivity, delivering more content, and supporting more comprehensive services than any other single medium. Computers can be used to transmit texts and graphics, connect users in a variety of real-time and asynchronous dialogues, deliver messages between users, and receive both audio and video transmissions. There are several commercial software products available to help educators construct online courses for students to access through personal computers. These products are basically a template of a blank course website, offering a choice of many of the technologies common to such courses. The instructor is then free to fill in the site with content, and to choose which of the available options she wants to incorporate. Despite the use of these common templates, there is no "typical" online distance education course.

When the concept of a class is transported to a virtual context, it is no longer constrained by the attributes of a physical classroom, such as the duration of a lesson, the ways in which materials can be used in class, and the schedule of the teacher and students. The virtual classroom can be defined by its ability to be tailored to the needs of different instructors, students and subject matters. The commercial templates are designed to be customised by each instructor. In addition, many instructors, or the information services of their institutions, build their own courses from scratch. Factors such as the technological sophistication of the target student body, and the level of technology available to these students, will influence how many of the available "bells and whistles" are used in a given course. There are constantly new products produced for this market, and numerous tools that can be employed in an online course. Although no list can be exhaustive, the technologies listed below are some of the most commonly used today:

i) *E-mail:* Electronic mail is a very common form of online interaction, and is present in virtually every distance education package. It is also used as an adjunct tool for communication between teachers and students in many "face-to-face" courses. E-mail is a delivery and receipt mechanism mostly for textual material, although other files, which could be textual or any other type, can be "attached" to the message. It allows educators and students to communicate with each other asynchronously, sending messages to individuals or groups easily and quickly. Messages can be written at any time, and can be read and responded to at any time. A file of e-mail messages sent and received is typically archived on the individual's computer.

ii) *Threaded discussions:* Threaded discussions are another form of asynchronous textual communications. An educator or student may post a message pertaining to a certain subject in a forum accessible to the whole class. Other participants can respond to that message or any of the responses, and so on. The evolution of the threaded discussion is displayed in hierarchical form to allow a participant to follow the discussion. A student or instructor can read the original message, the responses it generated, and the further comments generated by each of those responses. In this way, it seeks to recreate, in a time-independent environment, the flow of a classroom discussion while keeping a record of the discussion's progress. This record is usually stored on the class website for the duration of the class.

iii) *Chat*: The chat function provides a synchronous meeting place online. Students and instructors who are online and in this programme can write messages back and forth in real time. As one student types a message, for instance, the text appears on the computer of all the other students present in the chat room. This technology allows for live discussion similar to classroom experiences. It is possible for the participants to keep copies of the chat session.

iv) *Whiteboard:* A whiteboard programme is one that provides a common space in which students and instructors can work synchronously. Similar in use to a blackboard in class, whiteboard technology can be used for display or collaboration. During a whiteboard session, each participant has a blank application on their screen, a "whiteboard." Any participant can then cut, paste, draw or write anything into this common space, and it will be immediately displayed on the boards of all the other participants. This technology is useful for group projects or planning sessions, which require students to collaborate on creating something. It can also be used in connection with a lecture delivered through streaming technologies, permitting the instructor to display images or text to the class as she lectures. Participants can save the contents of the board to their computer at any time.

v) *Shared applications:* Like the whiteboard, a shared application can be used for display or collaboration. A shared application is a computer programme like a word processor or drawing programme that permits several people to use the programme at the same time from different locations. The participant with the programme to be shared opens it and specifies that he wants to share it. Demonstrations can be accomplished this way or, if the instructor specifies that the application can be used for collaboration, anyone in the class can also use the shared application. For example, all participants in a class session might have access to the same word processing programme or graphic design programme, and would work with each other within the application to create a product. In some implementations, the work that is done in the application can be saved or printed only from the computer of the person who shared it. For someone else to obtain a copy of the final product after collaborating, the person who shared it must send the file to the other participants.

vi) *Streaming video/audio:* Streaming video or audio is similar to broadcast technologies, except that the transmissions are sent over a computer network. Instead of the receiving computer's waiting to receive an entire file of audio or video information before playing it back, the receiving computer begins to play back the file while it is still arriving over the network. Playback is done "on the fly," in other words. With enough network capacity ("bandwidth") the result is comparable to radio or television. In practice, however, the limits of the internet's capacity today result in video images appearing small, with jerky movements. Sound quality is often quite good, though here again, the speed of one's connection to the internet, and the congestion on the internet at the time, make substantial differences in the quality of playback. In common implementations today, streaming audio and video do not result in a complete copy of the entire transmission being placed on the user's computer, although a different implementation could be created that would do so. With appropriate equipment, such as cameras and microphones, the audio or video can also be two-way. This technology is used to deliver lectures to students, or hold class sessions with interaction.

vii) *Video/audio files*: Video and audio files can be used to illustrate lessons or teach specific subjects. For example, a foreign language class might contain sound clips of different pronunciations of words, or a history class might integrate video clips of recorded interviews of war survivors with the lecture material. These files reside on the class network site for the duration of the class, and can be copied and downloaded by the students.

viii) *Course management*: Course management describes the infrastructure of the instructional content of the course. This could include the syllabus, written or recorded lectures, assigned reading, tests, and homework assignments. It generally involves posting material in common spaces on the network site, together with directions on how and when to access different portions of the material. For instance, an instructor might post a new lecture every week, with reading assignments, and a subsequent threaded discussion on the lecture. Or, she might choose to post all lectures and reading material at the beginning of the course, allowing students to read ahead, and organise chat sessions or threaded discussions every week on a different lecture. This information, once posted, generally remains on the course site for the duration of the class.

ix) *Links:* Links provide a way for students to quickly access material not present on the course site itself. Links to other websites can be embedded in the text, or listed separately. For instance, a lecture on computer programming might include a link to an internet website rating different types of software. Links may also transport the student to the university's library, where a student may access electronic reserves of material put aside by the instructor for that particular class.

x) *Interactive CDROMs and DVDROMs*: Some classes furnish students with a CDROM or DVDROM that interacts with the course website. These store large files, such as video, audio or animation, that would otherwise be posted on the websites. When the student clicks on the graphic or video clip in the course site, his computer obtains the file straight from the CDROM or DVDROM, instead of downloading it from the web page. This saves time, and also allows large files to be viewed with higher quality.

These tools are generally used in classes that involve some form of instructor-student interaction. There are also tools available for self-paced independent learning — the latter-day parallel to video and audio tape courses that can be taken home and used at the student's convenience, with no interaction with a teacher. In the digital environment, computer-based training is a common form of distance education. Programmes on a variety of subjects can be obtained by the student from commercial vendors or in the course of instruction at an educational institution.

The student reviews the material at his own pace, and tests himself on computer-generated exams. The programmes themselves may contain a mixture of media, including video, audio, graphics and text. They could be contained in a CDROM, for example, downloaded from a network site, or accessed online. The student has little or no interaction with a teacher, although the student may send the results of the computer testing to an educational organisation for grading or credit.

Many technology companies and content-provider groups are working to develop technologies for protecting works in the digital environment that will be viable in the marketplace. Industries are also collaborating among themselves in an effort to develop broadly-based, effective technological standards. Technology can protect copyrighted works in many ways. It can restrict access to the work, restrict uses of the work and identify the terms and conditions of using the work.

In some circumstances it can also find copies of the work on the World Wide Web and report their existence to the copyright owner, who can determine whether the copy is authorised. While there is a substantial degree of overlap in these technologies, they can be separated into technologies that limit access to works, and technologies that prevent or detect uses of works after access. Each method of technological protection varies in its cost of deployment and degree of security. As a general matter, there is a correlation between these two factors: the more expensive and complex the mechanism, the more inviolate the material. If the expense is high, the material to be protected may not warrant the outlay. As a result, the stronger protections may be used to protect only high market value works.

Although many of these technologies are highly effective, none provides absolute certainty. Any code can be broken, and any mechanism can be circumvented, with enough effort and investment. The effectiveness of access control technologies in particular depends on the behaviour of users, such as a student who is careless with his passwords or intentionally shares them with others. The goal of most of these technologies is to provide a high enough level of protection that the cost of circumvention outweighs the value of access to the material protected.

Educational organisations may limit access to students enrolled in a particular class or at a particular institution through several different methods used separately or in combination. Following are the most common methods used in the educational environment:

i) *Password protection*: Password protection is probably the most common type of protection in educational settings, and most educational institutions seem to use some form of password protection to ensure that their distance education classes reach only registered students. Access is restricted by use of passwords or "logins," assigned codes used to identify an authorised user. These protection devices allow the institution to act as a gatekeeper, permitting only authorised users entry to shielded systems or select data. Each student can be issued a single password, which opens access only to a course for which the student has registered, or the student can be provided a different password for each class. Passwords typically expire at a predetermined time — the termination of the class, the semester, the school year, or the student's enrolment in the institution.

ii) *Firewalls*: Both intranets and firewalls are common methods of protecting computer networks, and are used in many educational institutions. An intranet is an internal network cordoned off from public access by use of a firewall. Firewalls are created by a server, located between the intranet and the public network, which has been programmed to prohibit unauthorised users from accessing internal data. The firewall itself is not an access control mechanism; rather, it prohibits users from accessing the internal data by any means other than whatever access control mechanism the university has in place.

ii) *IP addresses / domain names*: By screening for only specific IP addresses or domain names, it is possible to restrict access to a website or other content source to only those computers that are attached to a specific set of networks. This allows content to be restricted to machines on a specific campus. These methods of access control are somewhat limited in the distance education environment. Restriction by IP source address or domain name can be used to restrict access to members of an institutional community, but not to students registered in a specific class, since class registration does not correlate to either IP address or domain names. In addition, many distance learners do not work on campus computers, but work from home or some other place. Because they will not be working from addresses on the campus network, they would not be able to access the material.

iii) *Hardware connections*: Physically connecting hardware is another way to restrict the access of unauthorised users to transmitted data. In the digital environment, connecting computers together can create a system similar to the "closed circuit" television systems in which cables connect the transmitting sites to the receiving sites, effectively limiting reception to within the circuit. This manner of transmission is still being used for both broadcast and digital network transmissions. Where computers can be physically connected to each other, unauthorised access to the transmission can be avoided.

iv) *Encryption*: While the use of intranets and passwords limits those who may enter or log on to a system, encryption technology limits access to information by protecting the information routed between a sender and a designated receiver. In an educational context, encry-ption allows instructors to send protected information which can be read only by students with the authorised decryption key. Encryption technologies are commer-cially marketed at a range of prices, depending in part on the level of protection. Encryption technology, in essence, encodes information from a sender into an unreadable form. Only an authorised receiver who holds the key to decode the information can access it.

v) *Physical control*: Putting the content into a physical object, such as a CDROM, which is given only to authorised users is another method used to control access to information. A CDROM is a physical copy of digital information that is inserted into the computer when the user wishes to access such information. The work may be viewed on the screen, but resides in the physical disk. Access to that work is therefore limited to students who are in possession of the CDROM. Although the use of a CDROM has not traditionally thought of as a technological protection, using a CDROM as a delivery mechanism is more restrictive than posting a work on a website.

Technologies cannot control what happens to the work once it has been accessed. After an encrypted work has been decrypted, or a password-protected site has been logged into, the material is available for further use, including printing, downloading to computer memory, or electronic distribution.

Technologies that affect the downstream uses of protected works are intended to address this gap. Some restrict use of the work, and others allow unauthorised uses to be detected. Several alternatives exist for restricting use of a work once it has been accessed. Few of these technologies are yet in common usage.

Several have just been released on the commercial market; others are expected to be commercially launched in the very near future; and still others are projected for release in the next year. The state of flux of this type of technology is high. As these technologies all represent different methods of addressing similar problems, it remains to be seen which, if any, will gain widespread acceptance and use with consumers and content providers.

There are a number of proprietary viewer technologies currently in the market or in development, and some copyright owners are considering them as viable alternatives for selling and controlling works of high market value in the digital environment. These technologies are often designed for a specific type of work, and allow copyright owners to set rules for the use of their works. These rules are attached to all digital copies of the work, regardless of how they are further copied or distributed, and prevent anyone from making a use of the work that is not in accordance with those rules.

Basically, the technology works by encoding the digital work and wrapping it in a proprietary file format that can be opened only by software that reads and abides by the usage rules contained in the file. The file format contains the conditions of access and rules of use for the work. The conditions of access specify which users are allowed access.

The complementary software identifies the user and responds to the rules embedded in the container. It also acts as a viewer, allowing the user to see or use the content, filtered through the viewer, in accordance with the embedded rules. However, the content is never subject to distribution or copying in decrypted form. If the work is further disseminated, the proprietary file format moves with it, and the work cannot be accessed or used by anyone who does not have the proper viewer and authorisation.

There are several examples of such technologies currently on the market, or in late stages of development. Most are designed to handle one type of content, although there are products which offer protection for all type of works. Some examples are listed below:

— *Adobe Acrobat Reader*: Acrobat is a system that includes a proprietary file format called PDF (Portable Document Format), a reader and software to create the secure documents. The most recent version was released in late March 1999. The format is widely used in scientific and technical journals and many other electronic publications. Using Acrobat, the publisher can set privileges in the file that the Acrobat Reader obeys. The publisher may require the user to enter a password to view the document, and can permit or restrict printing, modification and cut and paste. The file format can accept text, graphics, Powerpoint slides and spreadsheets, and the new version allows more advanced access control mechanisms. The reader software is free and is often distributed as a plug-in for browsers. Acrobat Reader is widely used today. It is primarily designed for printing high quality copies of documents rather than as a mechanism for viewing documents on-screen.

— *Liquid Audio*: Liquid Audio is a secure container technology currently used to sell recorded music files over the internet. Liquid Audio both delivers content and accepts payment. It does not, at this point, allow specialisation in the types of uses it permits or restrict. A customer using Liquid Audio has a limited number of choices — he can hear a sample, see the album cover, and sometimes read the liner notes. Then, if he decides to buy the recorded music, it is downloaded, marked with the buyer's unique player ID. Only software obtained from Liquid Audio and installed on the user's computer with a serially numbered identifier can open that file. After purchase, the buyer can listen to the recording as often as he chooses, but cannot copy or distribute it further.

— *InterTrust*: InterTrust is one example of a secure container system for protecting all types of works. Works come in secure containers called "digiboxes" which are accessed and used through proprietary viewing technology on the user's computer, called the InterRights Point. Although

> not yet in commercial deployment, InterTrust began shipping system developer kits in June, 1998, and is in an advanced stage of development. The technology incorporates a permission system for obtaining authorisation to use a work, a payment mechanism if a charge for such use is assessed, and a tracking mechanism, if desired and consistent with privacy agreements, to monitor usage for the purposes of metered payment. It also allows a highly nuanced set of rules to be enforced.

These technologies could be used in a digital distance education context. For example, the rules attached to a work through a secure container technology might provide that protected material could be accessed only by a registered student at a particular college, and that the student could view the work, and print out one hard copy, but could not save it to disk or distribute it to others electronically. A license fee, if any, could reflect these restrictions.

The student's viewer could then identify the user as a registered student, allow the student to see or print the work, but not allow the work to be sent through the viewer to the student's hard drive or e-mail system. If the information was being provided based on rules that required the institution to pay per use, the software could monitor the use for future accounting. This protection would apply to any kind of work and would persist in the work. The rules could also provide that after a certain time period, for instance a semester, the material would no longer be accessible. Secure container technologies that protect a range of works are not currently in use in distance education, however.

As these are relatively new technologies, it is difficult to predict the level of investment required to create and operate such technologies within an educational system. Some developers indicate that pricing could be geared for educational institutions. Streaming technologies for video and audio are not technically mechanisms to protect content, but rather to deliver it. However, using advanced streaming formats for video or audio, no copy of the whole work is created on the user's computer. Because these technologies do not facilitate the making of copies, they can hinder downstream uses by the receiver of the transmission. Therefore, a byproduct of the properties of the delivery mechanism is that it offers some degree of protection against redistribution.

Low resolution digital copies can be provided to the user with less than the full complement of digital data, creating a copy of lower quality. Such a copy can be adequate for on-screen viewing but does not print well. This technology is currently used for marketing graphic images online, allowing a prospective user to view a low resolution copy of the work, but requiring a purchase in order to obtain a high-quality image. It does not appear to be in common usage in the distance education environment. This may be because it is difficult for instructors who rely on graphic images, such as graphic design or art teachers, to teach their classes effectively using low-quality images.

In addition to technologies that restrict the use that can be made of a work, technologies for embedding information in digital works to identify and track usage are also in development and use. Information may be attached to a work in a number of ways, from adding it to the image visually to integrating it invisibly in the digital data.

Since it is fairly easy to remove a visible identifier, the practice of digital watermarking, which does not permit easy removal, is growing. Digital watermarking is the technology of embedding information within the content of a digital file in a manner that is not ordinarily perceptible without the use of special software. A digital watermark does not hinder copying of a digital file, but the watermark will be present in the copy. Although it is possible to remove watermarks, it generally involves more than trivial effort and inconvenience, and some types are harder to remove than others. Digital watermarks are typically used to embed information in a digital file about the copyright, such as the identity of the copyright owner and the terms and conditions of licenses. Users with the appropriate software can display this information and contact the copyright owner to clear rights to use the work embodied in the file. In general, it is easier to watermark some kinds of content, such as music and video, than others, such as text.

A number of technologies exist today that can provide effective technological protection for different types of works. Access control measures such as password protection are already common in distance education. Sophisticated technologies to prevent post-access uses of material are also a reality, although few are yet widely available. Some are in use in limited markets, some are in trial, and many are the focus of ongoing investment and development. The use of open standards is beginning to emerge. In the near future it will be technically possible to protect works against both unauthorised access and dissemination with a high degree of effectiveness.

REFERENCES

Garrison, D.R., "An analysis and evaluation of audio teleconferencing to facilitate education at a distance", *The American Journal of Distance Education*, 4(3), 16-23, 1990.

Horton, W., "How we communicate", *Paper presented at the meeting of the Rocky Mountain Chapter of the Society for Technical Communication*, Denver, CO, June, 1994.

Johnston, David, et.al., "The e-learning e-volution in colleges and universities: A Pan-Canadian Challenge", Ottawa: Industry Canada, 2001.

Keegan, D., *The Foundations of Distance Education*, London: Croom Helm, 1986.

Kerry, Bob et al., "The Power of the Internet for Learning: Moving from Promise to Practice", Report of the Web-Based Education Commission to the President of the United States, Jessup, MD: U.S. Department of Education, 2000.

Millbank, G., "Writing multimedia training with integrated simulation", *Paper presented at the Writers' Retreat on Interactive Technology and Equipment*, Vancouver, BC: The University of British Columbia Continuing Studies, 1994.

Pea, R.A., "Seeing what we build together: Distributed multimedia learning environments for transformative communications", *Journal of the Learning Sciences*, 3(3), 285-299, 1994.

Perraton, H. (ed.), *Distance education: An economic and educational assessment of its potential for Africa*, Washington, DC: World Bank, 1986.

Porter, David (ed.), New directions in distance learning: Interim report, March, 1994, available: David Porter, Manager, Schools Curriculum Programs, 4355 Mathissi Place, Burnaby, BC., Canada.

_______________, *Learning in a Wired World: Moving Beyond the Course as the Unit of Learning*, Vancouver: Open Learning Agency, 2000.

Pournelle, J., "An Educational Trip", *Byte*, 197-210, July, 1994.

Prawat, R. and Floden, R.E., "Philosophical perspectives on constructivist views of learning", *Educational Psychology*, 29(1), 37-48, 1994.

Report on Copyright and Digital Distance Education, US Copyright Office, May, 1999.

Scardamalia, M., Bereiter, C., "Computer support for knowledge-building communities", *Journal of the Learning Sciences*, 3(3), 265-283, 1994.

Schlosser, C.A., and Anderson, M.L., "Distance education: review of the literature", *Association for Educational Communications and Technology*, Washington, DC, 1994.

Sherry, L., "Issues in Distance Learning", *International Journal of Educational Telecommunications*, 1 (4), 337-365, 1996.

_______________, Morse, R.A. , "An assessment of training needs in the use of distance education for instruction", *International Journal of Telecommunications*, 1(1), 5-22, 1995.

Shneiderman, B., "Designing the user interface", *Reading*, MA: Addison-Wesley, 1992.

Simon, H.A., Interview, *OMNI Magazine*, 16(9), 71-89, 1994.

Sponder, B., "Distance education in rural Alaska: An overview of teaching and learning practices in audioconference courses", *University of Alaska Monograph Series in Distance Education*, No. 1., Fairbanks, Alaska: Alaska University, Center for Cross-Cultural Studies, 1990.

Talab, R.S., Newhouse, B., "Self-efficacy, performance variables and distance learning facilitator technology adoption: Support for the teacher needs hierarchy", *In Proceedings of Selected Research and Development Presentations at the convention of the AECT*, Research and Theory Division, New Orleans, January, 1993.

Tapsall, S. and Yoni Ryan, "Virtual Education Institutions in Australia: Between the Idea and Reality", In *The Development of Virtual Education: A Global Perspective*, Vancouver: The Commonwealth of Learning, 1999.

Taylor, James C., "Distance Education: The Fifth Generation", *Paper presented at the 19th ICDE World Conference on Learning and Distance Education*, Vienna, June 20-24, 1999.

White, M.A., "Information and imagery education", In M.A. White (ed.), *What curriculum for the information age?*, Hillsdale, NJ: Lawrence Erlbaum Associates, Inc., 1987.

Willis, B., "Instructional development for distance education", *ERIC Document Reproduction Service* No. ED 351 007, 1992.

2
Open Learning Issues

The world is changing at a scale and pace and with a level of interdependency to which we are previously unaccustomed. This phenomenon of 'hyperchange' is a combination of linear, exponential, discontinuous and chaotic change. Several forces, including the proliferation of information and communication technologies, the rapid production and flows of information, the globalisation of fragile financial markets coupled with the parallel growth of informal local economies, the decentralisation of governments and bureaucracies, the intense marketing of certain cultural fantasies and lifestyle preferences, and the rise of new political actors, are contributing to the intensifying, complexifying and churning of these change processes.

The current global environment is filled with a great deal of tension, frustration and conflict that is closely linked both to real and perceived shifts in power, glaring inadequacies of 'modern' institutions that are being continually revealed, and a nagging uncomfortability which is tied to the inherent unpredictability and uncontrollability surrounding hyperchange. Over the past three hundred years, the paradigm of modernity has played a significant role in shaping dominant notions of development, progress, growth, freedom, democracy, and social justice. However, several sacred intellectual spaces that have been closely linked to modernity are currently being contested and renegotiated on various terrains and at various levels of our day-to-day lives. These challenged spaces include: the mechanistic/ reductionist views of systems vs. complexity, the objective vs. the subjective, the modern vs. the traditional, the universal vs. the culturally specific and pluralistic, the public vs. the private, the real vs. the virtual, the secular vs. the religious, the urban vs. the rural, individual vs. the community, the male vs. female vs. gender, the nation-state vs. the supra-national vs. local, and the individual vs. community. Such contestations, on one hand, provide several reasons for optimism by opening up opportunities for shifting power and resources, generating new discourses and language, remapping borders, creating new identities, and liberating relationships. They also at the same, however, place tremendous pressure on the paradigm of modernity which can be expected to result in a multitude of skirmishes, shocks, bumps, dislocations, breaks, and ruptures as we try to come to grips with a messy world.

The levels of violence and destruction underlying these will no doubt be influenced by the global threats of militarisation, environmental degradation, and socio-psychological alienation. What should be viewed as particularly worrisome though is that the phenomenon of hyperchange places a severe strain on our present abilities to make sense of, contextualise, adapt to, negotiate, and influence the opportunities and conflicts taking place around us.

The basic outlines of what we must do to avoid self-destruction as a species have long seemed clear to many of us. If survival holds no larger meaning for us, avoiding extinction is not enough to draw us to the difficult changes we must make. To make a choice for life, we must be drawn by a compelling vision of new possibilities grounded in a sense of meaning. The narratives of the past have either collapsed, been deconstructed, rejected, or have fallen into self-preserving isolationist modes. Many societies lack both relevant shared narratives and a respect for and understanding of other peoples' narratives. Many individuals and communities around the world today lack the ability to generate, link, and evolve multiply interconnected personal narratives which provide them with a sense of meaning beyond themselves.

The ability to generate new meanings in socially constructive, pluralistic and non-violent ways can be seen to be constrained, to a large degree, by a breakdown of several social self-referencing mechanisms and feedback processes. The complex crisis we are confronting today include:

i) *Seemingly paralysing inability to introduce, interact around and utilise new ideas.* Anti-intellectual approaches masked under the rhetoric for 'pragmatism', 'practicality', 'implementation', and under false dichotomies of academic vs. practitioner and theory vs. action, are dramatically reducing the spaces for engaging in more critical, constructive and participatory forms of intellectual discourse which are essential for reflecting upon and challenging the ideological basis of how societies are being forced to conceive of their development. The results are the we are unable to generate new visions to give context to our ideas and new ideas to give greater context to our visions. In addition, dominant analytical frameworks, methodologies, discourse, and interactions are not robust and dynamic enough to help us understand and respond in creative and diverse ways to the complex challenges that face the world. Furthermore, most 'educated' people have been socialised to only see narrow immediate realities and isolated contexts which tend to be mired in the logic of functionalism, economic efficiency, cost-effectiveness, and risk averseness. Their ideas and positions are reduced to specific places, fixed periods of times, and rigid definitions of identity and social roles such as low caste, women, minority, left/right, etc.

ii) *Breakdown in our 'institutions of reflection' i.e., the multiple socio-spiritual spaces in which we engage in ethical self-reflection, sense-making, and dialogue about our attitudes and priorities and their links to our behaviour and actions.* Such institutions are critical to enhancing our awareness and consciousness, to continuously rejuvenating our optimism and hope, and to supporting our engagement in a process of radical transformation. However, having been simultaneously attacked by both the nihilistic forces of liberalism/post-modernism and preserved/hand-cuffed by the forces of conservatism, these spaces are either disappearing or becoming antequated and irrelevant. Many of our surviving and emerging institutions prevent us from having the time to think about the different changes taking place around us and our relationship to these.

iii) *Crisis of leadership*. Conventional notions of leadership have typically been framed in terms of those people who are in the elite ranks of governments, business, other organisations, rather than, in terms of all of us being leaders in different facets of our lives. This has created a situation in which individuals are easily allowed to defer their personal responsibility for actions to the 'other.' Many practised models of leadership are still grounded in notions of authoritarianism and hoarding of power with the guiding metaphors of self-preservation and manipulation. Many of our leaders have tended to adopt and hide behind positions based on the real-politik, partisanism and cynicism, and lack the courage and confidence to take bold risks in new directions. Preferring to preach dogma, they lack the ability to inspire others to create meaning in their lives.

Our responses to these problems have thus far disappointingly consisted of models that assume simplistic linear causalities which, on one level, have led to calls for more schools, formalised non-formal centres, and distance education modalities; and, on another level, have invoked and glorified a fool's paradise based on ever-increasing levels of economic growth/consumption and technological innovation.

These responses, for the most part, have lacked a deeper understanding of and commitment to supporting the processes of change that are required to radically transform systems.

They have been narrowly framed in terms of advancing the agenda of the economic and material rather than in terms of a more profound struggle to discover what it means to be 'fully human.'

The dialectical lifelong processes of discovery and self-realisation, both on individual and collective levels, should serve to guide a much broader philosophy of learning which extends far beyond the conventional classroom and one-dimensional standardised tests.

However, much of what we do today in education and development actually contradicts what we know about this broader understanding of learning. Many of our existing methodologies and approaches, for example, suppress or teach us to ignore our 'meaning needs'. i.e., the impulses that stimulate in us desires to create meaning. The suppression of these meaning needs prevents us from moving from modes of unconscious adaptation to conscious anticipation and from engaging in authentic fully humanising development.

Responses to the crisis of meaning by the international development community have thus far centered around schooling with increasing calls for more 'basic education,' 'functional literacy,' and 'skills training' opportunities.

Much of what we assume and do today in the field of education contradicts a larger heterogeneous vision of people-led development. Research from diverse fields such as cognitive sciences, applied linguistics, psychology, neurological sciences, ecological sciences, biological sciences, social anthropology and semiotics, indicates that the way schools are presently configured goes against much of what we know about learning — about the diversity and complexity of learners, learning styles and learning processes, learning relationships, learning cultures, and spaces where and conditions under which learning takes place.

Our current educational solutions, still grounded in the metaphors of yesterday, continue to view learning as a mere preparation for life - with a discrete beginning and end — not as an integral part of life. Such a recognition demands that the international development community's vision be expanded beyond merely trying to do more of the same.

Today, we recognise the tremendous value and need for organised learning spaces where adults and children can come together but argues that such spaces need to be radically different in terms of their ideological and philosophical goals and assumptions, structures and mechanisms, processes and practice. Some learning spaces have managed to undertake this process of transformation, however, constituted as such, it would be both imprecise and inappropriate to use the same term i.e., 'schooling', to describe the experiences linked to these new spaces.

Several generalisations can be made concerning how the institution of schooling has been developed and, in many cases, continues to be reproduced around the world. Schools have been shaped by ideological and philosophical traditions of development which are increasingly being challenged. The inter-connected logics of colonialism, industrialisation and human capital theory, modernisation, nation-building and globalisation have played significant roles, at different points in history, in shaping the values, goals, structure, timing, processes, and activities of schools. Schooling is predominantly driven by the development imperatives of the state. Thus, the rationale guiding schools has been strongly biased towards supporting the urbanised formal sectors of government and large scale industry. Schooling has served to 'mainstream' and socialise people into fitting into the dominant culture with the focus on maintenance learning. The acquisition of fixed outlooks, methods and rules for dealing with known and recurring situations. It enhances our problem-solving ability for problems that are given. It is the type of learning designed to maintain an existing system or an established way of life. There is virtually no ideological space provided for challenging existing knowledge frameworks and constructing alternative ways of seeing, believing, and doing.

Three mechanistic metaphors have historically contextualised our view of schooling and learning: the universe as a clock, the brain as a computer, and learning as blank slate. Assumptions derived from these metaphors, and further elaborated through theories of Skinnerian behaviourism, Piagetian developmental psychology and Darwinistic individualism, still underlie dominant structure and practice in conventional education systems. Schools and the processes of teaching and learning are predicated on the institutional desire to instill control and discipline. The effect is that the institution of school, with its daily lesson plans, fixed curriculum, standardised tests, and other such paraphernalia, tends constantly to reduce learning to a series of technical acts and the teacher to the role of a technician.

Education systems have tended to be conceived of as rigid and isolated entities. Schools have been developed as compartmentalised, closed systems that are delinked from their external communities. Learning in schools is seen as separate from and unconnected to the learning that takes place in non-formal and informal environments. Most schools have refused to acknowledge that learners spend more time in the informal environment than they do in schools. The validity of other spaces for learning, other knowledge systems, and other partners in the learning/teaching process has often been neglected, and even, devalued. Furthermore, there has been very little flexibility within the system. It has been organised along strict linear levels of education i.e., the 'stages' approach, with artificial separations such as primary, secondary and tertiary. Schooling takes place within inflexible blocks of time which require learners to be present on a year-long basis.

Parents and students' objectives for engaging in schooling have been narrowly centered around obtaining a job with the primary focus on doing well on the examination and obtaining a certificate. In this setting, there has been little value attributed to learning as an essential process in the wider context of life. Schooling has been conceived of as taking place only in the early years in one's life, and learning is thought to be completed when one graduates and receives a diploma i.e., signifying that one is 'educated.' Furthermore, the exam-orientation has tended to lead towards approaches tied to memorising a large repertoire of facts and routines with little concern over whether the learner actually understands and can apply different information and skills in constructive ways. Learning has become a ritual. Schools have, for the most part, failed to establish a culture of learning that extends beyond the walls of the classroom.

Schooling has been primarily framed in terms of knowledge and value transmission. In the outmoded view of learning that dominates our institutions, knowledge is regarded as an objective substance that can be deposited directly into people's minds. Education is seen as the process by which knowledge is transferred into the learner's minds, and teaching is seen as the packaging of knowledge for efficient transfer. The focus has been on teaching rather than supporting learning and understanding. Learners have been regarded as 'empty vessels' and the range of knowledge and cultural experiences that they already come to school with is hardly acknowledged.

There is very little sensitivity to the diversity of learners. The system has been constructed along the lines of factory in the tradition of Fordism. Within this framework, learning interventions have been typically designed for the imaginary "mean" learner. There is very little flexibility for catering to the specific differences of learners — their individual personalities, culture, linguistic, learning styles, family background, motivational levels, interests and special needs. Furthermore, the system fails to take into account the physical, emotional, social and cognitive abilities of each learner.

Many educators mistakenly believe that intelligence is a static, unmodifiable trait, and that potential and capability are finite. The IQ way of thinking says that people are either smart or not, are born that way, that there's nothing you can do about it, and that tests can tell you if you are one of the smart ones or not. Under this scenario, the 'smart' students enter into a virtuous cycle of praise, support and achievement, while those deemed as 'dumb' enter into a vicious cycle of self-doubt, neglect and failure. Closely linked to this notion, is a general fallacy that success in learning depends more on pure ability than on effort.

Curricula have been framed in tightly compartmentalised and fragmented disciplines, with content and materials that tends to be irrelevant to most learners, often favouring a strong urban and middle-class bias. Indeed, as currently constituted, our educational system is heavily biased towards linguistic modes of instruction and assessment and, to a somewhat lesser degree, towards logical quantitative modes as well. Several critiques have also been raised about the propensity of schooling to alienate individuals from their rural, ethnic and linguistic communities. The focus of curricula has been on developing abstract, academic, and generalised learning, with little attention to contextualised, reflective, emotional learning. Curricula have been conceptualised with the understanding that learning takes place in chunked, linear stages starting with notions like 'functional literacy' and 'basic education' constituting the first stage with later stages focusing on higher order levels of thinking.

Learning in the classroom has been seen as a predominantly individualistic activity. Competition has been viewed as a far more powerful motivator than cooperation. Sharing with, assisting and collaborating with fellow learners on projects is typically called 'cheating' and is punished. Fear and mistrust have shaped most schooling models. To support this, there is a strong hierarchy built into the school. The learner is seen to be subordinate to the teacher, who is viewed as the omnipotent expert, with classroom roles largely fixed. In turn, the teacher is subordinate to the principal and inspectors. The learner, the teacher, and communities have very little opportunity to participate in the identification of learning goals and the development of curriculum. The processes by which learners learn from other learners, their parents and communities, and in other environments are also not encouraged. Furthermore, by isolating learners into age groups, schooling has not fostered activities that would involve both adults and children learning together and geared towards building greater understanding between them.

The liberal democratic tradition has argued that 'schooling for all' serves as a mechanism for the creation of a democratic and egalitarian society. Schooling is supposed to be a great equalising and empowering force. However, schooling and its claims towards producing meritocracy has been strongly critiqued on the grounds that it reproduces hierarchical socio-economic relations and reinforces existing notions around the distribution of power. Many countries today, for example, still have education systems that feature different socio-economically biased tracks of learning, such as academic and vocational/technical, which tend to lead to different predetermined roles, opportunities and power in society. According to I. Illich, the feelings of 'psychological impotence' i.e., the inability of people to fend for themselves, are cultivated in students in relation to the dominant socioeconomic institutions. Those who drop-out or are forced out of the system are labelled failures and leave feeling humiliated, bitter, frustrated, and demoralised. J. P. Naik has analysed this process at work in India which is equally applicable to many countries of the South, "The main achievement of the system, therefore, is to condemn the bulk of children of common people as dropouts and failures and to consign them to a life of drudgery and poverty which has hardly any parallel in the contemporary world or even in our own earlier history."

The extent to which this generalisations applies to any particular context can, of course, be extensively debated. Positive examples can be found in the education system, but these occur in spite of the system rather than because of it. Most educational systems today still remain insensitive to the widely diverse needs of learners of all age groups and ignorant to the complexity of learning processes. Furthermore, the institution alised intervention of schooling has provided little space and empowerment for both individual learners and learner groups to engage in the construction of alternative visions of development.

Many current efforts by the international development community as part of the Education for All movement are primarily geared towards extending the system "to the unreached" by expanding existing delivery mechanisms and improving the management and financing of these. Distance education, commonly defined as "an educational process in which a significant proportion of the teaching is conducted by someone removed in space and time from the learner", is gaining immense popularity among these modalities.

While distance education serves to provide an added element of flexibility, most efforts do not address the deeper problems that confront education systems as they have tended to be conceived of as extensions of the school. Such activities fail to confront the ideological contradictions and systemic conservativeness of schooling. Formal schooling, whether in person or at a distance, is an inappropriate solution by itself for dealing with the development challenges and opportunities of the future.

OPEN LEARNING COMMUNITIES

The term 'open learning communities' is presented here in order to deliberately challenge the reader to think of learning beyond the conventional school-teacher-textbook modalities — to facilitate a shift from a culture of schooling to a culture of learning. The term should be seen as a symbolic descriptor representing the dynamic convergence of several ideological vectors from around the world. What this convergence provides is a set of principles, experiences and commitments that not only serve to challenge some of the basic assumptions and goals around how education systems have been conceptualised and implemented in the modern world, but also start to form a legitimised space for constructing new alternatives.

The concept of open learning communities is motivated by three sets of inter-connected goals:

i) To assist individuals in engaging in diverse processes and contexts which allow them to develop their full human potential — as individual persons, as family members, as member of different communities, as part of humanity as well as at a spiritual level. This requires us to recognise the diversity of both individuals and communities, their particular needs and aspirations, and the different roles and capacities which people are required to play in diverse cultural settings.

ii) To assist each individual and community in participating in meaningful ways to the decision-making and management functions of society. This implies that people must be empowered to access various participation opportunities as well as to contribute to the creation of new participation opportunities: They must continually learn to play new roles in different settings. They must be empowered to read the world with various relational lenses.

iii) To assist individuals and communities in engaging in the processes of creatively, responsibly and non-violently constructing alternative paradigms for development that are consistent with the ideals of mutual respect, compassion, trust, fairness and sacrifice. Such alternative paradigms should envision the renewal of human relationships and the rebuilding of families and communities, the transformation of institutions, the fundamental redistribution of resources and reconceptualisation of power along more equitable and sustainable lines, and the creation of respect for all forms of life and our natural environment.

There is no such thing as a simple, replicable "open learning community" that provides all things to all learners. Rather, there should exist a multiplicity of diverse, layered, interconnected open learning communities. Each particular open learning community can be seen to evolve out of specific cultural and historical processes, out of a response to a specific set of local/global problems, and out of dynamic interactions with its environment, other open learning communities and the contributions of the individuals who choose to participate in it.

While there is no one pre-defined or pre-fabricated model of an open learning community, we can, however, begin to articulate some principles which contribute to envisioning open learning communities. To better explain the concept, the phrase will first be taken apart in order to lay out some of the key dimensions and implications of the terms "open", "learning", and "community."

Although this approach may appear to be a bit artificial or fragmentary, transforming the world of learning requires us to question and rethink the basic underpinnings of how we see the world in terms of problems and opportunities, how we engage in processes of learning, and how we interact with each other. The phrase will then be re-assembled and discussed as a dynamic whole. The vision of open learning communities is continually growing and evolving.

Concepts of 'Open'

The concept of 'open' is grounded in systems thinking — a discipline for seeing wholes. Frameworks and approaches linked to the term open seek to liberate us from mechanistic approaches, reductionist thinking, rigid hierarchical structures, linear processes, isolated modalities, and bivalent thinking. Several dimensions of the term 'open' merit further elaboration:

Open can be used to describe dynamic systems and the interplay between them. All things that evolve in the real world, be they physical, chemical, biological, ecological, or even social systems, are dynamic open entities that continually interchange energy, matter and information with their environment to stay alive. The boundaries are seen as semi-permeable rather than absolute. Flows occur horizontally among units as well as vertically between different layers. Open systems are thus vulnerable to change within their own structures and also have the potential to change other systems.

Open thinking involves being able to see underlying structures and inter-relationships rather than linear cause-effect chains. It is closely linked to the notion of deep ecology which sees the world not as a collection of isolated objects, but as a network of phenomena that are fundamentally interconnected and interdependent. Deep ecology recognises the intrinsic value of all living beings and views humans as just one particular strand in the web of life. Within this context, there is a change in emphasis from viewing entities and organisational relationships in terms of hierarchical modes towards promoting more heterarchical linkages, i.e., systems in which each element is equally ruled by others.

Open thinking involves the ability to shift analyses and reference points back and forth between different levels of systems and across systems. It involves being able to move between different contexts and across different disciplines of knowledge. It also entails being able to connect different contexts and disciplines into more holistic frameworks.

Open thinking involves seeing change in terms of processes rather than as isolated snapshots. Such processes often take place in dynamic non-linear and unpredictable ways. This implies that we be willing to view conceptions of time differently. Time is conventionally perceived as being monochromatic in which events and acts follow in a certain definite sequence. Polychronic conceptions of time are used to describe different phenomena occurring simultaneously. Time is not understood in a linear way but rather as a set of certain points of mutual reference.

Open thinking involves fuzziness — seeing the world in infinite shades of gray between black and white, not only in black in white terms. The fuzzy principle states that everything is a matter of degree. Fuzziness means multivalence i.e., three or more options, perhaps an infinite spectrum of options, instead of just two extremes.

The above mentioned points have many implications for how we currently see the world of learning. For example, they suggest that the artificial divisions of formal, non-formal and informal education have little relevance as categories in isolation of each other. It calls for us to recognise that we all live in "mediatised environments where education is simply one of many different cultural experiences". It asks that we think in multichannel terms — designing approaches based on our understanding of the multiple channels that support different types learning processes and that learners engage in within a particular environment. This also involves discovering new ways to link these individual channels together. Within this context, it is important to understand how information flows between channels and environments and seek to stimulate different flows of information.

Open thinking also questions the value of using nation-states and geo-political borders as the primary unit of analyses for discussing learning systems. It pushes us to see institutions and policies in terms of horisontally and vertically overlapping layers ranging from the local to global. In addition, the idea of open calls for the introduction of more flexibility by moving away from constrictive and debilitating linear levels/grades, divisions of education, and rigid time frames.

The notion of open questions the value of using bivalent categories to describe complex realities such as: educated and uneducated, literate and illiterate, enrolled and unenrolled, developed and developing, rich and poor, modern and traditional, and so on. It pushes us to think beyond using isolated categories of race, class, gender. It strongly challenges the use of development strategies that target specific groups in isolation of each other such as out-of school and unemployed youth, drop-outs, street children, marginalised women, the poorest of the poor, unreached, etc.

Open encourages us to think more holistically and moves away from highly compartmentalised and isolated disciplinary approaches towards more integrated frameworks. It encourages the building of linkages across sectors, for example, between learning, health, culture, politics and economics. It also requires that we acknowledge the validity of other knowledge systems. There is a heterarchical space for a plurality of voices.

The idea of open challenges us to look at our work in development and education in terms of dynamic, continuous processes rather than as discrete projects which will result in easily definable end-products. The international development community must come to recognise that the future can neither be predicted nor manufactured.

Concepts of 'Learning'

Learning has implications for how people search for, acquire, analyse, synthesise, use and share information and skills from a variety of media; how they perceive themselves, reflect on their condition and negotiate their identities; how they connect with others and their environments; how they seek to express themselves, grow, and develop their own capacities to continue to learn; and how they construct meaning and evolve their consciousness.

Because of its inherent "ephemeralness and unpredictability" and the diversity of contexts in and purposes for which it takes place, learning is extremely difficult to describe. Rather than attempt to provide an extensive overview of learning, this part will merely serve to highlight a few aspects of learning that are particularly relevant to the concept of open learning communities. There is a wide range of goals that exist for learning which are culturally, systemically and learner defined. A few goals which incorporate both individual and societal dimensions for why we learn are discussed. We learn both for survival and in order to give greater meaning to our lives.

The Delors Commission suggests the following broad set of goals: Learning to Know, Learning to Do, Learning to Live Together, Learning to Be. Imbedded in these is a long-term dimension of learning as well as a perspective that cuts across all domains of life i.e., the goals of learning are not limited to only succeeding in the economic or formal sectors.

These goals are also not seen as static and are given meaning through the interpretations of different communities and individuals which allows them to go beyond being words on a piece of paper. Within this context, there is an understanding that spaces must be provided for interacting around the goals of learning in a pluralistic and participatory manner, in which there is strong respect and value given to different belief systems, knowledge systems, cultural values, and languages. We can also see the goals of learning in terms of processes which provide for the varying cognitive, emotional, psycho-social, health and nutritional, moral/ethnical, cultural/artistic, technological, participation, ecological and spiritual needs of individuals and communities.

Within the framework of open learning communities, there is a conscious attempt to link understandings and lessons from the past and the present towards actively constructing the future. This implies creating contexts in which we are expected to make mistakes and in which we are encouraged to learn from our mistakes. This also involves a shift in emphasis from status quo-based approaches which have supported maintenance learning. Rather, there should be a concerted effort to promote innovative learning which prepares individuals and communities to deal with new situations through the integration, synthesis, and the broadening of horizons. Its meaning derives from dissonance among contexts. It leads to critical questioning of conventional assumptions behind traditional thoughts and actions, focussing on necessary changes.

Innovative learning advances our thinking by reconstructing wholes, not by fragmenting reality. Underlying the idea of innovative learning is the belief that learning involves interacting, meaning-making, reflecting and creating. In the context of open learning communities, learning is conceived of as a continuous, asynchronous lifelong process that individuals and communities engage in through a variety of experiences and interactions. Lifelong learning no longer refers simply to recurrent education or to a second chance for those who missed out in the first instance. Rather, it is a genuine lifelong endeavor, from the cradle to the grave.

The notion of learning challenges popular thinking which believes that learning is the prerogative and responsibility of the young. It argues that one is never too old to learn. Active learning can and does take place at all ages. The brain is remarkably plastic, constantly learning throughout the span of one's life.

The notion of learning to learn is essential if individuals and communities are to actively engage in the processes of discovering and creating the 'for what?' of learning. Advances in neuroscience tell us that there is no limit to growth and to the capacities of humans to learn more. Neurons continue to be capable of making new connections throughout life. Every human being can learn to be more intelligent. There are no longer categories of 'smart' and 'dumb' learners. All people can learn to become more effective, flexible and organised learners. What becomes important in this context is our ability to continually develop the capacities to tap into our potential. "The deeper meaning of learning to learn is associated with learners learning to extend and master their own capacities for learning".

Learning to learn also calls for extending the notion of literacy beyond its functional definition to include multicultural literacy, technological literacy, democratic literacy, ecological literacy, critical media literacy, and so on. Learning to learn is also linked to empowerment. Each person develops a concept of 'self-as-learner.'

Learning to learn involves developing oneself: to engage in critical reflection and creative thinking; to open up to other people's ideas, attitudes, and feelings; to become aware of and access learning resources through a variety of media; to recognise and question one's implicit assumptions; and to become less fearful of change.

Learning to learn is also closely associated with processes that encourage us to think about our learning. Metacognition is used to refer to an awareness of thought processes, and metamood is an awareness of one's own emotions. The term self-awareness reflects an ongoing attention to one's internal states.

Though we all have the same set of physical systems, we must begin to recognise and appreciate the diverse, complex, multifaceted nature of each human learner. Some of this difference is a consequence of our genetic endowment. Some of it is a consequence of differing experiences and differing environments. The diversity is expressed in terms of personality and interests, cultures and family background, differing talents and intelligences, learning styles, motivation levels, and special needs. Vast ranges in diversity are characterise what it means to be fully human. Several theories related to intelligence have emerged, for example, to support the notion of diverse learners and learning processes.

According to Gardner, there are at least seven different human intelligences that allow us to engage in learning in order to make sense of the world:

i) language;

ii) logical-mathematical analysis;

iii) spatial representation;

iv) musical thinking;

v) the use of the body to solve problems or to make things;

vi) an understanding of other individuals; and,

vii) an understanding of ourselves.

Robert Sternberg has put forth categories of componential intelligence, creative intelligence and practical intelligence. Perkins offers the neural, reflective, and experiential aspects of intelligence. Goleman raises the dimension of emotional intelligence which includes: "abilities such as being able to motivate oneself and persist in the face of frustrations; to control impulse and delay gratification; to regulate one's moods and keep distress from swamping the ability to think; to empathise and to hope."

Every human being has his or her own complex portfolio of intelligences. Learners' abilities to engage in learning are derived from these different intelligences which are called upon in different contexts. It should be clarified that the idea of a portfolio of intelligences is not fixed. Learning also involves processes for allowing us to continually develop, connect and enhance our different human intelligences.

Each individual learner has a set of preferred ways of taking in and processing information and expressing themselves as well as their own paces at which they do so. They also have their own preferred learning environments. Learning style researchers, for example, point out that individual differences exist such as the preference for learning alone or in groups, concretely or abstractly, through books, charts, computers, video, oral stories and debates, etc. At the same time, different senses, different mind/brain attributes and different media/channels influence how different learners process information, construct meaning and express themselves. Different multisensory interactions and modes of communication and expression allow us to see the world in different ways.

The challenge that emerges from this understanding of the diversity of learners is the need to both appreciate that learners are different and need choice, while ensuring that they are exposed to a multiplicity of contexts. Underlying this is the critical issue of motivation and support i.e., encouraging learners to take learning risks and assisting them when they 'fail'.

Addressing this issue in meaningful ways starts with attempting to value the knowledge, information, experiences, interests, needs, aspirations, and Active Learning Capacity that each individual learner comes to a learning process with. It also involves understanding and validating the sorts of natural learning processes that learners are involved in various aspects of their lives. Several other dimensions are important to note when seeking to create learning contexts which nurture learners. Approaches should support situated learning i.e., learning should be placed within a culture of needs and practices that gives the knowledge and skill being learned context, texture and motivation. This involves making concerted efforts to understand, promote and link to the various potential learning channels that learners interact with on a daily basis.

In addition, we should to support the creation of educational settings with thinking-centered learning, where students learn by thinking through what they are learning about. The processes of learning should be conceptualised as being inherently social. All learning involves socially organised activity. Continually learning together is critical to building social relationships, negotiating difference and resolving conflicts.

Approaches of collaborative learning and active participation are crucial in this process. Michael Schrage defines collaboration as an act of shared creation and/or shared discovery. In addition, it is important to support different groupings of learners e.g., multi-age, inter-generational, multi-cultural, cross-gender, cross-class/caste, cross-professions, etc. Within the context of open learning communities, the notion of an omnipotent and omniscient teacher as "expert" is strongly challenged. Classic roles around who is the teacher and who is the learner become mutated and enter into a perpetual state of flux.

Learning is closely linked to different ideological positions and has political, cultural and socioeconomic dimensions. The international development community, however, tends to discuss education as if it were something quite neutral. Very rarely, has this group been required to make explicit its ideological biases.

Inherent in the processes of learning is a deeper struggle over discourse and power. Discourses are not just about what can be said, and thought; but also about who can speak, when, where, and with what authority. We must therefore continually be aware of the various ideological implications of learning and seek to make explicit our positions and actions within these.

The learning that takes place in schools has been used to reproduce inequities of society or to exclude people from power. What the dominant educational philosophies want is to educate people to adapt to those social forms. Rather than critically interrogate them. Under a different philosophical orientation, however, learning can be seen as a set of processes to lead society. This is the case if learning is seen as processes of actively constructing knowledge rather than a mechanism for transmitting knowledge.

The processes of learning become a means for negotiating identity and redefining attitudes, challenging the dominant social order, and reconstructing power, roles and relationships, and reappropriating the social, political, cultural forces that shape the existence of individuals and communities. Authentic participation in learning leads to a freeing; it is an emancipatory experience, resulting in actual liberation.

Concepts of 'Communities'

Element of 'communities' is critical to consider as it constitutes the socio-cultural context for bringing individuals together to engage in shared meaningful experiences. Such interactions form the basis for learning and for our becoming more fully human. It should be noted that there is no single generic, homogenous, universal community; rather, numerous types of communities exist throughout the world. Although this may seem to be an obvious statement, the international development community's discourse often fails to reflect this understanding as we tend to use the term 'communities' to loosely refer to a widely divergent set of social groupings with different purposes, cultures, scales, etc.

Recognising the complexity and diversity of communities and their associated layers is important to supporting communities. There are alternative definitions of communities created for a variety of purposes, including those based on:

i) geographic affiliations such as a village, rural district or urban areas;
ii) ethnic, racial, linguistic and religious groupings;
iii) sex and age;
iv) common occupations, interests, or experiences;
v) a resistance to some outside force or threat;
vi) shared family concerns;
vii) a general shared philosophy.

Communities are formalised in the sense that they do have some structure, a set of rules and logic to them, and several dimensions of culture. They typically have several knowledge systems in parallel operation i.e., oral, public/private, male/female, religious, etc. and they are linked to different social, political, and economic institutions.

Communities, however, have different sizes and boundaries. They are open in varying degrees to different types of information and people. Throughout the course of their lives, each individual participates in many different kinds of communities, with varying roles and objectives. A particular community is an evolving space in which the community's own identity and culture and that of its members is continually being defined, challenged, negotiated, and recreated by both its members and by other communities.

Strong communities are important for learning, and learning constitutes an important process of building and linking communities. Communities provide a humanising setting for learning, which has been previously described as an inherently social activity. Communities provide an essential forum for making sense of the world, exploring and building natural historical and cultural ties, negotiating difference, drawing from and building moral and ethical frameworks, and creating development alternatives.

Learning is profoundly influenced by the nature of the social relationships within which people find themselves. Communities also provide the cultural specificity for situated learning. It is essential, however, that individuals be able to participate in different communities in order to develop different contextual frameworks. It is also important that efforts must be made to mediate and link the learning that takes place in different settings. In the context of open learning communities, a community must be a "safe" space where learners can explore, share and grow.

Complex learning is enhanced by challenge and inhibited by threat. The brain/mind learns optimally — it makes maximum connections — when appropriately challenged in an environment which encourages taking risks. Positive emotions such as trust, love, tenderness and humour can facilitate learning. However, the brain/mind "downshifts" under perceived threat. It then becomes less flexible, and reverts to primitive attitudes and procedures. Negative emotions such as hostility, anger, fear, and anxiety can downshift the brain. This implies that a community must be "personalised" rather than depersonalised i.e., looking at each learner as a special human being that belongs not numbers.

In recent times, there has been a great deal of romanticisation around the notion of traditional communities. In discussing communities, we must not overlook the harsh realities that sometimes exist in many communities such as, resistance to new ideas and problems of unequal power relationships around race, class, gender, sexual preference, caste, age, etc. Nor, should we ignore that communities are often formulated in exclusionary closed terms with membership being tightly controlled.

Within communities conflict is inevitable and what families and communities learn to do is manage the conflicts to arrive at some measure of agreement, or even to more fully understand what divides them. Healthy communities are premised on both the individual and organisation's ability to enter into dialogue and negotiate conflicts.

Learning is the process by which we begin to understand each other, to engage in different roles and relationships, to make sense of the conflicts around us, to see new opportunities for connection and create new identities. Learning is also about strengthening and evolving local knowledge systems and, at the same time, developing self-confidence in one's 'tradition, imagination, intellectual and organisations reserves.'

The continued growth of such local knowledge systems coupled with the construction of critical frameworks for viewing other knowledge systems underlie the levels of creativity and sustainability of people-led development movements. In addition, learning together helps to create the underpinnings of trust — a sense of mutuality, of reciprocal loyalty — between people.

Some communities have been created along more closed boundaries, other communities are sometimes hostile. By bringing in new energy and information and stimulating a process of dialogue, learning can be a force for opening up communities and facilitating meaningful gender-aware, inter-generational, and cross-cultural interactions within a community and across communities.

Concept of Open Learning Communities

The concept of open learning communities seeks to provide a dynamic alternative framework for seeing and acting in the world. Open learning communities represent a celebration of differences and a desire to construct pluralistic environments which promote and foster these differences. Many examples exist today of the wide range of social groupings that represent potential open learning communities, such as regional configurations, cities and villages; women's associations; youth clubs; workers' cooperatives or unions; corporations and their departments; academic circles; religious groups; extended families; television and radio audiences; and World Wide Web sites. Conventional schools, although currently not considered to operate as open learning communities, can potentially transform themselves into open learning communities.

The principle of self-organisation implies the continual spontaneous emergence of diverse new communities and, at the same time, collapse of other communities. Within this context, every open learning community is a learning organism with its own evolving consciousness. Viewed as a complex adaptive system, the open learning community is constantly revising and rearranging its building blocks as it gains experience. It changes and adapt according to the divergent needs and interests of individual learners who participate and contribute to it as well as in response to the broader needs of society. To do this, flexibility, maneuverability and adaptability are important characteristics. This implies that the scale/size of the open learning community becomes critical. Massive systems characterised by rigid hierarchies, rules, structures are ill-equipped to manage change, and even less able to support innovation. In this context, the "small is beautiful" concept takes on a whole new meaning.

Feedback loops enable a community to regulate itself, correct its mistakes, and reorganise itself. Such feedback loops are integrally linked to a process of being able to listen to voices from within and outside, to learn from them, and to allow the energies inherent in them to facilitate the process of social innovation and transformation. An open learning community is not only capable of adapting or even embracing change, it can generate change from within and can share this change with other open learning communities and their larger environment. In this sense, it is not simply a reactionary entity but rather a pro-active agent of change. It is important that open learning communities not be viewed as isolated parts. Rather, they should be seen as a set of relationships operating within a larger learning ecosystem.

A learning ecosystem is comprised of a larger physical environment and layers of environments, various open learning communities and their layers, and individual learners who enter into the environment. Within this context, open learning communities, vertically and horisontally layered upon one another, function as networks within networks. An important aspect of the learning ecosystem is that it optimally uses and distributes the intellectual, experiential, spiritual, and material resources available to it. Another important aspect of the learning ecosystem is biodiversity, both in terms of different forms of life and in terms of cultural and linguistic diversity.

A diverse community is a resilient community, capable of adapting to changing situations. Diversity allows learners and communities to see their problems from varied perspectives and encourages them to develop different ways of dealing with them. A particular physical environment is comprised of a set of open learning communities which loosely operate within it. However, because of the various layers that exist , a space can simultaneously be both an environment which is comprised of its own associated layers of communities and an open learning community.

The institution of UNESCO, for example, is both an open learning community which operates within a larger set of environments, and an environment which supports multiple open learning communities. Each environment has its own architecture and space, information and communication technologies, values, constructs of time, policies and rules, structures, roles, relationships, resources, distribution of power, etc. These are not necessarily the same as those of the open learning communities which they support and sometimes may even contradict them.

The environment plays a large role in influencing the organisation and culture of a particular open learning community and its relationship with other open learning communities while, at the same time, the environment is being influenced by the open learning communities. There is a dialectical set of relationships in place. The environment is also critical to supporting the notion of distributed intelligence. Open learning communities within the same environment also influence and are influenced by each other. The flows of resources, information and energy form the basis for these relationships.

Open learning communities are influenced by the individuals who choose to participate in them. Learners are viewed as active constructors of the various open learning communities. Within this framework, individuals are able to participate freely in many different open learning communities, moving in and out as they wish. Notions of membership are loosely defined. In the context of their participation in different learning communities, individuals are given the opportunity to play different leadership roles and engage in different sorts of relationships. These roles and relationships are continually evolving.

Open learning communities also serve as institutions of reflection for individuals by continually demanding that people critically reflect on their values, attitudes, feelings, behaviours and actions and by encouraging them to engage in creative dialogue and action.

The basic thrust of open learning communities lies in utilising much of what we already know about learning through research and experience, seeing new realities and opportunities, developing new roles and relationships, respecting and fostering diversity, and stimulating new activities in order to give space and life to various socio-spiritual spaces.

The implications surrounding the development of open learning communities are, however, immense and overwhelming. They will require that whole new methodologies and frameworks be constructed, new discourses be created, new organisational structures be conceived, new approaches to 'training' be developed, new mechanisms for assessment and evaluation be formulated, and new attitudes be nurtured.

Throughout all of this, what will be most important to continually emphasise will be the process of engaging with people around the world to visualise and operationalise their own personal vision and linking this to a complex shared visions of open learning communities.

The process of developing the vision of open learning communities is critical if it is to mean more than words on a piece of paper or slogans of good intention. The process should reflect the idea of ongoing participatory conceptualisation i.e., that individuals and communities should not only be responsible for designing, implementing and evaluating open learning communities, but also be integrally involved in a continual process of conceptualising and modifying the vision that guides them.

Each individual and community must seek to understand the ideological and practical implications for themselves and for others, as well as for the present and for the future. Such a process entails a fundamental shift in metaphor — from that of a book which is written and disseminated by the well-schooled elite to that of an interactive World Wide Web site that is constructed through more participatory and egalitarian methods.

The focus of the shift, to clarify, is not on the medium; but rather, on the sets of attitudes, processes and relationships that surround the medium. Botkin et al. describe the traditional metaphor of the book, The conventional, often unarticulated, conception of how societies learn usually starts with one or more centres of concentrated competence as the emanaters of new discoveries, theories, beliefs and solutions. These new ideas are then disseminated to larger circles of people and the public at large.

The role of society at large is reduced to adjusting to and consuming the discoveries and knowledge produced at centres of expertise. The production of books tends to be linked to elite power structures and centres of concentrated competence. The publishing and distribution channels for books are also tightly controlled. For example, the writing of books is usually done by someone regarded as an 'expert.' Knowledge tends to be seen as fixed and sacred, often regarded as a commodity. With the metaphor of book, the emphasis is on 'dissemination' and 'distribution' whereby readers are typically viewed as passive receivers. The book also, in certain ways, limits our interaction around the ideas that are raised; keeping a safe distance between the writer and the reader. The structure of the book is typically structured in a linear progression, and must be read in this way. There is very little flexibility for the book to evolve. As we read the book, we can scribble on the margins and underline the words but cannot fundamentally contribute to altering the meaning of the text. Nor, can we engage with the author around the ideas — the author is allowed to hide behind the medium. We are prevented from entering into constructive dialogue in order to learn from as well as to challenge and influence the author. Out of frustration or anger, individuals may refuse to read books and sometimes try to burn them, but these destructive forms of resistance come with great individual and societal pricetags.

In place of the metaphor of the book, let us propose the metaphor of a Web site that is continually under construction. This Internet has been described as a 'great democratising force'; a liberating and empowering tool. Under the metaphor of the Web site, there is a concerted effort to move from approaches of one-way dissemination to two-way sharing. Such a metaphoɪ is geared around encouraging us to see ourselves as actively constructing and unfolding our own vision of open learning communities, and linking it to the visions of others. Knowledge is seen as dynamic and evolving.

The construction of the Web site constitutes a profound shared social experience — seen as something that the various participants build together. Furthermore, power over the process is transformed. Each one of us can contribute to and modify the vision of the site with text, pictures, sounds, videos; we can interact with each other around ideas; we can hyperlink our sites to other Web sites; we can even create our own sites. We should, however, be very aware that the medium of the Internet is not exempt from attempts at social control.

Construction of open learning community Web sites calls for a special set of attitudes and commitment. It will require that one be willing to move beyond fixing, defending, rationalising or thinking solely in terms of the institution of schooling. It will mean exploring how to link learning back to the deeper social, political and spiritual problems that face our world. It will require a commitment to enter into the often confusing and frustrating struggle of asking some basic philosophical questions — who are we as human beings, where are we coming from, and where are we going to. It will involve optimistic risk-taking — "a willingness to initiate fundamental processes of change, even when all of their implications are not known with total certainty in advance". It will ask that we reconsider our own privileged positions and the power structures to which we derive our authority from. It will require that we be open to experimenting with new ways of sharing and redistributing power.

There are the vested interests of the educational establishment with its teachers' unions and textbook publishers and building contractors. There are the vested interests of the nation-state and resistance of politicians who are unwilling to make decisions which might jeopardise their political power. There are also the vested interests of the development industry which continue to see certain countries and groups as 'developed' and delinked from the problems of the South, and are fundamentally unwilling to challenge this deficit approach. Finally, there is the loosely aligned vested interests of modernity which rely heavily on the institution of schooling to reproduce its ideological frames of reference and socioeconomic relationships.

These various interest groups threaten to crush the concept of open learning communities. The world is a dynamic place where new discoveries are continuously being made, new institutions and relationships being formed, new opportunities are emerging. The edge of chaos is where new ideas and innovative genotypes are forever nibbling away at the edges of the status quo, and where even the most entrenched old guard will eventually be overthrown. Our challenge is then to identify and nurture those opportunities at the edges of chaos and to prevent their being co-opted by the various vested interests.

The Learning Without Fronties (LWF) unit, housed in UNESCO, is attempting to partner with others from around the world who are involved in developing different visions of how to change the world of learning. The LWF unit is also engaged in a perpetual struggle of trying to define and redefine itself and its environment as open learning communities.

Interestingly, LWF activities have far focused on areas which have tended to be regarded more at the fringe of conventional education systems e.g., certain forms of distance education, community schools, in-service teacher training, special needs education, and early childhood development.

There has been greater flexibility in introducing and developing innovative approaches related to open learning communities in these domains. LWF has also become heavily involved in activities centered around various information and communications technologies (ICTs) e.g., interactive radio and television, computers, and the Internet. These ICTs have considerable institutional and operational potential in shaking up rigid bureaucracies and changing organisational behaviour, introducing spaces for raising questions and supporting dialogue, assisting people in seeing new realities, and transforming thinking and practice around learning.

Policy Considerations

Policies can shape agendas, remove as well as create opportunities and barriers, legitimise or de-legitimise institutions, and define courses of action which will affect large numbers of people. They are powerful mechanisms for facilitating, sustaining and preventing broad-based change. However, educational policy making efforts over the last 40 years have been largely ineffective throughout the world. There exists today a profound crisis of legitimacy in the realm of educational policy making. This does not stem from not being able to get the policies "right" or weak implementation capacity, but rather, from a deeper struggle over discourse and power.

Constructed within the context of modern democratic systems and nation-state structures, educational policy making is subject to the larger problems, i.e. the breakdown of social contracts and relationships and partisan politics, that confront these institutions. Most people around the world do not feel that they can influence or shape policies at any level of society, particularly at the national, international and supranational levels. Leaders often appear to be guided by personal interests rather than broader public interests.

Just as the concept of open learning communities challenges us to think about learning and learning systems differently, it also calls for us to engage in thinking about educational policy making differently — to question dominant discourses and power in meaningful ways. Simply enacting policies on open learning communities using conventional assumptions, frameworks, processes, institutions, language, and relationships will not be a sufficient strategy for enabling or sustaining open learning communities.

The development of each open learning community is seen as being simultaneously influenced and defined by both its larger environment, its interaction with other learning communities, and by the learners who participate in it. Driven primarily by external political and financial considerations, the content and scope of education policies contradict much of what we know about the diversity of learning needs, learning styles and processes, and learner backgrounds.

While educators have always noted differences among learners, they have been strongly inclined to believe that all students can learn in similar ways . The bulk of educational policies in place today tend to narrowly focus on the institution of schooling and are still driven by notions of human capital formation, transmission-based processes, and mainstreaming learners into rigid tracking systems.

There is a strong need to re-focus educational policies to reflect new ideas about learners, learning processes, and learning systems. Educational policies fail to recognise the powerful, informal dynamic learning environments that exist and are continually emerging, largely because of the spread of various information and communication technologies, and the growth of informal networks.

Educational institutions which used to have control over knowledge and over its dissemination now find themselves in mediatised environments where education is simply one of many different cultural experiences. Most ministries of education have failed to make clear policies in relation to various media such as newspapers, radio, television, and the Internet. In addition, traditionally grounded in the primacy of the nation-state, current educational policies fail to reflect the dual forces of globalisation and localisation which are sweeping across the world. This implies that learning communities are potentially much larger than boundaries of the nation state and at the same time are much smaller than these boundaries.

However, several implications for future policy directions begin to emerge. Two important priorities for widening the scope and content of educational policies include:

i) recognising the diversity of learners and that learning processes must take place at both individual and organisational levels, and

ii) seeing learning as taking place within mediatised environments.

A heuristic framework comprised of three sets of policy objectives that advance these priorities is proposed below. This framework attempts to incorporate several elements through which learning is mediated — language, technology and tools, values, human relationships, and information and images. It is shaped by belief that rigid distinctions between formal, non-formal and informal learning experiences are becoming increasingly irrelevant.

The framework deliberately does not assign responsibilities to any specific institution as it tries to flexibly allow for the multiple roles that any institution must play e.g., a distance learning organisation may simultaneously serve as an environment supporting several different learning communities, as an open learning community, and as an actor within a wider learning community. The exact scope and content of a particular policy framework vary according to the specific situation.

i) *Encouraging more winds to blow and building hallways, sidewalks, and bridges*

   a) Promote greater diversity of learning communities. Policies, for example, are being developed to accommodate the home schooling movement in the United States. In many Islamic countries, policies have been developed to promote madrasas as learning spaces;

   b) Create more flexible connections and pluralistic interactions between learning communities;

   c) Remove geo-political and spatial boundaries between learning communities.

d) Promote and value learning for a broad range of life activities;

e) Encourage respect for diverse knowledge systems and languages.

f) Develop literate environments. In this respect, the notion of literacy should be interpreted quite broadly beyond its typical functional definitions. Policies should seek not only to stimulate the provision and use of reading and writing materials e.g., through libraries and local newspapers, but also to facilitate the development of environments which encourage demand for music, art, sports, nature, etc. The environment is also critical to the idea of distributed intelligence.

g) Stimulate the development and use of technologies for learning purposes. This would involve policies for accessing technologies for learning purposes such as subsidies and tax exemptions for hardware, lower telecommunication tariffs, and free/reduced-rate satellite broadcasting time.

h) Facilitate the responsible sharing of information, ideas and experiences, between learning communities. The free flow of information will require that existing policies related to copyright laws and intellectual property rights be reviewed. Policies should also be developed which dis-incentivise the spread of or warn of potentially socially harmful information, i.e. pornography, violence, drugs.

i) Develop distributed networks rather than central source providers. Policies which support standards for open architecture and connectivity to distributed resources should be developed;

j) Create new spaces for experimentation and systemic learning.

ii) *Opening more windows, creating additional rooms, unlocking doors*

a) Develop the learning community into an inclusive entity. In the Phillippines, as part of a movement towards inclusive education, efforts are being made to link special education and regular schools more closely. Blended classrooms are being encouraged which mix learners with special educational needs to non-impaired students;

b) Increase the permeability of the boundaries of the learning community;

c) Create continuous and flexible opportunities for learning any time and anywhere. In many communities linked to farming activities, policies have been instituted to allow for flexible scheduling of the school calendar year in accordance with crops;

d) Removal of formal requirements to access learning communities;

e) Build multichannel learning modalities;

f) Regulate the selection and availability of instructional resources.

g) Enhance the social dynamics within a learning community by developing an atmosphere of trust and cooperation;

h) Support collaborative and interactive learning across generational groups;

i) Remove discriminatory biases related to race, ethnicity, gender, class, sexual orientation or age, that limit access to certain learning communities;

j) Support the construction of local knowledge and the evolution of local knowledge systems;

k) Encourage the institution to engage in organisational learning.

iii) *Distributing drafting tools, hammers, chisels, paintbrushes*

a) Encourage learners to be actively involved in building the learning community;

b) Support the diverse needs of learners, their individual learning styles and their ability to access and create different learning communities. Many interesting policies are being developed in the field of Special Needs' Education that recognise the continuum of learners with differing needs and abilities;

c) Validate different types of learning and learning experiences. In some countries, policies are being developed to support the recognition of prior learning methodology which accredits learners for knowledge and skills that they might have acquired through informal means;

d) Reduce barriers of age and circumstance (social/ cultural conditions, financial constraints, individual constraints (psychological/physical)).;

e) Assist learners in developing positive attitudes and feelings of motivation toward learning. This would involve developing policies which provide health, nutritional and psycho-social support to learners. It would also involve creating culturally-appropriate counselling services;

f) Encourage learners to develop their own learning projects and to build their own learning communities.

Policymaking

The policymaking process is about human and institutional relationships, self-interests, power, money, information, and survival, and for these reasons, it is fundamentally political and it is always changing. The process of educational policy making is extremely complex, filled with contradictions and uncertainties, and influenced by many dynamic and powerful forces.

Traditional assumptions underlying educational policy formation have failed to reflect this. Policy making was viewed as taking place within a closed system. It was believed that the process could be controlled and predicted using mechanistic procedures and centralised institutions. It was also assumed that policies could be standardised and transferred along a wide spectrum of beneficiary groups, disregarding the fact that people differ from one another and their circumstances also differ.

There was little attempt to understand the political economy of a situation. This resulted in a linear model of policy formation that was based on an input-process-output-outcome policy cycle. Such "stages" models have since been critiqued. Porter argues that "we should not assume that policy making is a highly coherent and rational process, with a beginning, a middle, and an end — that each part leads logically and inexorably to each succeeding part." According to DAE , policy making is a messy, fluid process which cannot be reduced to a simple linear mode. Crouch et al. describe one incarnation of this messy process: "Policy change usually takes place in a crisis mode. Policy itself is often nothing but the accretion of responses to past crises and half-hearted attempts to implement donor recommendations, operationalise vague ideological concepts from other sectors, or copy reforms from other countries." Under such conditions, Crouch et al. see policymaking more as a negotiation/bargaining process which takes place in the setting of a policy marketplace. It is comprised of diverse, competing groups, each trying to preserve and further their own vested interests i.e., state-affiliated bureaucracies, certain industries, political parties, teachers' unions, international donors. Porter attempts to capture the processes with a multiple streams model. "There are three process streams through which participants affect agendas. People recognise problems, generate proposals for policy change, and engage in such political activities as pressure group lobbying and election campaigns." The separate streams of problems, policies, and politics each have lives of their own and are developed according to the rationale of the institutions to which they are linked. Solutions, problems, ideas, people and choices are all mixed together. Alliances, preferences and perceptions of policy actors are continually changing.

We must move away from models that view policies in terms of top-down governmental declarations that are "officialised" in documents such as reports of special national commissions; the country's educational plan; the Ministry of Education Acts, Orders or Circulars; and reports of international agencies. Change should no longer be viewed solely as being centrally stimulated. We should see multiple policy processes in operation at institutional levels ranging from individual learning communities to local, district, regional, national, international, supranational groupings.

Rather than being forced to adopt policy blueprints, each of these institutional formations should be encouraged to initiate and develop their own policies on learning. This requires a different framework for thinking about who are policy makers, what their roles are, and what their area of jurisdiction is. The role of educational policymaking should no longer be the sole domain of sectoral ministries. Institutions concerned with supporting learning, whether they be schools, NGOs, media groups, distance learning providers, etc. must increasingly see themselves as important policymaking entities. Policy processes must be continually concerned with creating spaces for allowing alternative voices to be heard.

Policy formulation and implementation should not be viewed as discrete activities but rather as a continuous learning and experimentation effort. Rather than looking at policies from a fixed-state point of view, we may wish to conceive of a system of rolling policies which are continually monitored, reflected upon, discussed and appropriately modified as time progresses. Policy processes must play a dual role of implementing a vision as well as continually creating the vision. Underlying this policy learning system should be a strong emphasis on active, ongoing policy learning by organisational entities at different levels, including the citisenry at large, who are involved in the process. Such a system should be supported by data, analysis and dialogue. To make this exercise meaningful, however, would imply some dramatic changes in these tools. Data on learning would have to move beyond simply looking at the formal sector.

If policy makers really want to understand what is going on in a learning system, they will need not only a comprehensive system of indicators but a full research portfolio which is capable of looking at mediatised environments, information networks and the diversity of learners and learning processes. Analytical tools must also be reworked to take into account more dynamic multidisciplinary relationships and to discourage the tendency to settle for first-order solutions. These should be geared towards continually raising difficult questions rather than providing quick-fix answers. Institutions that wish to become involved in policy and decisionmaking processes should also become involved in data collection and analysis activities, rather than having this work done for them by others.

Participation must go beyond mere invitations to accept given solutions or ingenious attempts to capture goodwill and support for given products. Participation is not simply about expanding the range of stakeholders; rather, it should be geared around encouraging participatory conceptualisation. To encourage innovative societal learning, true participation must enable people to open and inspect the 'black boxes' of knowledge, to question their relevance and meaning, and to re-design, re-combine, and re-order them where necessary. Those involved in policy discussions must be encouraged to frame their own questions. Dialogue should also be seen as ongoing, not only as a one-time process. Media should be used to encourage this continual reflection and debate, and not just to transmit top-down declarations in mindless sound bites.

Policy development is a continuous process that should not be circumscribed by artificial political or operational time frames or fiscal years. Part of the challenge is also identifying the right timing for catalysing policy change processes. This may require the development of special policies that support an ongoing process of identifying opportunities.

We need policies that continually allow us to find out that change is needed. He says that we need policies that allow us to bend existing rules. There is also need for temporary authority structures that allow us to experiment and modify what we are doing. Such structures should be comprised as intersectoral work teams. Organisational learning also requires a different framework of incentives. In order to seize opportunities and learn, we often have to take risks, make errors, and correct them. Few organisations currently reward those who take risks and make mistakes.

It is also important to encourage the continuity of actors who are involved. Effective dialogue is premised on trust, understanding and a willingness to compromise, which can only happen when actors know each other. Continuity is also particularly important for building up an institutional memory. Many things go unwritten or are understood in the policy formation process.

Opening up the policy process fundamentally involves redistributing and sharing power, which is itself a messy process and will make many people uncomfortable. In addition, supporting a good process is expensive and will require significant budgetary shifts. However, if learning and social justice is a priority for humanity, then we must push strongly for spending more than 4% of the global government budget on learning. We can also expect significant resistance from people who continue to focus on yesterday's solutions and are unwilling to look towards the future. Under such resistance, facilitating a shift in policy direction will require a new type of commitment from all of us.

Establishing policies and programmes to enhance innovative learning are dependent on at least one premise: a willingness to initiate fundamental processes of change, even when all of their implications are not known with total certainty in advance". This requires that we are willing to question our own privileged roles as "experts" and "authorities." It also means that we must see ourselves as learners - building a vision, not simply implementing one.

Many positive experiences have taken place with new opportunities emerging every day. Many changes are already dynamically taking place. Our task must then start with continually linking these experiences into a coherent vision and building a critical mass of partners around the world. We must also focus on developing more robust frameworks and methodologies that both integrate our understanding about learners and learning processes and complex systems, and allow us to continually "see" new realities.

REFERENCES

Botkin, J., et al., *No Limits to Learning: Bridging the Human Gap*, Club of Rome, Oxford: Pergamon Press, 1979.

Bouton, D., "Learning to Learn", *New Horizons for Learning Newsletter*, XIII(2), Winter, 1992.

Burnett, R., "Networks of knowledge/networks of learning", *UNESCO Learning Without Frontiers (LWF) Advisory Task Force Meeting, held at UNESCO*, Paris, 25-26, November 1996.

Candy, P., "How People Learn to Learn", in: R. Smith (ed.), *Learning to Learn Across the Lifespan*, San Francisco: Jossey-Bass, 1990.

DAE, Association for Development of African Education, Formulating education policy: Lessons and experiences from sub-Saharan Africa. Six case studies and reflections from the DAE biennial meeting held in Tours, France, in October 1995. Paris, France: Association for the Development of African Education, c/o UNESCO (IIEP), 1996.

Delors, Jacques, *Learning: The Treasure Within*, UNESCO Commission for the 21st Century, Paris: UNESCO, 1996.

Gardner, H., *The Unschooled Mind*, New York, Basic Books, 1991.

Land, S., M. Hannafin, "A conceptual framework for the development of theories in action with open-ended learning environments", *Educational Technology Research and Development*, 44 (3), 1996.

Longworth, Norman, "Creating and Building Learning Communities", *European Lifelong Learning Initiative*, Eus, France, 1996.

Naik, J.P., *Equality, Quality, Quantity: The Elusive Triangle in Indian Education*, New Delhi: Allied Publishers, 1975.

Perkins, David, *Smart Schools: Better Thinking and Learning for Every Child*, New York, The Free Press, 1992.

Postman, N., *The End of Education: Redefining the Value of Schools*, New York: Alfred A. Knopf, 1986.

Psacharopolous, G., "Why educational policies fail", *World Bank Discussion Paper*, Washington, DC: The World Bank, 1990.

Visser J. and M. Jain, "Towards Open Learning Communities: Recontextualizing Teachers and Learners", *Learning Without Frontiers Unit*, UN, 1996.

3

Learning Without Frontiers

We live in a world of change. Individuals and societal entities are in constant need to adapt to change. While they do so, they generate change themselves. Learning is not only an essential requirement to allow people and groups of people to adapt to change, it is at the same time the most effective mechanism to ensure that change is being generated in a way that takes into account the ecological dimensions of its impact on others. Change occurs at a pace which has brought an essential dimension of unpredictability in the lives of people. It has become impossible to foresee one's life and thus to plan one's education accordingly, as if it were part of a linear sequence of events.

Adaptation to change can no longer be managed as a generational process — it has become intra-generational. Most of the existing educational establishment is out of tune with this reality. The notion of learning as an essential condition of growth of complex adaptive systems is currently perhaps best exemplified by the learning organisations. Survival, gaining and retaining competitiveness, are obviously much more immediately felt urgencies in the business environment than in the traditional closed school environment and its supporting institutions. It is there that one sees complex adaptive systems in action at a scale that may generate interesting models for the reconceptualisation of learning environments in general and the diffusion of organisational learning beyond profit making institutions. This should lead us to think of learning communities — rather than just learning individuals — as crucial elements in the conception of facilitating environments for learning.

Most schools, and for that matter also the traditional distance education institutions, are not learning communities. They are simply closed organised structures designed to turn uneducated individuals into educated ones. They do themselves, as social entities, not learn and are not designed to do so. Learning communities interact and are in dynamic equilibrium with their environment, i.e., with other learning communities. They are not fixed. Individuals may be part of different learning communities depending on context and circumstance.

The main conception underlying education continues to be that learning is something one does once in a lifetime and that it is essentially undertaken in preparation for the rest of one's life. It is thus best done during the early stages of one's life. For those who, for whatever reason, missed the boat, there are second chance opportunities, often via the distance education mode. Whatever is done in addition to this boils down to learning every now and then in the course of one's life in response to specific needs to maintain or upgrade professional skills or to adapt to new demands of the work environment.

There is no strong notion of lifelong and lifewide learning as an essential ingredient of life itself, as something which is more than, for example, a simple means to acquire a particular skill or to become familiar with a specific area of knowledge. To respond to the dual challenge to on the one hand overcome the failures of the past and on the other to be responsive to the demands of the future, the world needs to move beyond fixed modality delivery options based on the teaching-learning dichotomy. It needs to put learning and the learners at the centre of its concerns. It needs to break through the barrier of looking at learning as the consequence of something that is being done to people instead of something that is done by and with people.

Learning leads to empowerment, but it will do so only if the learning process itself is premised on the notion of the empowered learner. The learning-through-delivery-of-teaching model, whether face-to-face or at a distance, is contrary to that notion. Until a couple of decades ago, learning in preparation for the rest of one's life was still generally a valid option. School systems provided the main mechanisms to put that option into practice. A ministry of education could claim it had things under control if an adequate school system existed and people pertaining to the various socioeconomic strata of the population felt they had access to that school system according to their aspirations and needs. People could be reasonably sure that, after completing their education, they were well prepared for the rest of their life. The time to learn was over, and real life could begin. This, however, is no longer the case. In today's world, and that of tomorrow, the notion of learning to earn a living, and even that of learning for life, is no longer a valid one

Referring to education as a major bulwark of conservatism has become a mere cliche. No wonder that any alternative to the mainstream modality of educational provision, the teacher-classroom-textbook modality, had to fight a hard battle to achieve even a minimum of recognition. Against this background, it is to the credit of distance education that it has been increasingly successful in positioning itself as a valid alternative.

The term 'distance education' is now often associated with that of open learning. Open and distance learning is thus frequently used as a single concept, suggesting that distance learning is by necessity an open process and that open learning is mainly accomplished in the distance education mode.

The use of terms such as 'open university' and 'open school' adds to the confusion. The dimension of openness of such institutions is often limited. In addition, both 'open learning' and 'distance education' are frequently presented in contrast to and as separate from so-called conventional or traditional education. Distance education has as such little to do with the notion of openness as it appears in the concept 'open learning community'. Systems that use it as a modality can be equally traditional as and no more open than many conventional systems, based on the face-to-face mode.

Open learning communities, are themselves the result of a constructivist learning process, involving a variety of partners whose roles can best no longer be dichotomised as either those of learner or teacher. The process of their construction is helped along by the existence of a facilitating open learning environment which contains the essential ingredients and building blocks that learning communities will want to make use of. It is such environments that we must build. To establish its validity, however, distance education had to model itself on the same ideological underpinnings that also condition mainstream educational provision and show that it was equally or more effective or at least nearly as good.

Thus it should be no big surprise that the probably best known definition of distance education as "an educational process in which a significant proportion of the teaching is conducted by someone removed in space and time from the learner" is based on the same assumption that underlies the mainstream educational process, i.e. that a main condition for learning is that there is someone who teaches.

Moore G. M. and Kearsley G., advance the following more elaborate definition of distance education: "Distance education is planned learning that normally occurs in a different place from teaching and as a result requires special techniques of course design, special instructional techniques, special methods of communication by electronic and other technology, as well as special organisational and administrative arrangements." While this definition clearly puts the emphasis on learning and while it does not explicitly refer to a person who teaches, it is no less based on the notion that teaching is a necessary condition for learning to take place. For this very reason, the two authors express a clear preference for the term 'distance education' over that of 'distance learning'.

In building up propitious environments that are conducive to the generation of open learning one faces a dilemma. There is important existing infrastructure and practice that one would like to build on. However, part of that same infrastructure and practice reflects much of what is in urgent need to be changed whereas another important part of it has hardly received recognition as belonging to the learning environment.

It is perhaps in the first place necessary to consider the broadness, complexity and unpredictability of learning. At the theoretical/conceptual level, J. G. Greeno, A. Collins and L. Resnick note the complementarity of views on the nature of knowing, the nature of learning and transfer, and the nature of motivation and engagement offered by the behaviourist/ empiricist, the cognitive/rationalist and the situative/ pragmatist-sociohistoric perspectives. However different these perspectives, all three traditions emphasise the importance of organised patterns in cognitive activity.

A. Bandura's social learning theory stresses the observational nature of learning and thus the role of modelling of desirable and undesirable behaviours, an issue that has much relevance if one recognises how much learning occurs almost 'incidentally', by being part of the community and media context. The case for real-world based learning is made by authors such as Resnick, Collins, and Jonassen, Mayes and McAleese. Other authors have raised awareness about the thinness of learning processes that are mainly based on the recognition of but a small slice of a wide spectrum of intelligences. Yet others note the limitations inherent in the prevailing view that cognitive and meta-cognitive development terminate in early adulthood, an assumption which urgently needs to be reviewed in the light of research on life-span development. D. G. Perrin refers to the non-traditional learner as the biggest untapped market for education.

Most of what goes on in the educational establishment favours learners with a directive learning style and encourages the development of teachers and teaching styles that are effective for such learners. Yet others, like R. Burnett refer to the ephemeral and unpredictable nature of learning. However much we plan, or forget to plan, in the final analysis it is the learner who decides to derive from the learning environment what suits her or him best. In exploring to move from where we are to where we want to get, by moving away from an environment that was constructed out of a concern to deliver effectively fixed-modality instructional options to one that is oriented towards the demands of a multiplicity of learners and their varied range of goals and circumstances, one needs to have an open eye for opportunities.

TOWARD OPEN LEARNING

The spread of information and communication technology is helping many of us envision the practical potential and possibly inevitable proliferation of open learning environments to address all kinds of learning needs in all parts of the world. UNESCO's *Learning Without Frontiers* programme provides a perspective of collaboration to respond to the educational challenges of the global village in its present manifestation of social inequity. One of the key features of this perspective is the development of more open environments for learning.

There is a visionary quality to the idea of open learning environments as something qualitatively different from schools and training institutions as we now know them. Although the proliferation of opportunities for open learning will accelerate in the years ahead, they will not replace schools, particularly for children and adolescents and most certainly not in developing countries. The frontiers of the school wall provide security for the young and peace of mind for their parents. Schools provide important socialisation functions. Developing countries have invested heavily in the universalisation of primary schools, and there is good evidence that attending school has many social and private benefits — especially for girls.

However imperfect schools are as environments for learning, they will be with us long into the future. We believe that primary and secondary schools in developing countries can be assisted to provide more open learning environments. We believe that "openness" can be achieved in a kind of four-dimensional framework. These dimensions are not distinct categories, and development activities may be located in one or more dimensions at the same time. The four dimensions are as follows:

i) opening the environment to improve educational quality;
ii) opening the environment to enhance access/equity;
iii) opening the environment to expand the range of resources for learning;
iv) opening the environment to provide stronger learner control and linkages for learning.

Opening the environment to improve educational quality: Learning environments are typically ones where teachers and students are locked into interactions that are not conducive to effective learning. The dynamics of the teaching-learning process are marked by strategies that view students as passive recipients of poorly organised and de-contextualised pieces of curricular information.

Educational objectives, to the extent they are explicit, tend to call for getting students to memorise this information, and the road to memorisation is having students pronounce correctly, repeat, or copy the information given. It is infrequent to find students being asked to interpret information, to think critically or creatively, to predict or elaborate, to solve a problem, or to engage in any number of activities to assist students in making meaning of the information before them. The orienting stimuli in the instructional process are usually boring and devoid of relevance to the lives of students. As a result, there is little engagement in the learning process.

One of the most successful approaches to improving educational quality in the face of conditions encountered in schools in developing countries is that of Interactive Radio Instruction (IRI). IRI is a methodology that has evolved through twenty years of experience in more than a dozen countries. It differs significantly from other forms of radio instruction because:

ii) radio plays a primary rather than supplementary instructional role and

ii) lessons are designed to follow proven principles of learning, are subjected to systematic formative evaluation, and are developed to engage learners in active learning.

Interactive radio instruction audio programmes are delivered by radio or cassettes with accompanying printed materials. Interactive radio instruction has shown that it consistently and significantly influences learners' performance in a variety of educational subjects. It was first developed in the early seventies by the Nicaraguan Radio Mathematics project.

During the past twenty years, interactive radio instruction has been used to teach mathematics, language, science, health, environmental studies, civic education, child development, and adult basic education. Interactive radio lessons to teach English developed recently in the Republic of South Africa are now being broadcast nationally, and efforts are underway to use IRI to teach mathematics in that country.

Opening the environment to enhance access/equity: Too often, various factors impinge on a young person's chances to attend school. Especially affected are those who must work for a living, persons living in remote or underpopulated communities, girls, and various ethnic groups. It is often the case that distances to schools are too long, the school schedule is incompatible with work at home or a job, or other constraints make it difficult to attend regular school programmes. Developing countries are showing greater interest in exploring distance education methods to reach these groups of learners. There are also instances where distance is not an issue and school facilities may be opened in such a way as to permit greater access/equity for those unable to attend regular school programmes. This kind of openness will be especially important for countries hoping to expand the cycle of basic education to include junior secondary education.

There is a number of examples of attempts to open up secondary education by establishing study centres or making alternative use of existing facilities. A particularly interesting example is Indonesia's SMP Terbuka. This model makes possible junior secondary education for students who would not otherwise take part because of geographic or socioeconomic obstacles. Students are attached to study centres near their homes, which are linked to a nearby secondary school. Students engage in self-study and group learning, interact with teacher aides, and receive occasional face-to-face instruction from teachers at the nearby secondary school. There is flexibility built into scheduling to make it possible for young people who work to attend school.

Opening the environment to expand the range of resources for learning: Schools in developing countries can do to open their windows to the world —to enrich the learning process by going beyond the resources for learning that are typically available in the classroom. We see striking examples of learners in schools throughout the world making use of the Internet and other electronic networks to connect to sources of information not available in the classroom or to work collaboratively in joint projects or information exchange with learners in other schools.

Such activities are excellent routes to developing communication, information gathering, and problem solving skills and providing practice in dealing with multiple perspectives. Computers and electronic connections from schools in developing countries to outside resources are likely to become more common in the future. Already some developing countries are making good use of computers to enrich learning. For the near future, access to computers in schools will remain out of reach for many. But there are possibilities for opening and enriching the learning process through a wider range of learning resources that are available to schools in poor communities.

Adoption of "best practices" for teaching and learning will make learning environments more receptive to strategies and resources that go beyond the lecture/recitation/seatwork paradigm that characterises so much of traditional teaching in schools. The benefits of inquiry, discovery, and group projects need not involve electronic mediation or expensive resources - they can be achieved through thoughtful organisation and resources that can be found in the community.

Students in Costa Rica, for example, learned much about science, the environment, and the local economy by getting outside the classroom and tapping the knowledge of community members. Similarly, in schools where reading materials are scarce, effective learning materials may be generated that draw upon the experience of students and their parents. Experience stories are part of best practice even in schools where reading materials are abundant. There are other examples of how learning can be assisted by making more deliberate and imaginative use of what is available.

Opening the environment to provide stronger learner control and linkages for learning: One of the important dimensions of openness in learning environments that is achievable by schools in developing countries right now has to do with affording learners stronger control and linkages for learning. What this involves is ensuring that students are provided the opportunities for learning in such a way that it will assist them to function as well as they can as lifelong learners when they leave school.

Unfortunately, most schools in developing countries do not have this as a goal. Education is seen as years in school, with content broken up into bits to be hammered by teachers into students for demonstration on examinations. As a result, students leave school having had few chances to develop a meta-cognitive awareness of how to direct their own learning as they approach the challenges of work and daily life. Few have had the opportunity of learning in group-supported rather than solitary endeavor. Few have had the opportunities to make even the most basic choices of what to learn or how to learn it. Most have memorised facts about democracy; few have had the opportunity to practice it. This kind of opening of the learning environment can occur through a commitment to best practice that can be found throughout the world. Colombia's *Escuela Nueva* provides a good example of how schools may contribute to a greater participation of students in the management of the schools.

BUILDING OF OPEN LEARNING COMMUNITIES

Learning is an essential basis for both action and reflection and thus for creativity and problem solving. It is a pursuit in its own right which goes beyond the utilitarian conceptions that have for a long time related it almost exclusively to the world of work. In developing and industrialised nations alike, change, and consequently the need to respond and adapt to change and to manage ensuing conflict, are fundamental ingredients of life.

Learning is the mechanism through which human beings cope with — and in turn contribute to — change. The possibility to engage in learning throughout one's life and across multiple dimensions of life is thus essential for survival as well as a condition for continual quality of life. The traditional perceptions regarding education, based on the assumption that learning is the prerogative of the young, and that adult learning is at worst a response to failure and at best a marginal supplement, an exception rather than the rule, are becoming rapidly outdated. Learning is increasingly seen as a lifelong and lifewide requirement.

The emergence of the information society is also the need to rethink the priorities accorded to work-related activities *vis-a-vis* activities not directly related to the world of work. This is particularly relevant considering that in many societies people now spend decreasing proportions of their active life on what traditionally would be called 'work' and increased proportions of it on activities that would traditionally have been seen as pertaining to 'leisure.' Quality of life, then, becomes less a function of self-realisation in the work environment and more a dimension of, for instance, social, cultural and political participation in society. This things led to the rethinking of traditional learning goals, such as literacy.

Literacy has long been seen as a gateway to the world of learning. However, its definition as the ability to describe and interpret the world in terms of alphanumeric symbols is no longer adequate. There are many literacies and, consequently, illiteracies. Technological illiteracy, political illiteracy, ecological illiteracy, intercultural illiteracy, and so many other ways in which people are hindered in their ability to act and reflect upon their environment are just as important as the inability to read and write. Across these various literacies there is a growing problem of information overload which threatens to paralyse us. The inability to process and critically analyse information is increasingly a concern. Learners must develop the ability to access and process huge volumes of information so as to create meaning and generate new knowledge.

The important perspective on learning is the question of unmet learning needs. The world has known unmet learning needs as long as education has been a conscious concern of societies. What is new now is that such unmet learning needs can no longer be seen as isolated phenomena within the boundaries of particular countries or distinct parts of the world. The world is increasingly becoming a global society and a learning place in its own right.

Global learning depends on the ability of societies to turn themselves into learning societies and of communities within societies to constitute themselves as learning communities. In turn, learning communities exist to the extent that their individual members are learning individuals.

School systems, reflect the requirements of the formal economy and, besides their obvious role in serving the learning needs of new generations, they also serve as channels for the socialisation of human beings into the pre-existing socioeconomic hierarchies pertaining to the formal system. They are ill-equipped to respond to the learning challenges and opportunities of the future. Schools are burdended with a great deal of pressure due to increasing demand. In the past, they served a smaller and less diverse clientele, often already in many ways pre-selected. Today's schools are expected to carry out the almost impossible task of meeting the diverse needs of many more students. In its advice to UNESCO's Executive Board, the '*Ad Hoc* Forum of Reflection on UNESCO's Role in the Last Decade of the Twentieth Century' concluded in 1993 that "education is increasingly necessary and less and less possible, due to its cost."

Teaching is essential to the learning process. The emphasis of the teaching process has been centered around the teacher rather than the learner. In recent history, the tendency has been to view the teacher as an impersonal "expert" in the classroom whose only role is to transmit knowledge, facts, skills to the "empty" learner. The teaching process can be seen as providing prompts for engaging, stimulating, structuring, and encouraging learning in individuals and communities. While transmission of some types of knowledge and skills is part of this process and will continue to be important, the complexity of society and demands made on the problem-solving capacity of human beings will require that teaching be seen as fundamentally going beyond the transmission of information.

The teacher must challenge the thoughts and ideas of learners and stimulate them to engage in critical thinking and self-reflection. Essential to the process of facilitation is the ability of the teacher to link the appropriate set of interactions with the individual learning styles, interests and experiences of each learner as well as with the profiles of the communities that the learners perceive themselves as being part of.

Centralised curricula around the world have often been unable to take into account the rich diversity in society and suffered from lack of imagination, flexibility and relevance. The result is that many learners find themselves "lost" in the learning process. Given the broad range of learning styles, needs; interests, backgrounds, and aspirations of learners, teachers must adapt and develop new curricular approaches, content and language to ensure that curricula are, on one level, linked to the daily life of the learner but, on another level, push the learners to explore beyond the mundane aspects of their daily lives into undiscovered possibilities. The movement towards decentralisation provides an opportunity for allowing teachers greater control over the curricula.

However, with curriculum innovation, there must be greater efforts to conduct decentralised and participatory field research in order to understand the strengths and weaknesses of different strategies. Engaging in such research allows teachers to interact constructively and flexibly with the curriculum on a continual basis.

Learning is an individualised effort, it is also a social activity. Teaching must be conceived of in terms of a larger social exercise of connecting learners to each other and to the world around them. The process of connecting learners involves creating dialogue among diverse groups of learners that allow them to understand and appreciate the differences as well as the similarities that bond us as human beings. This means that teachers must be committed to understanding their learners and the communities that they come from. As part of this on-going process, they must also be willing to question their own internal biases and stereotypes.

Learning is a process that is filled with success and failure — often times involving great struggle and perseverance on the part of the learner. In many cases, failure can lead to great disappointment and withdrawal. However, if well managed, failure can also be turned into an important prompt to learning and thus can become the basis for success. It is the role of the teacher to provide positive inspiration at critical junctures of the learning process to ensure that learners stick with the laborious task of learning. However, the teacher should not take on this role in isolation, but rather seek to build a learning community in which other learners provide motivational support to each other as well.

A good teacher is a continual learner and must remain connected with changing societal frames of reference as well as with changing needs and interests of learners. They must be able to learn from their environment. But more importantly, they must be able to learn from their learners. This involves constantly trying to understand how learners react to, interpret and create meaning from different activities. It also involves a willingness to experiment with and adapt new approaches. In addition, the process of teaching involves modelling a love of learning.

Learning is a natural human process that occurs wherever human beings interact with each other and with their environments. Much of society's effort to create the conditions for learning concentrate on the school system. However, learning can take place in formal as well as informal settings. It is not uncommon that some of the best instances of learning occur outside a formal setting as the learners tend to be more at ease and learning tends to be more contextualised .within a relevant socio-cultural setting.

The teachers must be learners ("teacher/learner") and the learners must be teachers ("learner/teacher"). This is an essential element of the idea of open learning communities. Recognising this duality and supporting it requires that we reformulate many existing institutions, approaches and processes which were conceptualised along linear roles and relationships. At this juncture then, it is appropriate to shift the discussion to the means.

The teacher education is an integrated part of a broader conception encompassing the education of both learners and teachers for their new roles in open learning communities. Teacher education, particularly focusing on how information and communication technologies can be used to facilitate the process of change. But first it is necessary to reframe a few key conceptions around teacher education. The emergence of new

ICTs provides an opportunity and a necessity for pursuing this exercise.

Pre-service teacher education is best to be seen as a preparation not only for a predetermined role as teacher but particularly also for effective interaction with a continued learning-teaching process. The new ICTs help negotiate a hybridisation between formal and distance education so that face-to-face teaching is no longer only for the pre-service education and distance education is no longer only reserved for in-service education. Throughout the teacher education process, there should be a strong integration of both face-to-face and distance learning approaches.

The relationship between teaching and learning is fundamentally a dialectical one, based on a partnership between human beings to jointly create meaning. This partnership is no longer solely dependent on the physical proximity of its constituent members, nor is its quality necessarily determined by it. Separation in space and time is a mere matter of option, in many cases based on convenience or appropriateness in context rather than sheer necessity. What matters, and what needs to be validated, is simply the quality of the dialogue between partners —"teachers" and "learners" in the traditional sense of the word, but also other members of the learning community.

This implies that teacher education must put greater emphasis on developing in "teacher/learners" the skills required to become better learners. In addition to encouraging teachers to become learners, teacher education must also support the process of "learner/teachers" in becoming teachers, both in terms of how they can teach each other and how they can teach the teacher. Thus, teacher education may seek to involve "learner/teachers" in parts of the process.

ICTs are sometimes seen as a means of "fixing" this problem, particularly as they allow bypassing the assumed weak link, the traditional teacher trainer. This view, however, is erroneous. It was argued above that, in a context of different media, including the human being as one of them, the most striking characteristic which distinguishes the human medium from non-human ones, is the capacity to learn.

"Teacher/learners" can thus best be prepared for their new roles in an environment which models the behaviours they are expected to acquire. Such an environment should therefore be profoundly human and humanising and technologies need to be incorporated in it so as to enhance, rather than to detract from, this human aspect.

The use of information and communication technologies within a distance learning context is often advocated as a way to overcome such weaknesses. Excitement has been generated around new ICTs as it is assumed that they can bring the best expert directly to the teacher and facilitate two-way communication between the teacher and learner. Unfortunately, these are very narrow applications of the ICTs and we do not foresee them to result in any significant shifts in learning and teaching as they are simply extensions of existing approaches and processes. These "benefits" only serve to reinforce the teacher-over-learner hierarchies. However, the ICTs, if properly applied, possess the ability to unleash revolutionary changes in the field of teacher education.

Teacher education should be geared towards building a link between the various "teacher/learners" in society. Selected joint training sessions may be organised to do this with ICTs being utilised to facilitate greater communication, collaboration and reflection among the various partners. Initial sessions could start with discussions on how to work together, sharing of roles, and ensuring overlap. Such a process of dialogue should be geared towards discovering a basis for partnership in building open learning communities i.e., identifying strengths and weaknesses of each partner, formulating an understanding of the needs and interests of various learners, negotiating points of compromise, and team building.

More importantly, it should be focused on developing a shared consensus around learning and how it relates to broader objectives of social change and development. In addition, the ICTs provide an interesting opportunity for involving "learner/teachers" in selected teacher education activities. They can play a role in facilitating increased communication and sharing between "teacher/learners" and "learner/teachers." The ICTs potentially provide a way for not only the "learner/teacher" to understand the "teacher/learner" better but also for the "teacher/learner" to understand the "learner/teacher" and for the "learner/teachers" to understand each other, and sometimes even themselves, better.

The ICTs allow for the development of specific training models that are sensitive to the different needs, working conditions, learning styles, language and backgrounds of individual "teacher/learners." Such individually-tailored approaches of teacher education are better geared towards addressing issues of motivation and morale. However, this should not be taken to mean that a group of centralised training designers try to design hundreds of specialised training programmes, but rather that they should utilise the ICTs to support a process in which "teacher/learners" take on a greater role in generating and designing their own training programmes.

The ICTs allow the potential for teacher education to be moved out of centralised training institutions and into the "teacher/learner's" own working environment. In addition, they open up the opportunity to think of teacher education as a career-long career-wide activity rather than as a pre-service phase with bouts of in-service training merely for refresher purposes. Such an emphasis on on-going training is essential to allowing the "teacher/learners" to continually reflect on critical aspects of their own teaching as well as critical aspects of their own learning.

Teacher education content should be re-oriented to focus on learning and learners with subject matter and pedagogical/andragogical elements integrated around this focus. In addition, the ICTs should be used to make teacher education more consistent with the pedagogical/andragogical concerns being advocated, such as active learning, critical thinking, collaborative processes and creativity.

The role of the new media are already playing in the provision of education and cognisant of how this role will undoubtedly expand, it is critical to recognise the importance of media literacy among "teacher/learners." Such media literacy requires a strong understanding of the strengths and limitations of each medium and familiarity with strategies to reinforce the effect one medium can have on learning through the use of other media.

However, the idea of media literacy should be conceived beyond the glitzy hi-tech schemes available on the market. "Old" technologies such as print, radio, television will no doubt continue to make great contributions to the development of open learning environments worldwide, particularly if integrated in supporting community contexts. Furthermore, the "teacher/learner" should be encouraged venture beyond them and also make improved use of relatively unexplored media of popular expression such as puppet shows, local dances and music. Teacher education should ensure that teachers interact and experiment with these various media and creatively reflect upon how they can best be used in different learning environments.

REFERENCES

Bandura, A., *Social learning theory*, Englewood Cliffs, NJ: Prentice Hall, 1977.

Burnett, R., "Intervention during the first meeting of the Learning Without Frontiers Advisory Task Force held at UNESCO Headquarters, Paris, France on 25 and 26 November 1996". Reported in United Nations Educational, Scientific and Cultural Organization (UNESCO), 1996.

Collins, A., "Cognitive apprenticeship and instructional technology", In L. Idol and B. F. Jones (eds.), *Educational Values and Cognitive Instruction: Implications for Reform*, Hillsdale, NJ: Erlbaum, 1991.

Gardner, H., *Frames of the Mind: The Theory of Multiple Intelligences*, New York: Basic Books, 1993.

Greeno, J. G., Collins, A.M., Resnick, L. B., "Cognition and learning", In D. C. Berliner, R. Calfee (eds.), *Handbook of Educational Psychology*, New York, NY: Simon and Schuster MacMillan, 1996.

International Commission on Education for the Twenty-first Century, UNESCO, *Learning: The treasure within,* Paris, France: UNESCO, 1996.

Jonassen, D. H., Mayes, T, and McAleese, R., "A manifesto for a constructivist approach to technology in higher education", In T. Duffy, J. Lowyck, and D. H. Jonassen, *Designing environments for constructive learning*, Berlin, Germany: Springer Verlag, 1993.

Moore, G. M. and Kearsley, G., *Distance education: A systems view*, Belmont, CA: Wadsworth Publishing Company, 1996.

Perraton, H., (ed.), *Distance education: An economic and educational assessment of its potential for Africa*, Washington, DC: World Bank, 1986.

Perrin, D. G., "The new knowledge society and higher education", *Paper presented at the International Conference on Reinventing Higher education*, Bangkok, Thailand, July 1996.

4

Implications of ICTs in Distance Learning

Information and communication technologies (ICTs) has been growing exponentially over the last few decades. Computers have become more powerful; satellite, fibre optic and wireless technology has increased transmission capacity; and software developments such as multimedia authoring systems have made it easier to create digital materials such as electronic games, computer simulations and educational materials. The increased capacity and supply has resulted in plunging prices for computer functionality, telephone services and software.

Nowhere has the impact been greater than on the telephone industry. Long distance charges in North America and between major developed countries have dropped by 90 per cent in the last 15 years. Some analysts believe that the internet will transform the pricing structure for telecommunications from charges by distance and time to a flat charge by capacity. Thus a client will pay according to the size of the "pipe," not by the distance or length of time for which it is used.

While the growth of the internet is one of the major drivers for change, it is only one of several different but converging technologies that are resulting in widespread capacity growth. The rapid growth in satellite and wireless technology, and in particular the growth in mobile phone technology, is resulting in some countries attempting to leap beyond previous or intermediate technologies. As there is a very wide range of different applications of ICT in education, any choice of case studies is somewhat arbitrary. For example, the Open University in the UK (UKOU) has been using communications technologies such as broadcast television and radio for educational delivery since the early 1970s, and in recent years it has also moved into online programming. However, print still remains the core delivery medium for the UKOU, even though it has expanded its programming into Europe and other areas of the world. Similar national open universities, such as Indira Gandhi National Open University in India, the Chinese Central and State Radio and Television Universities, and the Korean National Open University, have operated for many years, primarily on a mix of broadcasting and printed materials. Other dedicated open universities, such as Athabasca University in Canada, have moved more aggressively into web-based delivery. Many institutions that offer both campus-based and distance programmes, such as the University of British Columbia (UBC) in Canada, Charles Sturt University in Australia, and Penn State University in the USA, have begun to move their former print-based distance education courses online. For instance, UBC has over half of its 110 distance courses now online. In Korea and several other countries, campus-based universities are forming consortia for the delivery of online distance learning programmes.

Most dramatic change in the use of ICT has not been in the traditional distance education market. The biggest impact has been on campus-based teaching and in the private sector training market. John Chambers, the CEO of Cisco, one of the world's largest ICT companies, has stated that the next big killer application for the internet is going to be education. WebCT, a course authoring software platform, has over three million student licences in over 1500 institutions, and it is growing at a rate faster than 500,000 new student licences a year. However, WebCT estimates that over 80 per cent of the use of its software is to support classroom teaching rather than "pure" distance education. Thus we are seeing the emergence of "mixed mode" teaching, combining face-to-face instruction with online learning. One of the best examples of this is the University of Central Florida, which has an extensive programme of web-based courses available both to on-campus and off-campus students.

A number of universities have formed consortia and partnerships with the private sector to commercially exploit their e-learning initiatives. Universitas 21 is a network of 17 universities in mainly Commonwealth countries, including Nottingham University, of Edinburgh, University of Melbourne, Hong Kong University, National University of Singapore and the University of British Columbia. Thomson Publishing and Universitas 21 have announced a partnership to found an "e-university." In 1990 there were 48 million people in higher education; by 2025, Thomson Publishing estimates that there will be 160 million. UNext, a US company, has established an e-university called Cardean that adapts its teaching material from that of the universities of Columbia, Stanford, Chicago, Carnegie Mellon and the London School of Economics. Degrees are awarded under the Cardean name, endorsed by the state of Illinois.

The London School of Economics (LSE) is also more deeply involved in an e-learning venture called Fathom, a global online library linking institutions such as the New York Public Library, the British Library, the Smithsonian, the Cambridge University Press and the LSE. Fathom's partners participate in the running of the service, and all must approve materials before they are published on the site. The UK government has established one of the most ambitious joint e-university projects. It has put the Higher Education Funding Council for England (HEFCE) in charge of attempts to create an e-university with a budget of £400 million, half of which will be public sector money. At first this was intended to be an exclusive arrangement, with universities bidding to become members. But now all UK universities are allowed to hold shares. The only human contact in the core programme will be with "navigators"—advisers who will help new students to select courses. Oxford University is linking with Stanford, Yale and Princeton to create an online college for alumni. The idea is to provide lifelong learning and support to some of the world's policy-makers and business leaders. Cambridge is exploring virtual learning in its £83 million government-backed link-up with the Massachusetts Institute of Technology (MIT). The project is known as the "bridge of minds" and is principally intended to foster commercial spin-offs from university research.

The University of British Columbia has been offering a fully online graduate level programme on technology-based distributed learning in partnership with the Monterrey Institute of Technology in Mexico, since 1996. The core of the programme is on the web, but UBC also participates by videoconference link from Vancouver to Monterrey in satellite television broadcasts to Monterrey Tech's 29 campuses across Latin America. Monterrey incorporates the five courses in its own masters degree in Educational Technology and has the rights to offer the five courses throughout Latin America. UBC has made the five courses available to both its own mainly campus-based master's students as well as to the rest of the world as a postgraduate certificate programme. To date, it has recruited students from more than 30 different countries.

In the private sector, there has been a rapid expansion of corporate universities, primarily in-house training organisations in the larger multinational companies making use of video-conferencing and the internet. In parallel, there has been the development of a whole new industry of online training contractors who provide online training services to medium- and smaller-sized companies. A number of private, for-profit organisations are trying to bridge the gap between centralised distribution and local support. For instance, TeltecGlobal is a business services aggregator offering corporations and governments a one-stop, turnkey solution for access to 21st century technology, services and education. The TeltecGlobal Centre of Influence is a last mile strategy that provides customers with products and web-enabled services available through membership in their Community and

TeltecGlobal Community Centres work in conjunction with multinational corporate sponsors, designing an offering of products and services to meet both community needs and corporate objectives. Business Centres license operations to local entrepreneurs and "global government-backed entities" in emerging markets. The TeltecGlobal works with the licensees to tailor the products and services to market needs and licensees' goals.

TECHNOLOGY USED IN E-LEARNING

The predominant technologies being used for e-learning in the developed world include the following:

World Wide Web (WWW)

According to authentic data, at the end of 1999, more than 196 million people globally were using the web and by the end of 2004, the number is expected to rise to 638 million. The major reasons for the rapid application of the web in education are:

i) Through the use of browsers and a relatively simple programming language, the web provides universal standards and interoperability between different machines and operating systems, which allows for global reach and access.
ii) The web can be transmitted both through already-existing infrastructure, such as analogue telecommunications networks, as well as through high-speed digital networks, giving it a wide range of technical flexibility.
iii) The web is a low-cost technology for education for several reasons. There is a relatively low cost of entry for educational suppliers. The cost of the technology needed for online courses is marginal compared with already-existing infrastructure costs for business and administrative purposes. Development of materials is relatively

low cost because of a simple computing language for creating materials and the development of intermediary course authoring software that enables web sites to be easily constructed. Through its use of the internet, there is no direct charge for independent packets of information; pricing is by volume, not by time or distance. Since most current applications use narrow bandwidths, the transmission costs per course for the supplier are virtually zero.

iv) The web's ability to combine text, graphics and a limited amount of multimedia gives it a wide range of applications in education.

v) The web enables free and global access to a very wide range of high quality learning resources located on web sites.

vi) The web offers opportunities for international, cross-cultural and collaborative learning.

vii) The web enables learners to study at any time and, increasingly, from any place.

viii) The web allows asynchronous interpersonal communication, not just between instructor and student, but more importantly, between learners and other learners, through e-mail, bulletin boards and online discussion forums.

The ability to enable students to communicate with each other independent of time and distance moves distance education away from a transmissive, teacher-dominated model of education to a more interactive form of learning where students can adapt and apply learning to their own needs.

In a knowledge-based society where information and knowledge are rapidly increasing, it is essential for students to be able to question, discuss and analyse their learning in a social context. However, there are several constraints that limit even greater expansion of the web as a learning technology, particularly in developing countries. In many developing countries, and in a small but significant number of communities and homes in developed countries, the necessary minimal technology infrastructure needed to support the web — a computer and a telephone — simply do not exist. Even where the minimal infrastructure is in place, many people do not have the necessary computer, keyboarding and literacy skills to make effective use of the web. Most applications of the web still have to fit into narrow bandwidths, limiting educational materials to text and static graphics. To fully exploit the educational advantages of the web, teachers need to adapt and change their teaching methods. Without adequate support and instruction, teachers will merely add cost to the current system by bolting on the technology to traditional classroom methods. Teachers also need technical support, both in terms of ensuring the networks, software and equipment work properly and are adequately maintained, but also in the design and development of web sites.

The interactive, participatory form of learning that has developed around the use of the web is culturally unsuited to the predominant mode of teaching and learning in traditional societies, which give great respect to the teacher, and where students are not expected to question the wisdom of elders. To justify the expense and stress of major changes in work methods, web-based learning needs to be used strategically and be adequately resourced.

Satellite Broadcasting

Satellite broadcasting for educational purposes has a long history dating back to the early 1980s. India was one of the first countries to use satellite television through the INSAT project, and today Indira Gandhi National Open University is still a major satellite user. The Chinese Central Radio and Television University is another major user, with over 800,000 students. Monterrey Tech in Mexico has four satellite TV channels operating 24 hours a day, seven days a week, covering large parts of Latin America. It is used primarily to deliver lectures from its headquarters in Monterrey, and it provides two-way communication through e-mail questions from students to the studio host in Monterrey. In North America, satellite transmission has become more and more integrated into a broader range of communications technologies, combining television, telephony and data transmission. There, satellite TV is now mainly used for educational purposes to cover relatively sparsely populated areas, or for special educational events, such as forums on topics of interest with highly respected speakers. It is rarely used as the main technology for formal education courses, although the National Technological University in the USA uses satellite TV to provide graduate engineering and business courses to corporations. One satellite application of particular relevance to poor developing countries is WorldSpace. Headquartered in Washington, DC., the WorldSpace business was founded in 1990 to provide direct satellite delivery of digital audio communications to the three-quarters of the world population that lacks radio reception and programme choice.

New digital technology combines low-cost radios with direct satellite reception using small, portable satellite receivers developed specially for the project by some of the world's leading electronic companies. WorldSpace obtains programmes from regular broadcasters such as the BBC. It started operations in Africa but has recently extended its services to Asia. Its potential audience is now approximately three billion.

The African Virtual University (AVU) is another initiative using satellite television broadcasting. AVU uses ICT to give the countries of sub-Saharan Africa direct access to high-quality academic faculty and learning resources in Africa and throughout the world. Professors from universities around the globe deliver classes in a studio classroom. The course is then beamed by satellite to AVU's learning centres all across Africa, each of which is equipped with an inexpensive satellite dish to receive the signal. During the class, students have an opportunity for real-time interaction with the instructor using phone lines or e-mail. At each participating AVU learning centre, on-site moderators guide the students through the materials and act as liaison with course instructors. All learning centres are equipped with internet access and at least 50 computers. Since the launch of its pilot phase in 1997, AVU has provided students and professionals in 15 African countries with more than 2500 hours of interactive instruction in English and French. More than 12,000 students have completed semester-long courses in engineering and the sciences, and more than 2500 professionals have attended executive and professional management seminars on topics such as Y2K, e-commerce, entrepreneurship, and strategy and innovation.

AVU also provides students access to an online digital library with more than 1000 full-text journals. More than 10,000 students and faculty have opened free e-mail accounts on the AVU web site. It has established itself as an independent, non-profit organisation headquartered in Nairobi, Kenya.

Satellite broadcasting has the following features relevant to education:

i) Because of the relatively high infrastructure costs, it has high fixed costs but very low variable costs; this makes it most effective when many students can receive a single programme.
ii) It provides a common standard of lecture or teaching to all students, wherever they may be located.
iii) It fits a transmissive model of education, where students are expected to remember and understand what is being taught.

However, satellite broadcasting suffers from some constraints. They include:

i) It requires very high start-up costs and a high level of technical expertise to launch and maintain.
ii) Despite the use of alternative technologies for two-way communications such as telephone and e-mail and the use of local teacher-supported discussion groups, it is difficult

to make satellite broadcasting very interactive for learners.

iii) Learners with internet access have less flexibility in terms of time and place of study from satellite broadcasting than from studying through the web, being tied either to the time of the broadcast or to a fixed location if they do not have personal access to satellite reception equipment.

iv) The need to provide convenient, secure and accessible local reception sites can add substantially to the cost, especially for satellite TV.

v) Satellite TV lacks the educational flexibility and the future potential for improvement that can be found in the web.

vi) Governments appear to be less willing to regulate and fund educational satellite TV initiatives, partly because of the high cost, and partly because of a move to more deregulated communications policies. In such a context educational users are usually unable or unwilling to pay full commercial rates for satellite transmission costs.

Satellite broadcasting has advantages for transmission of information to large numbers of students at relatively low cost per student. However, satellite broadcasting needs strong local support on the ground, through local centres or alternative two-way communication channels such as telephone or the internet. These ground costs and the constraints on learning considerably reduce the economic and educational benefits of satellite broadcasting.

Video-conferencing

Video-conferencing is widely used for educational purposes to link multi-campus colleges and universities, and for corporate training in companies with multiple sites. It makes use of fibre-optic cable or copper-based telephone networks and computerised compression technology to "squeeze" the high bandwidth requirements of full motion analogue television into a narrower bandwidth. It is used in education for the following reasons:

i) It saves instructor and student travel time between dispersed campuses, making possible the availability of some classes in sites away from the main campus.

ii) Teachers do not have to make significant adaptations to their normal method of classroom teaching.

iii) For corporate training the cost savings can be substantial, mainly due to savings on travel and accommodation.

However, there are significant constraints that have prevented a wider use of video-conferencing in education:

i) There are substantial installation costs, not so much for the video-conferencing equipment, but for modifications to classrooms to ensure adequate lighting and, in particular, good-quality sound. Transmission costs, especially with heavy use, can also be substantial.

ii) Students still have to be at a set place at a set time.

iii) While video-conferencing allows for more active participation by remote students than satellite TV, the larger the class the more difficult it is for all students to participate.

iv) The limited visual cues from the remote site and the often poor sound quality makes it a stressful environment for both students and teachers.

Video-conferencing can also be transmitted through the internet, but currently bandwidth severely restricts web-based applications. It is now possible to have real-time audiovisual communication between two desktop sites using relatively low-cost digital cameras and software. Picture quality is poor though, and there are still major bandwidth limitations preventing multiple site video-conferencing over the internet.

The technical constraints of video-conferencing limit its potential for use on a wide scale, but it can be useful as an additional resource for virtual education when used in support of the web. It can be particularly useful for language teaching and for areas where technical or interpersonal processes need to be observed.

Compact-Disk Technology

Compact disk technology, in the form of CDROMs or digital video disk (DVD), is being used in a number of interesting ways in virtual education. These disks tend to be used for applications requiring large quantities of data in real time, such as multimedia applications. The disks can run on the student's local computer in conjunction with the web; the codes on the disk are accessed from a web site, which can then call up images from the disk. Students can then seamlessly move between web site and disk, thus overcoming many of the bandwidth constraints of the web. The increased capacity of CDROMs and particularly DVDs facilitates a wide range of educational applications:

i) Large stores of slides, photographs or computer-generated images, each one digitally coded and catalogued, can result in the same CDROM being used in a variety of different courses.

ii) Video clips or learning objects often require too much time for downloading over the internet. Compression techniques now allow for high-quality video digital reproduction on CDROMs or the even greater capacity DVDs.

iii) Simulations enable students to enter data and see the consequences.

iv) A virtual lab can simulate many of the experiments and practices demonstrated in labs without the time required to set up experiments and equipment and with no worry about lack of convenient space.

v) Expert systems, somewhat like games, can help students make decisions and see the consequences. The outcomes are governed by rules and procedures based on expert knowledge.

The main constraints of disk technology are as follows:

i) The cost of development is very high. This means that compact disks need to replace otherwise very costly activities or be used on a large scale.
ii) Teams of highly skilled media producers and developers, as well as subject experts, are needed.
iii) Learners need a relatively high standard computer and disk player because of the memory and processing requirements.
iv) There can exist a lack of imagination and vision in thinking of how the technology can be used for teaching purposes.
v) There is concern that this a temporary technology that will be replaced when wide-band access is available over the web.

While CDs and DVDs indicate some of the possible future developments on a more universal scale over the internet, good-quality disk-based educational applications are very expensive to develop and require high skill levels. However, as more and more high-quality materials become available on disks, there will be opportunities for course developers to incorporate off-the-shelf disks into their own local programmes.

New Internet Technologies

Because of the rapid rate of technological change, it is important to look not just at what is existing now, but what is also likely to happen over the next five years. A number of related and interlinked technologies that could have major implications for teaching and learning are now clearly emerging. The increasing access to internet and web will widen as governments put in place national strategies such as linking all schools, providing community access and investing in infrastructure. As well, competition in a deregulated market will also widen access. Telephone companies, satellite operators, cable TV operators, and equipment companies such as Cisco and Nortel will all compete and market aggressively to provide the basic internet infrastructure in North America. A recent consumer technology study by Pricewaterhouse Coopers indicates that Canadian have the highest home use of the internet in the world, with 48 per cent having home access in 2000. It is important to note the trends in internet use as well as the static data. If the diffusion of computer use follows that of other domestic consumer technology trends, at least two-thirds of Canadians will be using the internet from home within five years. Nevertheless, research shows that the use of computer-based technology increases with education level, and the bias for home internet use tends to be towards high and upper-middle income families. Thus there will always probably be a small percentage of low-income or other disadvantaged individuals who will not have home access. While the majority of Canadians are still accessing the internet via telephone, broadband use is rapidly increasing.

The move to broadband applications and the need to develop sustainable business models for e-commerce could also have an impact on the current pricing structure of the internet. Its current flat rate pricing by volume may give way to pay-per-service use, especially once it becomes technically feasible to deliver on-demand television and movie programming over the internet. This may make the internet less appealing to potential learners, although it may make it more appealing to service providers. The rapid development of internet services and reach in North America is also fuelled by the relatively low cost of the services to the home and work place. This pricing, in turn, is driven by strong competition within the communications industry. Deregulation of telecommunications underlies this strong competition. Some countries may have strong national and social reasons for maintaining a single national telecommunications carrier or a closely regulated telecommunications system, but the cost of internet services will be much higher in those cases and, hence, the use of the internet much lower.

Such rapid spread of the technology and the increased bandwidth will have major implications for educational use. The issue then for most countries is not the direction of change, but the speed of that change. The internet is not going away; its use is going to increase in all countries. But how fast that increase occurs will be determined primarily by economic development capacity and by the technical ability within a country to develop and maintain the necessary internet infrastructure. However, some countries will try to manage the market and control access to the internet, through political means, which could slow down its development regardless of economic development and technical ability.

Wireless technology

Wireless technology is already manifested in mobile telephony and will increase to hand-held devices such as Palm computers and laptop computers. For instance, on arrival at the Monterrey Tech campus, students can obtain a small chip to put in their laptops to enable wireless internet access anywhere within their campus environment. The technology is cheap and will become cheaper and learners will have great mobility and be able to access learning while travelling or in a cafe without having to be hardwired.

Local power generation

The internet depends on a reliable and stable supply of electricity. The development of low-cost local power generation technology reduces the need for huge central investment in national power grids to reach all parts of a country. Small local power plants are springing up to offer neighbourhood users cheap electricity, thanks to not having to pay for distribution over a wasteful national grid. An added advantage of so-called "micropower" is that it will be much friendlier to the environment as well, when it is based on fuel cells that convert hydrogen direct to electricity without combustion.

Speech Recognition Software

Speech recognition and voice and text translation is going to be the most significant of all for computer use. Speech recognition software from companies such as Lucent, Nuance and Speechworks can now understand a wide range of accents and diction without having to be trained to a specific voice. Computer languages such as VoiceXML now make it possible to write voice services in the same way that HTML makes it possible to write web pages. With VoiceXML, the human voice becomes a substitute for a computer mouse and the spoken command for a click. The graphical user interface consisting of a keyboard and mouse is likely to disappear as a result. Full communication with a computer in the same way as with human beings may never become a possibility, but after many years of false starts and false hopes, speech recognition technology has now reached a stage where it has become reliable, cheap and useful. The importance of this development is that it will change the nature of interaction with computers. Word commands will make it easier to operate a computer, particularly for people with relatively low literacy skills.

Machine Translation

Developments in machine translation will have significant implications for the use of the internet. According to Global Reach, English is currently the predominant language of the internet, with 48 per cent of all internet users being English-speaking. However, the predominant internet languages are excepted to change dramatically over the next five years. The numbers of Chinese-speaking users, which now account for just 7 per cent of all internet users, is expected to surpass the number of English-speaking users within five years. It will become increasingly important for educational programmes to be available in a wide variety of languages if they are to be offered not just on a global basis, but also within multicultural communities. One way to do this is through joint course development between bilingual teams. This is the strategy of the UBC/Monterrey Tech partnership. The courses will not be translated, but will be designed in both English and Spanish, covering similar ground and as far as possible use similar readings, but will still be essentially different. Human translation is still too expensive at the moment, but so is joint course development of this kind. The alternative is machine translation. While it does not provide perfect translation, it currently speeds up the translation by humans by 50 per cent, and it is expected to increase in speed and accuracy within five years to the point where it speeds up human translation by 80 per cent. The importance of these new developments is not in their individuality but in their combined effects. The trend is all in the same direction: more powerful and cheaper technologies, wider access, and increased integration and convergence of technologies.

Controlling Forces of ICTs Usage

Technology is developed either for purposes of war or for business applications, and educational applications of emerging technology have followed on the coat-tails of military and business applications. For reasons other than education, in developed countries there is going to be increased and continuing investment in the internet and its underlying infrastructure by governments, businesses and individuals. This investment is being made to develop and maintain a new form of economy based on knowledge and information.

Globalisation is likely to lead to increased pressure on developing countries to invest in the internet and telecommunications infrastructure for business reasons. However, it is also critical for educational applications of the internet that the technical infrastructure be in place. Educational applications of the internet fundamentally depend on stable electricity provision, stable telecommu-nications networks, and a stable human resource capacity to build and maintain this technical infrastructure.

Another significant driving force for e-learning is the belief by corporations and investment banks that this is an area where a great deal of money can be made. Huge sums are being invested in e-learning initiatives. While many mistakes have been made, it is likely that sooner rather than later some corporation will develop a sustainable e-learning business. Another pressure on educational institutions to use ICT is coming from governments and the business community. They want technology-ready workers for the new economy, and they often believe that investment in technology will lead to reduced costs in education.

A major driver of the application of learning technologies is coming from within the education community itself. In those jurisdictions that saw major cuts in educational expenditures or increased student enrolments without balancing public investment over the last 10 years, teachers have seen their class sizes increasing, and hence their interaction with students diminishing. Web-based learning provides a hope for increased student interaction and access to resources that can free up the teacher's time for more direct contact with individual students.

Another driver for change, and one that will become more significant as time goes on, will be the students themselves. Many students now entering universities and colleges have lived all their lives in a computer-based society. They have been playing computer games, using the internet to listen to popular music and using mobile phone technology to communicate with their friends.

There are a number of strong pressures that limit the use of ICTs in educational institutions. Perhaps the most important and least appreciated is the newness of the phenomenon. The web did not exist as a public service before 1990. The first web-based educational course did not appear until 1995. It should be remembered that it took 50 years after the first book produced by the Gutenberg press before someone hit on the idea of numbering pages. It was over 200 years later before the University of Paris allowed students access to its library. We should not be surprised then that the web has not revolutionised education in six years.

The web and the internet are disruptive technologies. They require a fundamental rethinking of teaching practice. Students no longer are required to be at a set time and a set place to learn. Teachers are no longer the gatekeepers of knowledge. At the same time, schools, colleges and universities play a much wider role than merely transmitting information from one generation to another. They have social and cultural roles as well. Therefore educators are right to be cautious before rushing to adopt the latest technology. Education needs to match the needs of learners. Technology should be used only if and when it contributes to those needs.

Any move towards using new technologies requires significant up-front technical investment, even if for other commercial reasons the basic national infrastructure already is in place. Servers are required, computers need to be made available in classrooms, networks connected, software installed, and the technology needs to be maintained and upgraded to allow for technological change. Most public institutions, even in the richest developed countries, are under-invested in this area. As a consequence, the technology is often not conveniently available, is unreliable and requires a high level of competence and skills on the part of the teacher and often the students to use. Ironically, the inefficiencies caused by under-investment often cost more than properly investing in the first place. Nevertheless, even a well-planned investment requires initial additional spending from government and/or the institutions.

Most institutions have not provided adequate support and training for teachers to use the technology appropriately in an educational setting. As well as technical support, teachers need help with media production and instructional design. Without this, the use of technology is just bolted onto existing practice. As a result it increases not only the teacher's workload but also the students', for marginal results.

Because the application of the web to teaching is so new, there are very few convincing research and evaluation studies that indicate clear educational benefits for such an investment. Evidence is beginning to emerge, though, and the picture is not entirely positive. Studies on online learning have indicated the following:

i) Online learning provides the opportunity to reach out to new markets, particularly lifelong learners and international students.
ii) The flexibility of online learning is clearly of great value to many mature adults trying to balance work, family and study requirements.
iii) Many learners seem to appreciate the advantages of international courses and the opportunity to work collaboratively and closely with colleagues around the world and to have access not only to the course instructors, but to textbook authors and experts from other institutions.
iv) The opportunity to widen the range of potential students through online learning can make sustainable programmes struggling with small enrolments locally.
v) Online learning brings major benefits through the ability to work collaboratively with students from several different countries.
vi) Online learning can be as cost-effective as face-to-face teaching in the right circumstances, but it is not suitable for all students or all kinds of teaching.
vii) Online learning can be more than cost-effective; it can actually bring in net profits for an educational institution.

However, this requires a different approach to the development and management of teaching: it requires financial systems and financial management that, frankly, few higher education institutions have in place or are even ready to contemplate.

viii) There is a need for substantial start-up funds.

ix) Faculty require additional time to learn how to use these new technologies and students also have to learn to study effectively online.

x) Students need to be psychologically ready and financially able to embrace this method of course delivery.

There are important educational benefits to be had from the use of ICT in education. However, for these benefits to be achieved, a major effort is needed to provide suitable levels of investment, adequate training and a restructuring of the teaching process.

Policy Issues

If the internet represents a significant element of the future of education, the sooner that a nation or an educational system gains experience and practice in online learning, the more economically competitive that nation is likely to become. The reverse is also true: ignoring the impact of ICT on education could substantially reduce a nation's ability to compete economically in the 21st century.

However, few developing countries have the resources, the technology infrastructure or the skilled workforce necessary to make online learning available on a wide scale, at least for many years. When resources are scarce, they need to be concentrated and very carefully focused. It becomes then a matter of timing and priorities. We shall see that the decision to move to virtual education should to some extent depend on economic as well as educational goals.

One major issue is the balance between investment in the newer forms of ICT, and in particular in online learning, compared with investment in either traditional school or campus-based education, or older communications technologies, such as print and broadcasting.

The economies of scale of the mass media-based open universities, using print and broadcasting, offer considerable cost and sometimes quality advantages over conventional education. These cost advantages are not so apparent with high-quality virtual education. The big difference between virtual universities and open universities is the direct interaction between the instructor and the students in virtual universities, leading to more individualised instruction. This, though, comes at a cost. Although there are some economies of scale compared with conventional education, virtual education requires a reasonable student-teacher ratio to avoid instructors becoming swamped with e-mail and discussion forum messages.

What virtual education is offering is a more interactive education encouraging critical thinking, communication skills and flexibility for both students and teachers, compared with the one-way mass media of open universities. For countries with large numbers of students unable to access the later years of secondary or higher education, the open university, mass media model is likely to be the most appropriate, particularly if the aim is to develop a mass skilled workforce able to work in industrial or resource-based industries. Open universities such as Indira Gandhi National Open University, therefore, still provide the best route for mass education. For countries with already reasonable access to secondary and higher education, and a reasonable ICT infrastructure, virtual education will provide advantages over both conventional and open universities. These advantages will increase particularly for those countries wishing to move into a knowledge-based economy, but where there is a shortage of teachers in the new economy, since students can access such learning from anywhere in the world.

Virtual education depends on the appropriate technological infrastructure already being in place for commercial or administrative reasons. Stable electricity supply and reliable and moderately priced internet access is a necessary condition for virtual learning. Few institutions or governments have made the necessary investment in infrastructure for educational reasons alone. While in North America the university sector initially developed the internet, its rapid growth has been driven primarily by the business sector, although government policy can ensure more equitable access.

Government can certainly develop policies that will encourage rapid growth of the internet, as follows:

i) Deregulation of telecommunications services.
ii) Encouraging competition between telecommunications suppliers.
iii) Bulk buying of government telecommunications services through competitive bidding from suppliers.
iv) Encouraging internet use through consortia of educational institutions developing and sharing virtual education materials and courses.
v) Careful regulation to ensure access to all.
vi) Offering tax breaks to infrastructure suppliers to encourage investment and/or offering tax breaks on computers and internet services to end users to encourage greater use.
vii) Supporting open and corruption-free licensing practices to encourage genuine competition.

Many governments are decided to invest heavily themselves in the basic infrastructure because of lack of investment by the private sector. For these governments the trick is to know when to open up the management of internet services to the private sector once a market has been created. However, until there is a basic and reliable internet infrastructure in place, connecting at a minimum to most key businesses and universities, virtual education is unlikely to be a realistic or practical choice.

Even if the infrastructure is in place, there must be a national capacity to supply the necessary trained people to support and sustain virtual education. As well as having people who can install, manage and maintain the necessary technical infrastructure, virtual education also needs skilled media producers, such as web designers and instructional designers. Unfortunately, there is a global shortage of people with these skills. The danger is that a country will provide the necessary training, then the learners will emigrate to countries able to pay more for their services. Nevertheless, without such a skilled workforce to support it, virtual education will not work.

Today it is impossible for countries to ignore the potential of virtual education. At the very least, a country's leaders need to be computer literate, to know how to use and navigate the internet and to understand not just the technology but its importance for national development. The minimum, then, most countries should do is to ensure that key government offices, businesses and universities have internet access. The role of the university in particular is important.

A prestigious national university can provide a model of the benefits and services available through the internet and develop at least an elite with the skills needed to service national technical and educational needs for ICT development and for virtual education. This will enable the nation to build an affordable and targeted technology infrastructure, to participate in regional collaborative projects, to develop partnerships with institutions in other countries, to identify and adapt suitable programmes from other countries and to develop its own programmes where appropriate.

WWW-SUPPORTED OPEN LEARNING

The WWW provides many opportunities and supports in the delivery of such programmes and already has an established itself as a viable alternative to the conventional forms of course delivery. The popularity of the WWW stems mainly from its powerful delivery capacity for multimedia-based courses and programmes. But this delivery capacity is only one of its strengths and the technology provides opportunities to greatly enhance the quality of teaching and learning at a distance through informed use of its features and facilities. The WWW is an extremely expansive technology and often the use of the three letter acronym, WWW, conceals the scope and extent of the technology. When most people think of the WWW, they tend to imagine the vast network of connected computers of which it is comprised.

When WWW-based learning activities are imagined, they are mostly considered as activities where information is sought and accessed across this vast network. But another expansive aspect of this technology is the range of functional components that is the WWW. As well as information storage and delivery, the WWW is also an interactive technology, a communication technology and a construction technology. In some instances, it is these other functions which have the most to offer the innovative teacher in higher education.

When a similar continuum is used to place and compare the forms and roles of the different types of WWW-based learning materials, it is interesting to note that the applications appear to extend across the complete continuum. There seems very little that the WWW is not capable of providing. WWW-based materials which are used to deliver content. The common forms are WWW pages containing the course content which the students are required to read as part of their course work. An inspection of various online learning courses shows that most people who use the WWW for distance education and open learning build their learning programmes around these text-based WWW pages.

The key feature of WWW documents which have been designed primarily to carry information is that the materials and documents are usually electronic versions of existing paper-based courses. The reasons for delivering such materials via the WWW appear to stem mainly from:

i) information accessibility, teachers can post information and it can be accessed by students across many locations,

ii) reduced printing, teachers can reduce the level of printing required by providing electronic rather than printed documents for students,

iii) timely delivery of information, teachers can post materials before lecture and workshop sessions for immediate access by students, for example, to use in preparatory exercises.

The use of the WWW for the delivery of course information as described above usually involves minimal changes to existing teaching or learning processes. The advantages that are returned from WWW usage relate mainly to administrative efficiencies and convenience and are most often used in support of quite traditional forms of teaching.

Components of the WWW enable the production of documents with a range of interactive elements are coupled with an appropriate instructional design, the materials can serve specific teaching and learning purposes. Interactive learning materials result from the use of the interactive features and capabilities of the WWW in ways that engage the learner. For example, in presenting course content, one strategy would be to provide a page for the learner to read.

In an interactive learning environment rather than providing a page for students to read, they might be provided with a document containing a series of hyperlinks and a specified task to complete with them. For example, to gather relevant information through a process of linking, reading, comparing and information analysis. In such instances, students generate their own information and knowledge set, an activity many would argue as being more conducive to learning than reading alone.

There are many ways in which WWW materials can be used to engage learners. We use the title, interactive learning in relation to the WWW, to describe applications where the technology itself provides the feedback and responses in learning settings. Other forms of interactivity, for example, communications between learners, are treated as a separate category. The forms of interactive learning supported by the WWW are growing rapidly and more recent courses tend to include more interactive learning elements than those developed previously.

The WWW supports many different forms of communication which can be used in a myriad of ways in student-centred learning environments to support communicative, collaborative and cooperative activities among students and their teachers. There is a strong rationale supporting this form of learning activity.

Language plays an important role in the learning process and forms of communication and talk are integral component for learning. WWW-based applications and learning environments that are included and described by the category of networked communication include:

i) e-mail where individuals communicate directly with others with private or public messages sent between parties either in a one-to-one or one-to-many mode;
ii) bulletin boards where information is posted for public viewing and comment, where threads can be used to support detailed discussion of particular topics;
iii) chat sessions involving real-time text-based discussions between parties in both public and private domains; and
iv) real-time online audio conferencing and video conferencing where students can see and hear the teacher and others. Such settings often include shared software displays and files with which all class members can interact.

The use of the WWW for networked communication differs considerably from the previous two categories. Perhaps the most significant difference is that it does not involve the development and storage of specific course content and information. With networked communication, documents and content develop and emerge as a consequence of the communicative and collaborative activities of participants.

The WWW provides a forum for communication and discussion and a means for storing this discussion for subsequent use. Learning and knowledge development occurs through there search and reading that precedes the writing, from the negotiated meaning drawn from discussions with others and the exposure to multiple perspectives which this form of activity supports. This form of learning is not suited equally well to all discipline areas. However some, if not all, of the communicative forms of WWW interactivity can play a useful role of one form or another in most instructional settings.

WWW activity capable of supporting many learning outcomes is use of the presentation components of the technology as a learning activity. In this instance, the WWW is used by students as a display tool where they can create and publish documents. The learning is derived from the planning and access of the relevant information, its organisation into a publishable form and the collaboration that can be involved. Through the delivery capabilities of the WWW, other learners can participate in the development process at a distance. There is a large amount of research and writing that supports and demonstrates the learning potential of this form of activity.

Many WWW pages abound with text and have been designed on the premise that when a student reads he or she learns. This is clearly an assumption which cannot be sustained, especially in electronic texts. We know that reading from screens is difficult and tiresome. We know that WWW screens tend to fragment the content and to conceal structure and form. We also know the value of narrative as a learning strategy but continue to use hyperlinks within the text to distract and break flow. It would appear that much of what is known about how students learn from text is ignored in the development of WWW-based learning materials.

The real test of the quality of interactions in WWW learning environments is the level of critical thinking and reflection, which result. Too often the forms of computer-based interactivity which are used in today's WWW documents are limited. Common examples include drill and practice routines and simple question and answer feedback provided by simple CGI scripts. Better interactions from a learning perspective are those that involve such higher order thinking skills as hypothesis formation, testing, analysing and reviewing.

A common component of many WWW learning environments are communicative elements brought about through the use of such facilities as chat rooms and discussion lists. These have the potential to contribute significantly to learning outcomes by enabling students to communicate and collaborate. They are effective when they support and encourage such activities among learners as reflection; articulation, negotiation. But too often, the use of the chat room and discussion is an additional rather than integral component in the learning. Often discussions are started to which students must contribute. Many WWW-based communicative activities are teacher-led and directed dialogues. The situation often mimics a classroom discussion where individuals contribute and a broad but not necessarily deep treatment of salient issues. This is a trend we have also observed in other forms of computer and technology mediated communications.

The critical component in the design of effective WWW-based learning environments is to start by considering the form of learning environment that is required and then to mould the various facilities of the WWW to enable this. Too often people start the process with a limited view on how the content is to be delivered and on how the WWW can be used. This leads necessarily to a narrower set of opportunities. There is now a great deal of literature and debate to guide the development of effective WWW-based learning materials. It is interesting, but not unexpected, to find that within many descriptions, there is frequently no mention of particular WWW elements themselves. The WWW holds outstanding promise to deliver teaching programmes, but also to create enhanced learning environments. The challenge is for designers to approach the move to the new technologies from a learning perspective rather than being led by the lures of the technology.

Web-enhanced Instructional Development

Educational institutions worldwide spend large amounts of money each year developing, adapting or acquiring learning resources and courses. The development of electronic learning resources is particularly expensive and often produces course materials that are platform or operating system dependent. The internet and the web are seen as vehicles for lessening dependence on hardware platforms, but even in this domain there are competing standards and different flavours of web browsers.

With the development of the web as a viable medium for learning and self-directed study, education providers are increasingly able to provide learning opportunities in a more flexible and customer-aware manner. But many continue to replicate traditional educational models using the new medium. While the web world focuses its attention on knowledge management, customer profiling, and e-business practices, many education institutions continue to automate traditional instructional and administrative practices. For most institutions, courses continue to be the standard units of instruction, the "one-size-fits-all" building blocks of academic credit, even within the virtual education arena. Very few have considered the idea of component-based instructional units, "learning objects," and complementary business systems and student service models that have the potential to revolutionise instructional practice.

The growing currency of distance and distributed learning practices has instilled in learners the expectation that educational institutions can provide them with personalised study options to their homes or to their places of employment. Web-based environments that are accessible to the masses can build an enormous following of loyal users, provided they give users what they want in a convenient and web-centric manner.

The challenge for educational institutions offering virtual programmes is similar, yet few seem able to achieve the promise of education to the masses in a convenient and user-driven manner. Very few educators or institutions understand the concept of the learning object. Fewer still have even attempted to apply pure web-centric thinking in their approach to virtual learning. Too many traditional institutions present hierarchical views of their organisational structure to learners at the front doors of their buildings, through their academic calendars, or even through their web sites.

Instead of identifying a learner's goal and then describing potential pathways to achievement, many institutions deal more with their own institutional requirement to qualify the learner to be enrolled. This position can be attributed in part to the historically autonomous nature of institutions of higher learning, where the power resides in the hands of the institution. Many see no real need to change, even in the face of increasing competition from the private sector. In basic education situations, there are good examples of personalised and self-paced learning environments. These are geared to help individuals achieve their learning goals quickly and efficiently, often using a mastery learning approach.

However, very few systems store or manage their learning modules in a granular, object-based structure that allows them to be reused, re-purposed or repackaged in different media for different situations. Repackaging an online, computer-managed instructional system to service the needs of a rural population in the developing world with print-based modular materials is not a situation that many, if any, instructional management systems could handle with the development and delivery architectures that are embedded within their software systems.

What learners are typically looking for from a virtual education experience is to achieve their academic or work-related goals with a focus on access, choice, flexibility, recognition of prior learning and end-to-end service. As learners become increasingly informed about the possibilities for virtual education, and as the choice of programme options expands with new players in the virtual education arena, learners will likely begin to feel power in their hands and will be prepared to exercise it decisively with those education providers that respond to their needs. For educational institutions there are some object lessons from the web that they will need to learn if they expect to use the medium effectively. Building an educational repository that provides access to learning objects requires standards and structures that can facilitate object storage, retrieval and aggregation to suit the needs of learners or the pedagogical intentions of instructional developers.

Learning objects

Method for preparing learning assets for use, reuse, re-proposing and electronic commerce involve associating the structure of the educational materials with a standard classification system that facilitates the storage and retrieval of the learning objects. The IMS Global Learning Consortium, a group of hardware vendors, software vendors, publishing companies and educational organisations, is currently promoting a metadata standard for educational material that is gaining a following worldwide, both from industry and from educational organisations.

The implication of the IMS model is that educational organisations and institutions will need to begin to observe metadata standards to ensure that their databases and repositories for print, audio, image, video and computer-based materials are accessible both for internal and for external purposes. It is also imperative that they begin to inventory their learning assets and have a plan for converting any analogue assets for use within a learning object economy. The major attributes of learning objects are given below:

i) *Granularity*: The term 'granularity' describes the degree of precision with which learning objects (text, image, audio, video) can be described in a learning system. Granularity provides opportunities for customisation that can allow an educational institution to re-purpose its educational assets for individuals or for groups. A common database of learning objects that is accessible to instructional designers, producers and clients in different formats represents a new way of organising learning materials in an enterprise-wide fashion. When learning materials are organised in a granular fashion and accessible from a common database in different ways by different clients, a scalable model emerges that can be used to service niche applications as well as mass audiences.

Granularity and scalability are influenced by the degree to which technical systems observe common standards and the degree to which those systems provide desktop-level access to all members of the development and delivery community. For example, at the Open Learning Agency (OLA), grade 11 and 12 course content for the Information Technology and Media Arts curricula is re-purposed using the same metadata but with a different instructional schemas and learner profile for use as content in a teacher education programme. Instead of being offered as part of a course syllabus for grades 11 and 12, the content is offered in modular chunks that satisfy learning outcomes that teachers wish to pursue as part of a self-directed professional development programme called The Learning Lab.

ii) *Modularity*: Modularity in learning systems is key to providing flexibility for learners. When learning objects can be modularised at a fine level of granularity and can be described by metadata as competencies, learning outcomes, lesson text elements, assessment items and other instructional elements, they can be deconstructed and/or aggregated by a development and management system into a set of elements that might represent different instances of course modules for different audiences.

iii) *Interoperability*: Interoperability is a requirement for systems that manage granular learning objects. It is the retrieval and transfer of the media assets from within the systems to new delivery environments and to learners and customers that adds value to them. Learners and other education clients are in a better position to use an education provider's products when they observe platform-independent standards and can be confident that the learning materials that they acquire will work with their own systems. Content can be delivered for different client groups through open source delivery environments such as Linux, or be transformed electronically to proprietary systems such as WebCT or PLATO.

iv) *Customisation*: Customisation is the market factor that will affect an institution's access to the business side of learning in the future. Institutions that are able to customise their learning offerings to meet the actual needs of learners will prosper and grow. Customisation is a complementary attribute to interoperability, and it is related directly to the granularity of the learning assets that an organisation owns. The more content an organisation owns that is finely divided into granular components, the greater the opportunity for customising learning products or learning pathways for multiple purposes, new opportunities and new jurisdictions. If an institution wants to move away from packaging courses for single format applications and towards mass customisation, building a store of granular learning objects is the key step on that road. Observing standards like the metadata recommendations of the IMS Global Learning Consortium provides the additional opportunity to interchange, sell or buy learning objects from other institutions and publishers that observe a similar format.

v) *Common object standards*: Current rate of technology change requires that education providers use or have access to learning systems that meet standards and specifications commonly agreed upon by a range of institutions, publishers and technology vendors worldwide. Currently, the IMS Global Learning Consortium's metadata specification is the set of standards that has captured the attention of the education and training community because of its adherence to the principles of openness and interoperability. Within such a standards-based environment, institutions can follow the lines of development that best meet their client needs without compromising their ability to participate in the commercial exchange of learning objects with other educational institutions or vendors.

vi) *Instructional design options*: Learning objects provide instructional designers with enhanced opportunities to reuse or re-purpose granular components to suit the different pedagogical needs of individuals learners or programme offerings. For example, an instructional designer developing a very focused upgrading course in Mathematics might assemble learning objects for a particular set of outcomes in a systematic way that forms a coherent unit of study. These materials might be assembled for a computer-managed instructional system that works on the principle of mastery. Students must master developmental materials at a predetermined threshold before being allowed to move on to new materials. An adaptive testing system might present the student with a short test and then assemble a programme of study based on areas of weakness. Such a system could become a new business opportunity for an institution, or become a part of a normal challenge exam process that features flexible study opportunities prior to the exam.

vii) *Business systems linkages*: Discussions about customisation, flexibility and extensibility need to consider the instructional development and work flow management systems that institutions and educational organisations will use to gain access to a common pool of learning objects. They may need to model workflow concepts in relation to learning object databases in small-scale projects first, but ultimately they will need to deal with enterprise-wide initiatives. Such an enterprise-wide approach would be a key outcome for any educational organisation contemplating a major foray into virtual learning as a core function of its business. Accomplishing an "open" model for the development and sharing of interactive educational content depends on hardware and software vendors, publishers and educational institutions agreeing on a protocol on the standards for locating and operating interactive platform-independent materials.

The IMS Global Learning Consortium is the primary standards group that is promoting a structure for developing and sharing content and is based on emerging technical and metadata standards for the internet and electronic commerce. Document-type definitions and schemas based on the World Wide Web Consortium's extensible markup language (XML) standard will be the basis for the development of learning object content using IMS standards. The IMS group is also promoting standards for transactions between learning systems, student information systems, learning resource libraries and the business systems of education and training institutions and vendors. These administrative systems provide the business and student service back ends of instructional systems. As institutions and training organisations build their learning and technology plans, they must pay attention to metadata specifications, the work of the IMS Global Learning Consortium and similar standards-based initiatives. The ability for education providers to engage in collaboration or commerce in the future with learning systems from different institutions or content vendors may depend on the ability to comply with common technical standards for learning systems.

Learning object thinking is beginning to emerge in educational jurisdictions worldwide. In Canada, educational institutions and their faculty often own valuable learning assets in the form of print materials, audio, video and computer-based media. The ability to effectively use, trade or sell learning assets in the future will depend on the ability to match assets to the needs of learners, to those of other institutions and to those of vendors who may wish to purchase them. The Portal for Online Objects in Learning (POOL) is an example of a government-sponsored initiative in Canada that is leading post-secondary institutions in the direction of storing learning objects in a database environment objects, such as audio or video clips, simulation applets, and multimedia case studies, POOL provides organisations in higher education, workplace training, and continuing education with a gateway to learning resources and a distribution channel for their learning objects."

The Open University of the Netherlands is experimenting with Educational Modeling Language (EML), an XML-based notational system that allows the construction of course materials from their component elements.

At the University of Queensland in Australia, a research team lead by Jane Hunter is examining multimedia metadata modeling and XML schema design for incorporating rich media learning objects such as video, audio and WebTV into instructional systems Hunter's team develops tools, technologies and information management processes that allow organisations to locate, access, retrieve and manage information on highly distributed heterogeneous networks. Hunter's research team is providing metadata schemas to the CANARIE-sponsored POOL Project in Canada.

In India, 'Schoolnet India' is beginning to develop instructional content and multimedia resources for basic education and corporate training through its Learnet India subsidiary. Learnet India is building a software development kit (SDK) that can be used to construct and aggregate learning objects for the deployment in courseware and instructional materials. This SDK is based on the emerging XML standard and uses XML and Active X controls to integrate and author any multimedia-based title within Learnet.

The United States is the home of the IMS Global Learning Consortium, the Advanced Distributed Learning Initiative, and other standards initiatives focused on online learning. It continues to be a hothouse for learning object theories and practices. In April 2001, the Massachusetts Institute of Technology (MIT) announced an initiative that will further stimulate thinking in the learning object domain. MIT OpenCourseWare will make "course materials that are used in the teaching of almost all undergraduate and graduate subjects available on the web, free of charge, to any user anywhere in the world", A collaborative venture between MIT and Stanford University will make available to the educational community an object-based instructional delivery and management system, called the Open Knowledge Initiative. "The Open Knowledge Initiative (OKI) addresses what is perceived by many in higher education as a critical need: meaningful, coherent, modular, easy-to-use web-based environments for assembling, delivering and accessing educational resources and activities."

Information Structuring

The primary requirement for success in the virtual educational marketplace is the marriage of distinct product and service differentiation to high-quality execution. This requires a course development strategy that can provide multiple product and service streams and allow for custom designs to suit client needs. Underlying such a development process is a structured information model that applies a standards-based development and delivery framework that can align with the metadata systems such as those of the IMS Global Learning Consortium (IMS), Dublin Core, the Shareable Content Object Reference Model (SCORM) or others that may be available. But developing and implementing multiple course options from a unified development process is a problem for many educational institutions offering virtual learning programmes. A technology-enabled approach using a structured information can facilitate the production of courses that are web accessible and available in formats ranging from print to CD.

The key to understanding structured information is the concept of separating content from its presentation, which can be done using standard generalised markup language (SGML) or extensible markup language (XML). These are metalanguages can be used to develop print or web-based products that follow this separation. For example, in a course, an informal self-assessment item might appear in a particular font or format, or in a particular position within a lesson or unit, thereby cueing learners to its significance. To the human viewer, this convention is easily understood. But for a computer there is nothing significant about this string of characters apart from it being boldface, italicised, numbered or boxed, which may also be the style used to mark a section heading or some other structural component in the course document. In an SGML document, an explicit tag defines a self-assessment item. This tag informs the computer that it has encountered an informal assessment item, which can then trigger specific processing of this data. For example, instructional designers may wish to collect all the assessment items from a series of lessons and present them at the end of a unit as a review. If the same document is published on the web, specific processing for informal assessment items might draw upon a database in which randomly selected informal assessment items are presented to the learner for review purposes.

Formal separation of content from presentation allows content to be presented in multiple media from a single, unified source. The styles used in a specific medium are applied to the structural or semantic tags only in final presentation. The content is not bound to a specific presentational format and can be re-purposed with greater ease. Granular learning objects (text, image, audio, video) that are described by a classification system of metadata can be made available for product delivery from database environments using SGML and XML to describe and mark up content. At present, there are very few implementations of structured authoring processes that produce learning objects in practice. The Open Learning Agency's development model is one example of a structured information process that can provide multiple products from a common development system. It is used to illustrate some of the concepts behind learning objects and structured information.

IMS Global Learning Consortium project that has led the process for defining requirements for interoperability in learning materials. It is based on a metadata specification that permits structured information approaches to the authoring and packaging of content. While it has set the pattern for a reference model that can be applied widely, it is not alone in this work. The Advanced Distributed Learning Initiative (ADLI) of the US Department of Defence launched an implementation project in partnership with IMS in 1997 with the purpose of ensuring "access to high-quality education and training materials that can be tailored to individual learner needs and made available whenever and wherever they are required". The initiative was designed to "accelerate large-scale development of dynamic and cost-effective learning software and to stimulate an efficient market for these products in order to meet the education and training needs of the military and the nation's workforce in the 21st century through the development of a common technical framework for computer and net-based learning that will foster the creation of reusable learning content as instructional objects". The result of the ADLI initiative is the Sharable Courseware Object Reference Model (SCORM), an XML schema that describes the hierarchy for packaging course components using IMS metadata standards.

The Microsoft Learning Resource iNterchange (LRN) tool kit is another initiative that implements the IMS content packaging specification for a wider commercial audience. By providing a learning object tool kit to the education community, Microsoft further ensures that the IMS specifications will be accessible and potentially more widely adopted. Other hardware and software vendors such as SUN Microsystems have announced similar tool kits that are IMS compliant. The IMS Global Learning Consortium Web site lists directories of vendors and products that currently or will shortly comply with the IMS specifications in their product and service offerings.

When major hardware, software and product vendors get behind a standard, it has the potential to become the dominant specification worldwide.

Structured authoring tools such as Framemaker +SGML and document-type definitions were used in the Open Learning Agency example to produce content that could be rendered to print, to the web or to CD-based delivery media. The files were stored in a file management system, but no attempt was made to store object elements at a granular level in a database, where the real power of learning object models can be realised. Recently, more effective content management systems for object storage and manipulation have become available in the marketplace. Industry publications such as KM World have begun to feature content management systems that can structure and store learning objects in ways that allow them to be more easily manipulated at the object element level.

New content management systems can store the DTDs and XML schemas that are the keys to transforming objects into multiple distribution media. Systems such as the Vignette Content Management Server, eBT Engenda System, and Chrystal Eclipse/Astoria have the capability to store learning objects at a fine level of granularity. They can also be configured to automate workflow processes and to provide rich search capabilities. When these systems are matched with a customer relationship management and profiling systems, they can be positioned to provide self-service customisation. Vignette's Content Management Server product is optimised to power online periodicals such as Time magazine. A visit to the Time Web site will demonstrate the front-end capabilities of a content management system that has back-end workflows for writers, editors, graphic designers and page layout staff. The interface presents rich search capabilities and the ability for end-users to see almost instantaneous changes in object-based content.

Applying the same logic, it is possible to optimise a content management system to provide the workflows and self-service capabilities that would be required of a leading edge learning system. When the back-end database management systems are matched with authoring and media creation capabilities, a system close to the ideal of IMS Global Consortium begins to take shape.

Tools such as XML Authority can be used to design and edit XML schemas and SGML DTDs, the fundamental building blocks for granular learning structures. This is a highly technical process, but one for which instructional designers are well suited as team members. It is within the schema design process that the architecture for learning is created. Schemas and DTDs can be used to author instructional content and associated metadata in structured authoring tools such as XMetaL, Framemaker +SGML and Epic Editor.

Although these tools may be somewhat foreign to many content authors and instructional designers, they represent a way of thinking about instructional content production that reinforces the separation of presentation from content rubric. The tools require training to use, and they tend not to offer the opportunities for tinkering with presentation that can consume large amounts of development and production time. They are designed for large-scale content management problems where they interface directly with content management repositories, enabling version control, check-in and checkout workflows, reuse and re-proposing of content fragments or complete documents of any file or media type. When content authored using XML-aware tools is matched with an object-enabled management system, it is possible to leverage other tools in the virtual sphere to add additional value.

Many content management systems also come packaged with e-business applications and customer relationship management systems. These value-added tools provide the opportunity to profile customers and use the information collected to customise offerings to suit end-user preferences, as well to transact the financial details such as credit card payments for course modules or associated sales of books and media resources from other internet e-business partners.

Instead of seeing content or course authoring as a standalone activity in an educational organisation, the web-centric trend is to see the operation of an educational organisation as an integrated whole that can provide customised service to all of the organisation's learners and clients.

Learning content management systems (LCMS) that consist of a learning object repository coupled to an automated authoring application, an online delivery interface and an administrative application are becoming available from a number of vendors including Knowledge Mechanics, WBT Systems, and LeadingWay Knowledge Systems. These LCMS systems have the potential to highly automate the development, management and deployment of training content. They also signal the potential for the emergence of analogous systems optimised for the formal education sector.

Implications of web-oriented instructions

Instructional development environment enabled by a learning object model presents an enormous opportunity to educational organisations that are just now ramping up with virtual education products. They can design modularity and metadata into their products from the beginning with no legacy encumbrances. They can build systems that integrate business and customer support functions with instructional development and delivery functions. They can consider their instructional materials as true assets that will be archived, revised and upgraded over time. The object assets will be available for trade or sale in an e-commerce system that tracks their usage and assigns costs and royalties appropriately.

The metadata associated with the learning objects will make them easy to find on the web and provide streamlined paths for users, whether for instructional purposes or for commerce in the objects themselves. Examples of collaborative sharing models based on learning object attributes are already visible in the public education space.

The Multi-media Educational Resource for Learning and Online Teaching (MERLOT) is one example of a consortium approach to providing online resources for faculty and students. MERLOT was created in 1997 by the California State University Centre for Distributed Learning as "a free and open resource designed primarily for faculty and students in higher education. Information hosted in MERLOT is free to use for educational, non-commercial purposes, and materials linked to by MERLOT have a range of licence agreements from public domain to commercial".

For organisations with a longer history in virtual education, the challenge of the object economy is much more difficult. Decisions have to be made about identifying valuable instructional assets, modularising them, adding metadata and managing them in a format that allows for efficient storage and retrieval. For most traditional organisations, the move to a learning object model could be labour-intensive and expensive. A recent Goldman Sachs Equity Research report on the value of content in business-to-business (B2B) applications cited content management and the creation of "order from chaos" as the underlying routes to success for most existing organisations that want to be players in the content business.

Like educational institutions, content-rich organisations have massive amounts of unstructured instructional content that is not catalogued in any consistent manner and often not formatted in any consistent file type. The report documents processes that can be used to aggregate, cleanse and rationalise information so that metadata schemas can be applied before it is published in a catalogue or content management system where internal end-users or external commercial partners can get access to it.

While the Goldman Sachs (GS) report is aimed at publishers and commercial organisations, the same principles would apply to educational institutions. The GS report notes that XML is "a key technology in the B2B revolution." By using an XML tagging schema based on a metadata standard and coupled with a packaging specification for instructional materials, educational organisations empower themselves to participate in emerging shared resource consortia such as MERLOT or in commercial ventures with e-learning companies. It is imperative that educational organisations, particularly virtual education institutions, realise that a content management system is a requirement for success in this milieu.

Instructional developers in virtual education environments either act alone or as a part of a team. In a typical university scenario, courses that instructors or professors have offered in a face-to-face environment have been converted to online, web-based offerings, or have been extended to take advantage of unique features of the web such as asynchronous access to course materials for self-directed study. In many cases the instructor is given training in a particular online development, delivery and management tool such as WebCT or Blackboard and then the instructor proceeds to craft a course for online delivery.

The pedagogical structures embedded within the instructional delivery tool are tweaked to suit the needs of the class, the content or the particular instructional problem. In most cases, the courses are hand tooled and kept current through the intervention by the instructor over time. In large-scale distance education and distributer learning environments a more industrial model can be viewed.

Typically a team approach is used that includes subject matter experts, instructional designers, graphic artists, web designers, online delivery specialists and help desk staff. There is a specialisation in team roles that plays out throughout the development process. Instructional designers usually oversee a course through all stages of development and production, ensuring consistency and conformity with institutional guidelines for course production.

Courses in a large-scale environment tend to be reviewed periodically and are updated based on feedback from students, tutors or instructors. When taken to the web, instructional materials are either developed as standard HTML or they are produced in an instructional delivery and management system such as WebCT. In both cases, content and presentation become a blend that is difficult to separate into constituent parts after production has happened.

Updates and revisions occur across the entire work. Reuse or re-purposing of granular components is currently a labour-intensive process. Revision control is difficult beyond the level of the entire work. Use of modular components of a course for another purpose is difficult, if not impossible. If a new instructional delivery application comes along after many courses have been created, the change-over of all content to the new system would be expensive and time-consuming. The lesson here for instructional developers is a consistent theme: keep content and presentation separate throughout the life cycle of instructional materials. The advantages of this approach are all about opportunity:

i) Opportunity to produce instructional content at the course or modular component level from a common content source repository.

ii) Opportunity to deliver content in multiple media from a common content source repository.

iii) Opportunity to custom deliver content in any instructional delivery system now, or in the future, from a common content source repository.

iv) Opportunity to provide user-driven pathways through a common content source repository.

v) Opportunity to produce new products now or in the future from a common content source repository.

Instructional developers need to become familiar with learning object theory, metadata classification standards, instructional materials packaging schemes, content management systems, authoring tools and instructional delivery tools. And all of these related topics need to be enabled within an enterprise-wide system for the potential of the learning object approach to be realised in instructional development. If what learners are typically looking for from a virtual education experience is to achieve their academic or work-related goals with a focus on access, choice, flexibility, recognition of prior learning and end-to-end service, then learning object models can be used to facilitate such an experience.

NET-BASED TRAINING

The arrival of the World Wide Web signals the beginning of some fundamental changes in how teaching, training, and self-directed learning will occur at all ages and stages of life. Educators at all levels, from Kindergarten to adult training, are drawing a distinction between two fundamentally different approaches to teaching. The ultimate goal of distance education is to transfer, as effectively and efficiently as possible, a concise and coherent block of information from the teacher or computer into the minds of the learners.

Most existing computer-based training for adults has been designed with knowledge transfer in mind. Extraneous information is left out. The content is simplified. The emphasis is on individual learning and learners have a limited number of paths through the lesson. This approach works well for the training of basic skills in areas of knowledge that are well defined and stable. For most of us, though, the world just isn't that way. Adults face one ill-defined problem after another. They have to know change so quickly that some knowledge becomes obsolete almost as soon as we master it. The knowledge-transfer approach doesn't prepare adults well for a messy world in constant motion. An alternative way to think about teaching and learning is called constructivism. A constructivist trainer doesn't strip away the natural complexity of a subject. Instead, multiple perspectives are brought to bear.

The goal of a constructivist learning environment is not the accurate transfer of content from the instructor to the learner.

Instead, the learner is given tasks and opportunities, information resources and support, and is encouraged to construct their own version of the content, subject to revision through feedback. Many paths through the lesson are allowed and collaboration with other learners is stressed over lonely individual learning.

A constructivist use of technology presents information to the learner in multiple forms from multiple sources and invites the learner to make sense of it. The learner can acquire the information needed from several sources via the computer, and from off-line sources including his or her own prior experience, from information gathered while collaborating with other learners, and from references and other sources of expertise found somewhere far away from the computer screen. In general, a constructivist approach is more learner-focused, and less teacher-focused. The emphasis is on making a set of tasks and resources available to learners, and creating an environment in which the learners can actively create their own meaning in that context, rather than to passively absorb knowledge structures created by the instructor. In this approach, the instructor's role moves toward being a coach and orchestrator of resources, and moves away from being the sole source of information. This web technology has grown enormously in importance and accessibility lends itself beautifully to constructivist, active learning. The web is a part — the fastest growing part — of the internet. Before we get into the educational uses of the web, let us define some of the terms commonly used in discussing the web. Mosaic was the first of the graphical user interfaces to the web. Later on came another programme, Netscape, that added more features and faster speed. Both Mosaic and Netscape are what are called browsers.

A typical document of web page includes graphics both as a source of information and as decoration. Some of the text many be bold and underlined. These underlined words are called anchors or hot text. What happens when one click on an anchor? The browser sends a request off to a distant computer asking for it to send the information for a different page. If one had clicked on an anchor, the screen would have gone blank for a moment and then very quickly changed to a new page. The page that we are looking at resides on a computer called a server. A web server can be run on a personal computer or a UNIX workstation. The server need not be a fast, expensive machine. Setting up a server is a fairly simple task, and corporations, university departments, and even elementary schools are doing it every day.

Every document on the web has an address called a URL or Uniform Resource Locator. The web allows us to create anchors that download files for us or allow us to send e-mail to an individual. The web thus makes it easy to gain access to data, software and people. It is a user-friendly front end to almost everything on the internet. Within a year or so, the mechanics of creating documents on the web will become transparent. Most publishers of word processing software are adding the capability of saving documents in web format to their ever-growing list of features. So far, however, the end result of using a word processor to create web pages directly may not be exactly what you had in mind.

An active webwriter will want to know how to tweak the appearance of the documents and, for the moment, that requires some familiarity with HTML. HTML, or HyperText Markup Language, is easy to learn. To prepare a page for the web, you just embed special characters or tags in your document to tell your browser how to display a given word. An alternative method for displaying content on the web is the Adobe Acrobat format. This allows complex page layouts to be used, but users of the materials must all have the proper helper application installed on their machines.

Most medium to large-sized corporations have already established a web presence, and many smaller companies have as well. Whether one purchase space on the machines of an internet provider or set up his/her own webserver, he/she need not be physically near the server itself. To use web to distribute course materials, one should take advantage of all the material that is out there beyond the walls of his/her institution. The more he/she incorporate such activities into the course, the more it will become transformed into a learner-centered environment and the less often he/she will find himself/herself holding forth on centre stage. The resources which can be tapped include:

i) *External experts*. Though being brilliant, one probably may not be know all about the domain of course to be distributed. If one can get friends and colleagues, both in and outside of the enterprise, to volunteer to answer questions, he/she has broadened the pool of experience available to the students.

ii) *Newsgroups*: Newsgroups provide an invisible college of people helping people. They are a great source of up to the minute news about software releases, bugs, and workarounds. If one have his/her own newsserver, he/she can also set up internal newsgroups specific to the course to provide a space for students to exchange information on an ongoing basis.

iii) *FAQ files*: Most newsgroups maintain a list of frequently asked questions that have come up within that group. These can be a rich source of materials and pointers to other resources on the web.

iv) *Technical notes*: Most major software publishers have placed their technical notes on the web. One can wire these in as reference material and create activities that require the students to access them.

v) *Software archives*: There are many sources of useful wares such as patches, applications, utilities, documentation, ready to be downloaded. FTPing (i.e., grabbing) and decompressing this software is handled transparently by the web browser. One can place an anchor on a page that refers to a file and all the users have to do is click on it to have it delivered to their desktop.

vi) *Simulated people*: If one is teaching a course on desktop publishing and he/she want the students to have the experience of dealing with a difficult client. One way to bring that kind of encounter into the classroom is to set up an e-mail address with a fabricated name.

Having access to the web at one's institution/clssroom is like suddenly having the largest library in the world move in next door. For many people who are new to the web, the temptation to browse and pursue one link after another is so strong that they spend countless hours glued to the screen. In an educational or training situation, however, teachers does not have the luxury of spending all of their time that way. As much as they value curiosity and exploration, it is necessary for them to find ways to get the greatest learning benefit from the web in the shortest possible time.

There is a larger leap in sophistication needed to accomplish interactivity and automation. Think about all the things that you do as an instructor that are repetitious or clerical. If you could move those things onto the webserver's plate, you'll have more time to create a better learning environment in other ways. Here are several possible tasks that are appropriately delegated to the computer:

i) *Interactive FAQ's*: In any course, 20 per cent of all possible questions come up 80 per cent of the time. Instead of taking up class time dealing with these, place them in a database of pages organised by a branching tree of questions and subquestions.

ii) *Testing*: As you move towards distant delivery of your course, you lose the ability to sense who knows what among your students just by watching their body language. Frequent small-scale tests will provide the information you need and let you focus your attention on those who need extra help.

iii) *Tutorials*: The web lends itself well to the kind of one-frame-at-a-time tutorials that have been the staple format of computer-based training since the 1960s. For well defined stable content, you can move parts of what would have been a lecture into this more interactive format.

iv) *Meeting scheduling*: Outside of class time, you'll want to make yourself available by phone, videoconference, or in person. The web can provide a way for individuals in the class to sign up for a particular time slot so that your time and theirs is well spent.

v) *Course evaluation*. The best instructors don't wait until the end of a course to find out how it was perceived by the learners. Putting an anonymous evaluation form up on the web and encouraging its frequent use will allow you to make mid-course corrections quickly.

vi) *Feedback database*: In providing feedback to learners on their performance of complex skills such as programming, page layout, or spreadsheet design, you find yourself making the same kinds of comments repeatedly. A web-based feedback template would allow you do pick and choose from among common comments and edit them into a personalised reply efficiently.

It is a simple matter to place a form on the web that collects information from your learners. To actually send that information to the server and process it, though, goes beyond simple HTML into the realm of CGI: the Common Gateway Interface. It is here that most web developers stop because creating CGI programmes at this point requires the ability to programme in C, Perl, or AppleScript. As time goes on there will be ready-made CGI's available to accomplish most tasks, but for the near term there's a learning curve here that stops most people.

After putting the necessary course materials on the web, and by building in constructivist activities that make use of resources available in cyberspace, you could begin to allow distant learners to participate in your course. If you ask anyone who has conducted a course over the internet what it's like, the first thing they'll tell you is how much time they spend answering e-mail. Creating tools that allow for efficient testing, question-answering, and feedback will allow to scale up your course to many additional learners at a distance without breaking your back.

The net world is moving quickly towards greater interactivity and sensory engagement. There are several developments worth watching:

i) *RealAudio*: Some websites allow you to click on a picture and hear a greeting or introduction in the form of a sound file. You have to wait for the file to download before hearing anything, though, which tries the patience of all but the most fervent websurfers. RealAudio is different. It begins to stream audio to your workstation almost immediately. It's like radio on demand. For distance education, the usefulness of RealAudio is obvious. All of the spoken communication that makes up a bulk of a traditional class can be digitised and made available as needed. As long as this doesn't lead back to the "talk, chalk and a hairy arm" tradition, RealAudio could become a standard feature of distance education on the web.

ii) VRML: Virtual Reality Modelling Language is an embryonic set of tools and conventions for portraying three-dimensional space on the web. Instead of seeing a static picture, you'll be able to hold your mouse down over a graphic and see it from multiple perspectives, zooming in for detail and veering in any direction. For distance education, this allows for a more intuitive depiction of content: imagine seeing bubbles labelled with all the major concepts in your course. Lines linking the bubbles represent the relationships among them. Zoom in on a bubble and you've arrived at a webpage describing it in more detail. You might also use VRML to create a simulated learning environment with a reference room, laboratory, and help desk.

iii) *Java*: Most of what's available on the web is inert. You can admire it but not interact with it. Java is a language for writing small programmes (applets) that are downloaded as part of a web page. This will allow the web to take on most of the characteristics of the interactive multimedia you would find on a CDROM.

iv) *MOOs*: MOO stands for Multi-user dimension, Object-Oriented, which doesn't at first convey much about its meaning. A MOO is a shared virtual space that people can help create from their own computers. You can set up your conference room the way you like it and invite others to join you there. At present, most MOOs are text-based. When they begin to become more graphical, they will become the most popular places to be in cyberspace.

These developments, and others, will make distance education more and more practicable on the web as time goes on.

APPLICATIONS OF COMPUTER-MEDIATED COMMUNICATION (CMC)

The term computer-mediated communication (CMC) signifies the ways in which telecommunication technologies have merged with computers and computer networks to give us new tools to support teaching and learning. CMC describes the ways we humans use computer systems and networks to transfer, store, and retrieve information, but our emphasis is always on communication.

The computer network is primarily a mediator for communication rather than a processor of information. As it is currently used to support instructional purposes, CMC provides electronic mail and real-time chat capabilities, delivers instruction, and facilitates student-to- student and student-to-teacher interactions across a desk or across the world. These uses are enabling and promoting several paradigmatic shifts in teaching and learning, including the shift from instructor-centered distance education to student-centered distance learning and the merging of informal dialogues, invisible colleges, oral presentations, and scholarly publications into a kind of dialogic virtual university.

CMC is changing instructional methods in several ways, including:

i) generating improved technological tools that allow classes to use a fuller range of interactive methodologies, and
ii) encouraging teachers and administrators to pay more attention to the instructional design of courses.

Both of these factors can improve the quality, quantity, and patterns of communication in the skills students practice during learning—a change that requires, in many cases, both teachers and students to learn different roles. Educators often categorise the use of instructional CMC in three ways: for conferencing, informatics, and computer-assisted instruction (CAI). Computer conferencing provides e-mail, interactive messaging, and small and large group discussion. Informatics (repositories or maintainers of organised information) include library online public access catalogues (OPACs), interactive access to remote databases, programme/data archive sites (e.g., archives of files for pictures, sound, text, movies), campus-wide information systems (CWIS), wide-area information systems (WAIS), and information managers, such as Gopher and Veronica. In CAI, the computer is used to structure and manage both the presentation of information and the possible responses available to the human user.

Uses of computer conferencing, informatics, and CAI include:

i) mentoring, such as advising and guiding students
ii) project-based instruction, either within the classroom or in projects involving community, national, or international problem solving

iii) guest lecturing, which promotes interaction between students and persons in the larger community

iv) didactic teaching, that is, supplying course content, posting assignments, or other information germane to course work

v) retrieval of information from online information archives, such as OPACs, ERIC, and commercial databases

vi) course management, for example, advising, delivery of course content, evaluation, collecting and returning assignments

vii) public conferencing, such as discussion lists using main frame Listserv software

viii) interactive chat, used to brainstorm with teachers or peers and to maintain social relationships

ix) personal networking and professional growth and such activities as finding persons with similar interests on scholarly discussion lists

x) facilitating collaboration

xi) individual and group presentations

xii) peer review of writing, or projects involving peer learning, groups/peer tutorial sessions, and peer counselling

xiii) practice and experience using emerging technologies that may be intrinsically useful in today's society

xiv) computer-based instruction, such as tutorials, simulations, and drills.

One of the greatest benefits of CMC is its ability to liberate instruction from the constraints of time and distance. The convenience of access from home, school, or office permits many students and instructors to better meet travel, job, and family responsibilities. CMC promotes self-discipline and requires students to take more responsibility for their own learning.

Using CMC, instructors can vary a course's instructional design to include everything from structured projects to open projects in which students are free to work on "messy"—but authentic—problem solving. On the other hand, because students must manage their own learning, this newfound independence may be a hindrance to those students who need more structure.

We have entered an information age in which power comes to those who have information and know how to access it. If we consider which factors of CMC will be most important to education in the information age, it seems that our goals should be to develop self-motivated learners and help people learn to find and share information. If designed well, CMC applications can be used effectively to facilitate collaboration among students as peers, teachers as learners and facilitators, and guests or experts from outside the classroom. One of the more important aspects of CMC use in instruction is that it is text-based. Facility in writing is essential across the entire curriculum, and with the present technology one cannot communicate on a computer network without writing.

If used effectively, CMC encourages and motivates students to become involved in authentic projects and to write for a real audience of their peers or persons in the larger world community, instead of merely composing assignments for the teacher. At the same time, we must recognise that not all students can express themselves well in writing, and, even for those who can, the act of writing and using online text-based applications can be a time-consuming struggle.

CMC promotes an equalisation of users. Because CMC is, at present, primarily text-only, the consequent reduction in social cues leads to a protective ignorance surrounding a person's social roles, rank, and status. Further, it is impossible to know if another person took several hours to draft a one screen response, or several minutes. Responses are judged by the ideas and thoughts conveyed, more so than by who is doing the writing. As a result, the lack of social cues and the asynchronous nature of the medium affords those with physical limitations or personal reticence the possibility of participating fully and equally in communicative activities within a mainstream environment. However, researchers realise that when social context cues are minimised nonreticent personalities can be encouraged to become overly zealous in their responses, or to become publicly inflammatory and aggressive on a personal level in ways that generally do not occur in other media. It has been noted that some students prefer the social aspects of the classroom and are unsettled by the lack of face-to-face interaction in CMC, or the lack of a charismatic lecturer during presentation.

Another potential benefit of CMC is in promoting multicultural awareness. With the demographic make-up of many countries changing so rapidly, it is becoming increasingly important to develop communication skills for a culturally diverse community and world. Still, although CMC enhances some of these valuable skills for the 21st century, we must remember that because the bulk of CMC is conducted in English and in the written rather than in the spoken word, it may perpetuate some cultural hegemonies.

Responsible use of CMC means using it in addition to other media, not as a replacement. There are technical benefits to using CMC, such as the ease of circulating and archiving files and documents. The learning curve, with regard to learning the system and the technical "how tos" of the computer and telecommunications, can be steep. The cost of buying and supporting systems or accessing other networks is a significant "overhead" item in schools and colleges today, as is the cost and inconvenience of upgrading, repairing, or replacing hardware. Further, computer systems are not 100 per cent reliable, a fact that adds to inconvenience and wasted time. With so many systems to learn and sources to tap, information overload has become a problem as some users struggle with the lack of criteria to help them to decide what to keep and what to discard from the swiftly flowing stream of incoming information.

Researchers, information designers, and instructional developers can use CMC to promote collaboration, cooperation, the sharing of ideas, and as an equalising medium. No longer perceived as the sole experts and information providers, teachers become facilitators and guides. Conversely, students are no longer passive learners, attempting to mimic what they see and hear from the expert teacher. They become participants, collaborators in the creation of knowledge and meaning. Yet we must attempt not to reproduce or augment the problems associated with the gap between technology "haves" and "have nots" when we design CMC and computer conferencing applications and curricula.

Every software, networking, or curriculum innovation reflects, to some degree, the unarticulated assumptions about the world view of the culture that created it. We must be aware of this fact and strive to create and use CMC innovations that allow for multiplicity, for change, for difference. In response to increased pressure on universities and instructors to provide instructional delivery systems that go beyond the traditional "chalk-and-talk" form of lecture, computer-mediated conferencing has emerged as a tool for instructional communication not bound by prescribed meeting times or by geographic proximity.

Successful integration of CMC into the curriculum, however, depends on one's ability to design and use CMC applications that meet course goals, delivery goals, or both. As part of course planning, we must address issues such as course goals, hardware availability, and student readiness. Large expenditures on CMC for the classroom will not help unless teachers understand how the technology helps fulfil the goals of the course.

CMC's flexibility and variety allows instructors to meet numerous learning and personal needs, especially when working with individuals with special needs and those who are less mobile or shy. However, many CMC applications require that students first take the time to learn considerable information and skills and be provided with access to computers and software that can be costly. CMC enhances both the teaching and the learning process. In considering the major benefits of CMC, her students said that they appreciated the timely feedback, the accessibility of faculty and resources outside of class hours, and their ability to get more out of the class.

Networked Interactivity

Like face-to-face communication, computer-mediated communication has the capacity of enabling high interactivity. One postulated outcome of interactivity is engagement. Interactivity can lead to sociability. Interactivity is a theoretical construct that grapples with the origins of captivation, fascination, and allure that can be inherent in computer-mediated groups. It is a variable quality of communication settings. It expresses the degree to which communication transcends reaction. It is a cause in the social dynamics of group communication. Such interactivity is made possible, but not always exercised, by CMC.

The concept of interactivity is a likely candidate to help in explaining how groups, especially CMC groups, stick together. Interactivity is not a characteristic of the medium. It is a process-related construct about communication. It is the extent to which messages in a sequence relate to each other, and especially the extent to which later messages recount the relatedness of earlier messages.

Communication is mostly about and for the purpose of interaction. Interactivity places shared interpretive contexts in the primary role. Interactivity describes and prescribes the manner in which conversational interaction as an iterative process leads to jointly produced meaning.

Interactivity merges speaking with listening. It is a general enough concept to encompass both intimate, person-to-person, face-to-face communication and other forums and forms. Logically, it is indicated as a useful concept for mapping group CMC because it is a hybrid construct. The concept of interactivity directs our focus to the intersection of the psychological and the sociological, the bridge between mass and interpersonal communication, the meeting of mediated and direct communication, and the paradox of written vs. spoken.

Interactivity varies along a continuum. At one end is declarative (one-way) communication (e.g. most radio and television). Reactive (two-way) communication is further down the road. In reactive communication, one side responds to the other side. Fully interactive communication requires that later messages in any sequence take into account not just messages that preceded them, but also the manner in which previous messages were reactive. In this manner interactivity forms a social reality.

Interactivity is the condition of communication in which simultaneous and continuous exchanges occur, and these exchanges carry a social, binding force. The following are some additional qualities of interactive communication:

i) allowing for multiple types of cues,
ii) potential spontaneity,
iii) emergent progression of the content,
iv) the ability to interrupt or pre-empt,
v) mutuality, and
vi) patterns of turn-taking.

Interactivity in communication settings is associated with the attitudinal dimensions of acceptance and satisfaction. But it is also related to performance quality, motivation, sense of fun, cognition, learning, openness, frankness and sociability.

Interactivity operates in a supplementation mode. Quasi-interactive (reactive) media can allow people to use the media as a substitute for sociability. The human need for interaction, when satisfied, allows people to use interactive media to bolster their favourable disposition toward interacting with others. Interactivity can be shown to lead to more cooperation.

Networks are centralised distribution mechanisms that are both democratic and anarchic. Computer mediated groups can be viewed as an enigma in traditional, rational and economic terms. After all, the medium is owned by no one. The process is unmanaged in any traditional sense of motivation, profit, control or censorship. Joining and departing participants do so without so much as a required introduction or an agreed upon etiquette. CMC groups are neither mass nor interpersonal. If we count participants and symmetry, we find that CMC is the largest form of conversation, or the smallest form of mass communication.

REFERENCES

Bates, A.W., *Managing Technological Change: Strategies for University and College Leaders,* San Francisco: Jossey Bass, 2000.

Christensen, C.M., *The Innovator's Dilemma: When New Tech-nologies Cause Great Firms to Fail,* Boston: Harvard Business School Press, 1997.

Dirr, Peter J., "Distance and Virtual Learning in the United States." In *The Development of Virtual Educa-tion: A Global Perspective.* Vancouver: The Commonwealth of Learning, 1999.

Farrell, M. Glen, *The Development of Virtual Education: A Global Perspective,* Vancouver: The Commonwealth of Learning, 1999.

________________ , (ed.), *The Changing Faces of Virtual Education*, Commonwealth of Learning, Vancouver, Canada, 2001.

Huang, J., *Distance Education: A Key Strategy for Lifelong Learning in Chinese Taipei*, Taipei: Department of Research and Development, National Open University, 1997.

Hutton, L., "Distance Education: Players and Changes," *The Advising Quarterly* Summer, 1999.

Moe, M., and H., Blodget, *The Knowledge Web*, New York: Merrill Lynch, 2000.

Rose, E., "An Evaluation of Online Distance Education Course Databases," *DEOSNEWS 10*, no. 11, 2000.

Smith, P., and C.L., Dillon, "Comparing Distance Learning and Classroom Learning: Conceptual Considerations", *The American Journal of Distance Education* 13, no. 2, 1999.

5

Distance Education: Globalising Trends

The global environment has changed remarkably with respect to the application of information and communication technologies (ICTs) at all levels of education. Most educational institutions are developing or planning to develop web-based course delivery capability. A significant number of government, institutional, corporate and private websites have emerged to chronicle the burgeoning numbers of virtual education initiatives.

The provision of education is the biggest challenge for most governments as they attempt to attain the ideal of peace, freedom and social justice, while striving at the same time to position themselves to generate more wealth and compete in a global market. The governments and international development and aid organisations are experiencing a growing sense of urgency to respond to the challenge of providing education in a changing global market. They are recognising that it cannot be done effectively without substantive reform to their education systems.

A number of global forces are serving to raise the sense of urgency. First is the increased world population. In 2015 it will be 7.2 billion, up from the current 6.1 billion. Ninety-five percent of the increase will be in developing countries. People in most countries will live longer, which will add to the demand for access to education as well as for health-care and other services. The second force is globalisation, which is driven by the global networked economy, will enhance not only the demand for education, but create need for more diversified content and greater flexibility of access.

However, two trends running parallel to the globalisation process will have a significant impact on the development of global systems of virtual education. These are the creation of more small and medium-sized enterprises and an increasing desire to defend cultural, linguistic and religious identities. Each of these trends complicates inter-institutional collaboration and mitigates against the flow of globalised content across borders. Exponential growth of scientific knowledge continues to be accompanied by a widening gap between developed and developing countries, the latter being unable, single-handedly, to acquire the basic infrastructure necessary to access that knowledge.

Educational strategies that are being deployed in response to these forces may variously be called virtual education, distance education, distributed learning, online learning, web-based learning e-education, e-learning, or any one of a number of other labels. Current strategies typically involve the use of digital networks, either synchronously or asynchronously, for the delivery and tuition of courses and management of administrative services such as registration, records, fee payment, etc. However, whatever the label used to describe these current strategies, they all have their roots in the practice of distance education.

The new distance education force transforming higher education may not be controlled by the traditional structures or providers of education or by traditional academic policies. Not only do the new forms of education portend a change for student populations, but also they will force faculty to develop new modalities of teaching and administrators to provide a new infrastructure for support. As a result, the advent of distance education is forcing many institutions to review and amend many of their existing policies and procedures.

Change in education systems is always in pursuit of one or more of the following goals:

i) Improvement of access to educational opportunities.

ii) Enhancement of quality in terms of both standards achieved and the learning process.

ii) Improvement of efficiencies such as increased productivity, greater return on invested capital and cost reduction or containment.

Many authors have described the increasing use of ICT as an evolutionary process that has been underway for some time. In 1999, Tapsall and Ryan, described the evolution of delivery modes in terms of three phases: distance education, open learning and flexible learning. According to them, the first phase, distance education, emerged in response to the needs of learners who were unable to access campus- based institutions because of geographical distance and/or work and personal commitments. The second phase, open learning, while also responding to the problems of distance, is primarily focused on meeting the needs of those who are disadvantaged in terms of entry qualifications and, therefore, need to be served through "second chance" enrolment policies and alternative programmes and delivery models. The third phase, flexible learning, is less about distance or disadvantage than about providing more education to more students, anywhere, anytime, at less cost. Flexible delivery modes, using CDROMs and the internet, are being used as much as a solution to on-campus problems as they are to off-campus access. Tapsall and Ryan claim that, as a result, face-to-face and distance and open learning modes are converging.

Another view of the evolution of ICT applications in higher education offered by Peter Dirr claims that two features have characterised the process. One is that the technology application decisions have been driven primarily by technology, not by consumers. The other is that the applications have been to a traditional academic paradigm. He points to the widespread use of video-conferencing, which has enabled instructors to retain many of the old pedagogical methods, but has done little to accommodate the learner's need for flexibility. Dirr Peter argues that institutions have failed to employ the full potential of newer technologies and have not taken full advantage of the resources available to both learners and instructors.

Another perspective, put forward by Stephen Ehrmann argues that "many institutions are searching for a unifying vision to guide their investments in teaching, learning and technology. Some of them hear a thundering herd of innovations collectively referred to as distance education and learning anytime anywhere for anyone and are wondering if their campuses even have a future." Ehrmann contrasts the concept of the "campus- bound" paradigm with the "campus-based" paradigm. The former assumes that the quality of a programme depends entirely on the books, laboratories, faculty members, students, etc. that are on-site. But the latter, which he calls the new paradigm, assumes that some of the resources and some of the learning are off-site. Networks enable staff and students to use a web of academic resources and, as a result, they may only be on campus part of the time.

Application of ICT to education and training has increasingly allowed institutions to deliver learning in a variety of venues. The choice of venue is driven by the ability to access the learning materials using ICT. Many potential learners do not have ICT in their homes, so there is a need to find alternative ways to access such learning experiences. Institutions using ICT as the delivery platform for learning can be defined as virtual institutions.

It is estimated that about two trillion dollars or one-twentieth of global gross domestic product is spent on education. One-fifth of this amount is being spent by the private sector while the rest is spent by governments on the public education system. International and national campaigns such as 'education for all' have succeeded in drawing learners into the education system, but the development of distance education opportunities has also had much to do with the growth in numbers. Many students are attracted by the prestige of offshore degrees, and this trend it likely to continue as distance and virtual education continue to develop. The private sector has also supported and been a driving force behind the increase in participation in distance and virtual education. Employees who want to advance their careers, but who can't afford to take the time out to study at contact institutions, are attracted to virtual learning opportunities.

ICTs have made the walls of the learning space transparent, providing a freedom for the learner to explore sources of information outside his institution, even outside his country. While ICT has undoubtedly opened new avenues for increased numbers of learners, it has also opened new areas of research focusing on the role of pedagogical processes when using new technologies and on their impact on cognition.

Use of the new technologies are vital components of the new information economy and information society. The term 'knowledge society' has enabled a shift away from technology as a driver of change to a tool that offers new ways of combining the information available with people who will drive development. This shift pressures countries to develop education systems that enable skilled people to work within the knowledge society and within the global economy. The result of such pressure on both developing and developed countries has been a massive increase in education and the drive for qualifications. Rapid development of virtual education is most noticeable in the developed world where there is much greater access to educational institution and learning technologies, especially computers, CDROMs and the internet. In the developing world, limited access to ICT is apparent.

As access increases, in the corporate world, companies will focus on their ability to exploit internet and e-commerce opportunities. Employees will need to rapidly develop their knowledge and skills to use the technology and to redesign the business process. Many businesses will encourage in-house and distance education and training, and they will complement this with e-learning.

Current research indicates that while the education market has declined in tandem with other sectors that make up the internet economy, the sector encompassing corporate e-learning providers and companies serving higher education markets has not suffered more than other sectors anchored in internet technologies. Many companies view e-learning as a strategic necessity that is vital in today's knowledge economy. While ICT makes it possible for many potential learners in many parts of developing countries, including remote and rural areas, to have access to education, such access is very limited.

There are a number of technological constraints that restrict virtual education. For one, the telecommunications infrastructure outside many of the major cities in developing countries are limited and inadequate. For example, in Africa has approximately 12 per cent of the world's population, but only 2 per cent of the global telephone network. Telephone density is less than two lines per 1000 people. These figures become even more startling when compared with Asia, America, Europe and high-in-come countries. Internet reach in India doubled from a subscriber base of one million to over two million within six months in 2000. However, when this impressive figure is matched against the total population of India of one billion, you get the sense of the magnitude of the lack of access to computers and the internet. The situation in Latin America indicates huge disparities. In the mid-1990s, few people in South America, rich or poor, owned a computer or had access to the internet. The changes have been dramatic over the last few years. Now 35 million Latin Americans own PCs and 20 million use the internet, but the poor have been largely left out of this development.

Both developing and developed communities have responded in different ways to these and other constraining factors to virtual education. One key response has been to redefine the nature and function of learning venues that enable virtual education.

DEVELOPMENT OF INNOVATE LEARNING VENUES

Introduction of ICT to support virtual education has generated a range of discussion, generally focusing on the value of using the technology for this form of education delivery. Often such discussion illustrates a lack of unanimity on the issues that need to be addressed for the effective use of technology to support virtual education. However, there are three issues that seem to generate consensus by all people involved in education: costs, decision-making and access. The lack of access to learning venues and the lack of access to connectivity and learning technologies within venues was a major constraint, particularly in developing countries. And it is this element of education, the "place" of the educational interaction, that is increasingly being seen as crucial to promoting access to virtual education. Response of many developing and developed countries to ways of increasing access to virtual education has been to redefine the nature of learning sites. There are many terms used to describe these learning sites, including community learning centres, multi-purpose community centres, telecentres and derivations thereof.

Community Learning Centre (CLC)

Community Learning Centre (CLC) is a site where education programmes that are relevant to the needs of the community are made available to the members of the community. These centres are located in different types of buildings. The key characteristics of community learning centres are flexibility, responsiveness to local needs and the creative and efficient use of available resources and infrastructure. CLCs are often connected to various data sources and networks and use these connections to offer various opportunities such as: offering services and resources based on; local education and training needs; providing access to formal and non-formal training and skills development programmes; being a catalyst for communities to make use of their own resources; providing information and communication according to community needs; acting as access points for local and outside resources; providing a base for community development forums, etc.

Multipurpose Community Centre (MPCC)

The term 'multi-purpose' implies the various sectors that offer services such as information, housing, adult basic education and training, health, culture, small business development, various types of employment, welfare and social interaction. An MPCC is often seen as a "one-stop shop" that directly meets the education and training needs of both the individual and the broader community. A further derivative of the multi-purpose community centre is the multi-purpose community learning centre (MPCLC). The MPCLC is seen as that component of the MPCC that is focused on education and training services. An MPCLC delivers multi-sectoral education and training, with formal education at certain times and non-formal at other times.

Telecentres

The term, 'telecentres', has been derived to describe a centre that offers various communication services. Telecentres are communal facilities consisting of a physical space that provides public access to ICTs for educational, personal, social and economic uses. The services offered range from basic telephony, fax and e-mail to full internet connectivity. In their paper on telecentres, Gomez, Hunter and Lamoureux have developed a typology of telecentres that describe the five different types: basic telecentre, telecentre franchise, civic telecentre, cyber cafe and multipurpose community telecentre (MTC).

Basic telecentres

Basic telecentres are generally small operations that are either privately owned or run by non-governmental organisations (NGOs) as part of their services. The NGO operation is often funded by international donor agencies. Basic telecentres are usually found in rural, marginalised or peri-urban areas that support poor communities with high levels of illiteracy. They usually offer "a mix of services including telephony, fax, computing, internet, photocopying and related technologies". As well, they often have a small number of computers that use dial-up connections to an Internet Service Provider (ISP). The key to the success of basic telecentres is that they are linked to the local community they serve and their workers are drawn from the local community.

Telecentre franchises

Telecentre franchises refer to a number of interconnected telecentres that are independently owned. As they are based on a franchise model, there is a centrally located organisation that facilitates technical and/or financial support. Telecentre franchises generally have a small number of computers for public access and use dial-up connections to an ISP. While there is central support, the nature of the services offered differ according to needs of the community that is being served. In Egypt, three technology access community centres (TACCs) have been established in the delta. They have generated over 3000 community internet users and trained hundreds of community members to use the internet. This was done at a cost far less than the commercial cyber cafes. Brazil offers another example of the telecentre franchise model. At present there are 208 Computer and Citizenship Schools in Brazilian states that have been established by the Centre for the Democratisation of Computer Science.

The Global Distance Learning Network (GDLN) initiative of the World Bank has established 23 telecentre franchise operations in Africa; Asia; Europe; Latin America and the

Caribbean; Middle East and North Africa and North America. These centres use state-of-the-art technology to promote learning and information sharing. Each centre is run and managed by the institution hosting it and offers courses and capacity-building programmes aimed at government officials, private sector representatives, NGOs, students and others. While GDLN centres do not fit into the traditional model of telecentres, the services many of these offer reflect the telecentre functions, albeit at a higher level of technology. GDLN centres are designed to offer full multimedia connectivity and interaction, which runs independent of the local country telecommunications infrastructure. The centres are designed to have one room for live video and data interaction with a second room being used for computer and internet-based activities. Other rooms are for the network communications equipment, training, administration, etc.

Civic telecentres

Civic telecentres are probably the most common type of centre found in many traditional civic institutions (e.g., public libraries, schools, universities, community organisations that have buildings and community centres). These centres have traditionally offered services to a single group within the community. Recently, there has been a shift to offering multiple services to multiple groups at different times and in different spaces within the centre. Egypt provides one example of this type of civic telecentre. The Investing in Egypt's Future initiative focused on developing ICT-empowered libraries. The telecentres follow a business model that was structured to ensure sustainability. In the USA, the Community Technology Centres Network (CTCNet) has assisted in establishing hundreds of telecentres in low-income urban and rural areas. CTCNet brings together agencies and programmes that provide opportunities where people of all ages who lack access to technologies can use them to develop personal skills and self-confidence.

Majority of these centres' clients have used them to improve their skills, mainly in computer- related areas, and to find jobs. These organisations support lifelong learning opportunities, especially for people who have had limited and/or negative educational opportunities. Some of these centres are standalone while others operate as part of larger organisations such as museums, libraries, job training centres and shelters. These centres often offer limited services and do not publicise their services outside of the immediate community.

Cyber cafes

The rapid growth and popularity of cyber cafes, especially in urban areas, is worth noting and exploring ways for their use to support access to virtual education opportunities. Some community-oriented cyber cafes offer preferential rates or services to communities or local organisations while still maintaining their commercial business activities to the general public. An example of using a cyber cafe was recently illustrated by Niall McKay in which he focused on the computer science courses being offered by the Carnegie Mellon University. The courses are being offered worldwide, and in India the point of access is the internet cafes in Delhi. To offer support to the students, Carnegie Technology Education, a subsidiary of the university, has partnered with Sterling InfoTech, an Indian internet service provider, and local cyber cafes.

Multi-purpose community telecentres

Multi-purpose community telecentres (MCTs) are likely to have higher-end technologies, employ full-time staff, focus on specialised services and train a broad array of users in areas such as health, education, small business and local governance". Often these centres also offer postal and banking services, and given the high bandwidth requirements of the MCT, most have leased lines or ISDN (integrated services digital network) with a local network connecting the computers. Increasingly these centres are being used for tele-trading, support to small and medium enterprises and vocational training courses. In Brazil, the pioneers of the MCT sought to open telecentres based on a multipurpose model comprised of public service module, tele-office module, business module and educational module. The Australian Telecentre Network was established to enable access to tertiary-level students that were in rural and remote communities. Thus these centres serve as venues through which educational institutions can offer courses and programmes.

In India, the MS Swaminathan Research Foundation has partnered with the International Development Research Centre (IDRC) to implement the Information Villages Research Project in the Pondicherry region. This project is based on the argument that providing information and adding value to such information is vital to enabling rural families to access it. The project has established value-added centres where staff scans the internet for information on technologies, health, transport, public events, education, subsidies, prices of local commodities, etc. Thus the value-added centre acts as the hub site and uses VHF radio system for a local area network that connects the hub to village information centres. Each shop varies in the way it is operated and supported. One has a village development council; another has a non-formal trust established by the community; a third uses space allocated to it by the locally elected panchayat. The shops each have a pentium PC with multimedia software and printers. The PC is connected to the wireless network through a modem. Each shop also has a board to display bulletins and other village information. Given the range of information available via the hub site, various members of the village use the shop for different purposes.

To develop a telecentre, we should have the following technology options and requirements:

i) *Telephony services*: A telephone system is a vital part of telecentres. Phones need to include audio-conferencing facilities, answering machines and a call accounting system that can note the unit charge of the calls made and, therefore, calculate the costs of the call. Faxes are also important to communications, and telecentres are increasingly able to make use of low-cost internet-based fax services.

ii) *Computer systems:* The majority of centres have a multi-PC environment with one machine dedicated to administration with the others being available to the general public. Increasingly, many telecentres are using refurbished computers to add to their network.

iii) *Internet access:* It has become the selling point for telecentres. If telephone linkages are unavailable, then standalone computers, TVs and radios are able to provide services to the community. Internet access via dial-up to an Internet Service Provider (ISP) is often expensive, especially when it requires a long distance call.

iv) *LAN systems*: When more than one PC is being used, they can be linked together via cables into a local area network (LAN). Wireless LANs are becoming popular as they allow for expanding the networks to other buildings without the need for cabling.

v) *Community radio stations*: Some centres also have community radio stations that offer valuable information and support to education, health and community development. Other technology requirements include printers, modems, video-conferencing and various software for training, education and communications. Other equipment generally found in better resourced telecentres include photocopiers, binding machines, CD writers, scanners, laminators, paper shredders, cameras, VCRs, audio cassettes, and projection equipment.

There has been a massive increase in the number of students enrolled in various sectors of the education and training system. There has also been increasing demand for professional development opportunities that has resulted in the rapid increase in the number of private sector providers using technology to deliver education and training. This growth, coupled with the developments in ICT, has resulted in learning being accessed in creative ways. The concern to bridge the digital and information divide is also an important driving force in the development of innovative learning venues. This is best illustrated by the recent meeting of the world's richest nations at their G8 conference in Okinawa, Japan.

The Japanese prime minister announced that Japan is committing U.S.$12 billion in loans and U.S.$3 billion in grants over the next five years to ICT technology initiatives in the developing world. This announcement was coupled with a set of proposals constructed by a task force established at the 2000 Davos meeting that called for, among other things, the creation of a Peace Corps-style group called the Global Digital Opportunity Corps and the establishment of local technology community centres.

The need for individually tailored education has been helped by the development of resource-based learning, distance education and, more recently, the creation of learning objects for content aggregation. Enabling the individual learner to access education opportunities using ICT has ensured that there is an emerging market for education. This in turn has driven the development of innovative access points to learning opportunities. Access is not only about hardware and software; it is about creating an environment which attracts students by providing them with a place to meet their peers and teachers/ tutors and with access to resources necessary to complete their courses.

The need for more physical space in the form of traditional classrooms is often resisted in developing countries because of the cost. The notion of multipurpose learning centres offers a more cost-effective use of such physical infrastructure. A further driving force supporting the development of multipurpose learning centres is the potential to cater to diverse and varied community education needs over the wider age continuum. These centres have the potential of offering programmes directed at preparing learners for the world of life and work beyond school, and more specifically, to become competent citizens in the information age and knowledge society. These centres are able to be flexible and respond to changing demands for different learning options. Multi-purpose centres also allow learners to work on their courses at a time and place convenient to them. This flexibility allows students to engage with tutors and course developers via e-mail rather than having to wait for a time and place in a traditional space of the lecture or tutorial room.

By increasing access to the technology, greater demands are placed on the time of the tutor or instructor. These demands are for quick responses to queries, assignments and other work for assessment, for keeping the web site updated and for electronic discussions. This requires proper planning, both for the network that is being used to engage with students and with the response time for feedback to students. There are a variety of other constraining forces that hinder the development of innovative learning spaces:

Access to connectivity remains one of the major challenges facing many developing countries. Students would need access to computers that can send and receive messages using web browsers such as Explorer or Netscape. In addition, they would have to find on their computers word processors and other applications to complete basic assignments. Easy and inexpensive connections to internet service providers would be required. In addition, depending on the nature of the given course, students might be required to use a VCR to play videotaped instruction and perhaps tape recorded lectures. Textbooks and other printed materials would still be part of the curriculum.

Issue of costs is also a hindrance to developing learning spaces. Governments in many developing countries have stopped building schools and classrooms on any meaningful scale. It is left to donor agencies and the private sector to consider building classrooms. The costs associated with using

ICT are also prohibitive in many developing countries. While the unit costs of hardware and software are being lowered in terms of the US dollar, the worsening exchange rate of developing countries means that there is no appreciable drop in the costs.

The use of multi-purpose centres for virtual education relies on trained and professional support. Often learners require support, whether online or at the centres where they access the learning materials. This support, however, is often lacking in developing countries where, to date, very few scholars are familiar with teaching and support in an online environment. This situation poses a threat to being able to deliver online learning as well as to the development of online courses that are context-specific to a country or region.

Another concern is about the quality of the degrees being earned online. The American Federation of Teachers, which represents more than one million teachers, does not believe that an online degree equals the same degree as one where someone is meeting with other students and professors. This opinion illustrates the need for trained and professional support at the access points to ensure that the quality of support for online degrees and other courses increases the quality of those degrees and courses.

Development of Learning Venues

The four major considerations that need to be addressed if learning venues are to support virtual education are planning, management, education application and learner support.

Planning

To plan effectively, it is necessary to conduct an internal and external environmental scan. The internal scan should focus on internal practices to identify the strengths and weaknesses of the centre and the technological infrastructure required. The external scan should note the various factors that would support or hinder the centre. Some of these would include possible partners in terms of content, technical support and education institutions; organised user or client groups within the community; government; local businesses and the recreational needs of the surrounding community. This scan is crucial to determine the programmes that could be offered, to ensure that the centre is able to meet the needs being expressed by the community it is serving and to enable it to become economically self-sustaining.

Often these centres have been established by government departments, private sector organisations, development agencies, non-governmental organisations or a combination of these entities. There needs to be a combination of local ownership and management with external investment. The franchised-based model for the multipurpose centre offers the best option to enable sustainability. It allows for outside seed money, bulk services and rates, training, equipment and technical assistance to be provided to the centre.

The centre needs to be located in an area that has a relatively dense population with a strong small and micro-enterprise (SME) platform to enable it to be sustainable. If such centres are linked to existing institutions of good standing within the community, then the chances of being successful and sustained are greater.

The centre must meet real needs and develop specific content for local communities. The need for relevant, accurate information that can be applied to different sectors ensures that the users identify with the centre and the relevance of the services being offered. This approach displays a demand-driven list of services that meet needs.

The quality and commitment of the management and staff is vital. Training of a technical nature, personnel, financial and marketing is necessary to the success of the centre. A centre that offers a broader range of fee-for-use services to the local community is likely to generate revenue that could be used to cross-subsidise other services that are not revenue-generating.

While there is great value to offering a wide range of services and functions, this approach can also lead to the centre management and staff not having the skills and being unable to cope with the strategic planning and management required.

Management

The community-based telecentre model under experimentation in a number of developing countries may well represent a new organisational form for delivering quality educational services on a more equitable and cost-effective basis." Given the experimental nature of telecentres, their success is based on good management that interprets the mission, aims and objectives into deliverable programmes, projects and services that meet the needs and priorities of the clients and community. In this context, managing the planning process, staffing structure, recruitment and responsibility, financial management, quality assurance of the services being offered, administration and governance of the centre are important management issues.

Managing any centre should also include external components that include advocacy in terms of stating what the centre offers, providing information to client groups, marketing the services, assessing new needs of the various client groups and facilitating collaborative relationships with various institutions, both public and private, non-governmental and community-based organisations. The manager and staff need to understand the above requirements for a successful centre. All staff members should be able to clearly articulate the focus of the centre and display a high degree of skills and attitude that meets the needs of the client group and encourages them to visit the centre and use its facilities. The computer skills, together with strong management skills, are necessary prerequisites to making a telecentre work. Thus, training is a vital part for the development of any centre and should include management and other necessary skills. They list the following as possible key training components:

i) Communication and development.
ii) The role of telecentres in development.
iii) The role of the telecentre manager.
iv) Business and financial skills.
v) Needs assessment skills and evaluation methods.
vi) Training skills.
vii) Human resource management.
viii) Marketing and public relations skills.
ix) Communication and development.
x) Basic computer skills.
xi) Information production skills.

There are already a variety of course materials available in these areas for training.

Educational Applications

While noting the changes in technological and educational trends, the question of whether the concept of a school as a single-use building occupied for only part of the day by an age-defined group of people will not be entertained. It is clear that given the economic pressures, access pressures, the changing nature of the learning and teaching process and the developments in the technology, there will be a multiplicity of uses across different age groups and different types of education needs will be met. In determining such venues for a multiplicity of uses, it is important to ensure that all learning forms are catered to, including individual learning using different technologies as well as space to encourage collaborative work. The main technologies need to include telecommunications, computers, electrical power from different sources and broadcasting. Understanding the educational applications within the physical learning venue is important One of the most obvious strengths of the technology is its ability to offer up-to-date resources and information to a large number of learners, teachers and administrators immediately, easily and relatively cheaply. Using internet technologies, the following applications become possible:

i) Supporting the use of resources that combine more than one medium, namely multimedia resources, which combines video, audio, graphics and text, and have the potential of providing rich learning experiences.
ii) Bringing designers of online learning resources in contact with the huge resources base that resides on the World Wide Web.
iii) Supporting a range of communication strategies between the learner and teacher, between learners and between teachers. Such communication could be asynchronous or synchronous.
iv) Ensuring that the technology supports and creates efficient management and administration systems within the education system.

LEARNER SUPPORT

One feature of using technology for education and training is student support services of various kinds. This requirement has both organisational and costs implications and is often labour intensive, even when using different technologies. It follows that learner support is an important consideration when implementing virtual education interventions. Several types of support should be made available to learners. They include:

i) Support of all kinds on a regular basis offered by educators both through face-to-face contact and other forms of communication including telephones, the post and computer links.
ii) Interaction between learners on both a group and on a one-to-one basis.

iii) Provision of any necessary learner support in educational courses.

iv) Provision of access to the necessary facilities, including a space in which learning activities and interaction between learners can take place, as well as access to computers, laboratories and other resources that might be necessary within the learning process.

A fifth type of support necessary for centres to consider when supporting virtual education is easy access to administration procedures that are necessary when registering and paying for courses and when needing to enquire on matters.

The delivery of virtual education, that is the provision of an educational transaction for a formal certificate or for non-formal purposes, has shown tremendous growth and is likely to increase as the demand for education and training grows. However, this growth and projected increased demand has been and is likely to be uneven with the developed world being able to fully exploit the advantages of virtual education. The developing world, with its difficulties in education systems, education processes and practices, infrastructure, telecommunications infrastructure, lack of ICT infrastructure, etc. will constantly find itself at the lower end of usage of virtual education. To encourage access, the development of innovative learning centres has been occurring. Such developments have been experimental in nature and driven in large part by development agencies and the private sector. These centres face crucial challenges in terms of their sustainability, their effective management and meeting their target group's needs. Despite these challenges, such centres offer access to learners of various virtual education opportunities. The development of these centres need to be encouraged and supported if they are to be effective in ensuring that more learners are able to take advantage of virtual education opportunities.

In a traditional classroom of a simple education system, learner support is the provenance of the individual teacher.

Teaching and learning occur through direct instruction, from one to many, in a physical space which might contain other physical resources such as maps or books, designed to supplement the teacher's knowledge and extend student learning within a defined and constrained curriculum. As educational systems become larger and more complex, the various roles of the teacher and administrator are shared among other specialised professional roles, such as that of teacherlibrarian and academic counsellor. The teacher may remain a primary locus of support, and indeed i; expected to be so, but learners have recourse to services in the form of professional staff and resources collected for their benefit. Such a system implies that two forms of learner support are necessary: one related to development of the individual's potential and another related more to the needs of the system for accountability, although these obviously intersect in a society which values certification of an individual's achievements.

In developed economies, the late 20th century saw a swing away from the teacher-centred model which had characterised education. Pedagogical and social theories favoured a new "learner-centredness." This involved attention to the development of the personal potential of each student, according to his or her talents and ambitions. However, learner-centredness has since segued into learner responsibility. The explosion of knowledge in the late 20th century meant a greater emphasis on the process of learning, rather than on the content, which is, it is widely argued, rapidly superseded. This pedagogical theory of learner-centredness coincided with another trend: the "commodification" of educational provision as a service industry and the emergence of for-profit educational organisations, with a consequent emphasis on students as clients and customers. For-profit providers stressed not only the employability of their graduates, but also their level of "service" through attention to administrative ease, pre-enrolment advice, career days with prospective employers, streamlined enrolment and credit card payments. Traditional providers in all sectors had rarely considered such services important to their student base. Competition among providers has changed that attitude over the last 10 years, as on-campus and traditional providers discovered the niche market of adult learners, who have little time or patience for queues and delay.

The phenomenal increase in computer power and the associated development of equally powerful software applications have made record-keeping and learning management systems possible through relational databases; encryption devices have enabled students to directly access an institutional system with relative security. The 1980s saw the emergence of the internet as a communication device with the ability to manage both real time and delayed time interactions and one-to-one and one-to-many communication, an obvious boon to distance education.

Practitioners and managers have made variable progress in systematically addressing the issues of supporting their learners through various means:

i) improving the quality of print materials in terms of physical presentation;
ii) devising instructional design processes that involve both "content experts" and "learning experts";
iii) implementing borrowing policies that maximise student access to resources while minimising student mail costs;
iv) establishing student support centres where local tutors assist both face-to-face and by telephone.

Specialist distance education administration units have been established to deal with the inevitable problems facing the distance and adult student: inability to meet assignment due dates, lost assignments, enrolment and contact with the teacher. Design teams develop learning materials that aim to promote "active learning," to replicate in some sense the dialogue that Laurillard argues is essential to the learning process. In institutions with a distance education mission, learner support has involved systematic investigation and research into how students can learn in a non-classroom environment, how best to substitute for the informal and incidental learning that occurs on campus and the vast range of consumptive service benefits.

The extraordinary confluence of forces — technical, pedagogical, ideological, economic — which have stimulated the growth of distance education, in the last century have increased the potential of distance education systems to overcome many of the disincentives to off-campus study, especially through providing social learning opportunities and immediacy of access to resources, both human and digital. Off-campus study has never enjoyed wide popularity as a mode of education.

In the Australian higher education sector, despite being long-established as an alternative access mode for those disadvantaged by distance or circumstance, distance enrolment remained relatively stable as a proportion of the total enrolment in higher education, at 10 per cent to 12 per cent between 1989 and 1995. After fees increased in 1998, the number of mature students and part-time enrolment increased. This corresponded with a sharp upsurge in distance enrolments to 14 per cent in 2000, which was affected by the Asian financial crisis. Distance enrolments among Australia's Vocational Education and Training students remain at 10 per cent. It was reported that between 1989 and 1999, there was a 800 per cent increase in Australia's international distance enrolments, with international students constituting nearly 10 per cent of all external enrolments. The same report observes that failure rates among traditional school leavers are twice those of mature students in distance mode.

For an increasing number of students, it is obvious that distance learning is a convenient option, or the only possibility for gaining an educational qualification. Yet the attrition rate remains high, certainly much higher than the 17 per cent drop-out reported from all U.K. universities. J.Potter reports a 75 per cent non-completion rate at Athabasca University, a wholly external provider with an excellent reputation that uses mainly print. But for the U.K.'s Open University (UKOU), Potter quotes a Bates 1989 study on non-completion that show numbers between 25 per cent and 50 per cent. The difference is attributable to a much stronger support network, including face-to-face tutorials and assigned telephone tutors at UKOU.

Successful students in the University of Phoenix online programme reflect the social correlates of "connectedness" in the US: they come from a high socioeconomic group, are primarily male and are already attuned to a networked environment through their work place. This suggests a real challenge for online education in other than advantaged groups. We owe it to our distance learners to devise better support services and to avoid both the personal failure of students and the economic costs of wastage to the institution and the wider society. If online programmes are registering poor completions, institutions must increase their attention to learner support services rather than focus simply on providing technological infrastructure, as they have done to date.

Online Learner Support

Presently, much of what is provided in the form of learner support is systems-driven rather than student-centred. For example, Inglis et al. briefly explore three service areas: the helpdesk, the library and counselling. EDUCAUSE's criteria for the Award for Systemic Progress in Teaching and Learning 2001 advises that applicants must give evidence that the system is learner-centred, but there is no explicit mention of student support. A scan of online courses indicates that most are information heavy. Text is "shovelled" online, with embedded links to other resources, without any understanding that use of the internet is a "socio-technological practice." We need to envision it as not merely a tool, but as "constitutive of the educational experience itself or constituted by educational experiences."

Virtual education has been approached as a technical solution to distance, without considering that, for the student, the nature of the educational experience is a function of the opportunities for thinking and learning that the institution might provide. For many students, the technology is the least important aspect of their learning, if not a disincentive. Such considerations also raise the inevitable question of the degree to which learner support online for truly distance students differs from learner support online which complements or supplements face-to-face teaching. The distant student cannot easily borrow texts from the campus library, make a low-cost local phone call or take a faulty computer to a repair shop. Too often, developers of online materials assume that what works to complement and extend class-based teaching will open new markets at a distance, where online provision constitutes the entire educational experience.

There is clearly a need for further research into individual institutional populations, especially since internet-based courses deliberately target a new demographic of lifelong learners, those seeking the qualifications now demanded by a wired world and a shrinking manufacturing economy. In the U.K., for example, the University for Industry (UfI) is predicated on the use of the internet to enhance workers' skills for the knowledge economy. A Marchmont Observatory report argues that learner support is "crucial to the success of the UfI learning model," especially since non-traditional learners are likely to be discouraged by learning in the unfamiliar medium of the internet. In other regions, student needs may differ in emphasis from those reported by Potter's respondents. Learner support in developed economics differs vastly from what is expected and can be provided in less wealthy economies.

On-campus online students unfamiliar with the internet environment face problems which have rarely been subject to "systematically empirical or critical study." Firstly, technical problems predominated, especially for those without access to computer support or who lacked computer skills and for those who relied on on-campus laboratories for access.

Lack of familiarity with the equipment and the nature of online searching left students frustrated with the long hours spent attempting to fulfil assignment requirements. A second major frustration lay in the "lack of immediate feedback from the instructor and ambiguous instructions on the web and via e-mail". It appears that internet instructors and designers have to learn anew the very language in which they communicate, since the medium encourages hasty responses. Many online instructors, without distance education experience, have not learned the critical nature of clarity and explicitness. This is not the case in the classroom, where ambiguous messages relayed by a teacher can be immediately "corrected" when the puzzled expressions of students are noticed. Such difficulties illustrate how much successful learning depends on specific teaching skills in the online environment, and they raise the issue of adequate professional development for the internet teacher.

Learner support becomes more visible in the teaching process itself. Technical support is clearly critical, as is some degree of familiarity of the teacher with the systems being used, since student frustration rises when students are simply referred to technical support services. If online education is to fulfil its promise for distance education, it must clearly focus on providing quality learner support services which meet the particular learning needs of the institution's students. These needs will be compounded by distance and a new medium of delivery, one which brings additional support needs in both instructional methods and technical skills. Providing informational needs is relatively easy; most educational institutions already make much of their documentation available online. However, providing handbooks and course descriptions online is clearly far from sufficient. Nor can an institution simply provide e-mail packages and bulletin boards and expect students to master and enjoy this new form of learning.

The study of J. Potter, and research of N. Hara and R. Kling, provide a learner-centred framework for the form and content of online support services, beginning with information about the opportunists distance education can offer.

Pre-enrolment support

For the potential student, there are any number of commercial and agency sites that extol the virtues of e-learning and provide a database of distance and online courses and programmes. However, not all their links are to accredited providers, and it is often unclear if subject enrolments in commercial programmes attract credits to fully accredited providers. The notorious case of Greenwich University in Hawaii and Australia as well as the activities of other unscrupulous operators demonstrate the need for an authoritative listing of accredited online providers, and the nature of the qualifications gained, including their acceptance in other jurisdictions.

At the next level, Potter's students wanted information about the range of courses available. This would suggest not merely the usual brief description of a course and its potential benefits in terms of career opportunities, but all subject requirements, their sequence, any limitations in their offering, the nature of their delivery and the support mechanisms students could expect.

Most institutions are weak at providing such details in on-campus study, where informal communication between students, and between students and staff, substitutes for "hard information." For the prospective online student, these tacit knowledge sources are unavailable, so they have to be made explicit online and via telephone support. Jay Mathews's constant recourse to telephone advice shows how important this element is, along with embedded e-mail links to an inquiry service.

The University of London external programme has such links, along with an automated response for out-of-hours inquiries. It also has a frequently asked questions (FAQ) page, although this is limited in scope. The UKOU provides a good practice example of information at the course level.

Since distance education requires strong self-motivation and independent learning skills, pre-enrolment support ideally would include a checklist to help students decide whether this is an appropriate modality for their circumstances and learning style. Several providers have rudimentary self-assessment tests that are designed to help students realistically appraise their capacity to undertake an online course. Learning style preference checklists are useful to the prospective distance student: the student who prefers to learn through reading and reflection is likely to prefer print-based modes, even if they are delivered online, over a video-based course, for example. Checklists should also include a nominal weekly time commitment for each subject. For profit organisations currently excel in allowing students to "taste test" individual subjects online, even where they do not provide a checklist.

However, Learndirect, the network of the UfI, suggests prospective students "dip into our tasters for a flavour of the learndirect experience" and offers a wide range of different subjects for sampling. At this stage, it is also critical to provide details of equipment requirements, indicate the costs of purchase and ongoing connection, clarify the technical skills levels required and indicate the level of technical support provided.

Had Hara and Kling's students been informed that they had to know or learn HTML, they may have decided against enrolment, taken a preparatory course or accepted HTML as another learning objective of the subject. Students should also know whether the institution provides subsidised ISP services, and whether internet access attracts a long distance or local call charge. Potter's students also wanted ease of text-book purchase, and there is strong evidence that in this requirement at least, many institutions excel, since online book orders reduce provider costs and are therefore an attractive proposition. However, information about library resources and costs appears to be less well-handled. The University of Phoenix is exemplary here, although it has the advantage of a restricted curriculum which is largely confined to contemporary knowledge, where online resources are often sufficient. It informs prospective students that courses are supported by a digitised library service to relevant publications, and it even allows alumni continued access to those resources.

Institutions with a wider remit of programmes should provide links to local public libraries and indicate what, if any, borrowing arrangements can be made with other library services. Since distance education of its nature is an out-of-hours activity, telephone and e-mail help desks with restricted hours are not helpful.

Several institutions have developed imaginative solutions to the budget blowout that is likely to result from a 24-hour service, the ideal if online provision is to fulfil its promise of "anytime, anywhere, anyplace" learning. For example, Macquarie University in Australia and the London School of Economics have partnered to provide a 20-hour help desk, without adding to institutional cost, by utilising the different time zones between the two institutions to provide coverage of each other's students.

USQOnline, where fee-paying units are serviced by a commercial applications service provider (ASP), NextEd, provides all-hours support for technical and connection queries by routing e-mails to employees in different time zones in its Asia-Pacific-West Coast, US workforce. If immediate all-hours responses cannot be logistically provided, an automated response should give a guaranteed service level that the query will be attended to within 24 hours. Tuition fees and any available financial aid are also critical information, although distance part-time studies do not qualify in most countries for aid. However, some institutions are currently offering scholarships to induce students into fee-paying online courses, and details of these should be available online.

Most institutions have invested heavily over the last three years in the infrastructure of their online systems with varying degrees of success in integrating student management systems, instructional support systems such as library databases and course content and communication systems. Network platforms that support student-teacher communication and student-student collaboration, chat rooms, bulletin boards and the library have generally had priority, as the Computer Supported Intentional Learning Environment (CSILE) network project at the Ontario Institute for Studies in Education demonstrates.

But the urgent need is for an electronic "one-stop shop" for the individual student which provides transparent links to the many servers carrying different systems. Distance education providers must embrace e-commerce solutions to payment and admission procedures. Indeed, many vendors which began as ASPs providing optional institutional service levels have seen the advantage of adding an e-commerce strand.

It is also critical to provide telephone-based course advice by well-experienced academic advisers, at the pre-enrolment stage, One of the difficulties reported by Western Governors University (WGU) in their call centre operation, was that they employed poorly educated staff who had not themselves been to university and who did not, therefore, understand the nature of callers' questions. Further, they were paid on a time-on-query basis, inappropriate to the very specific and detailed queries they received from students concerned about investing their educational energy and dollars wisely. It is at this pre-enrolment stage that commercial providers like the University of Phoenix (UoP) excel in another element of support service which is generally handled poorly in the public sector: credit transfer. UoP, with its mission to provide convenient and speedy qualifications for adult workers, has generous credit transfer arrangements for prior learning in a variety of organisations, especially the military services. Credit transfer calculations for many organisations and subjects can be made online. UoP has also devised a software programme which calculates credits and equivalences, including those obtained in some overseas countries, and they inform students of the results in one-third of the time taken by the American Council on Education and at much less cost to the student.

At the post-secondary level also some institutions have developed prior learning assessment (PLA) procedures, but these are generally limited to assessing outcomes rather than formal courses. For example, British Columbia's Open Learning Agency (OLA) has a rather complex web site devoted to helping potential students determine how to claim credit via a number of modes: portfolio development, challenge examinations, assignments, etc., as guided by an adviser. Candidates are warned that credit claims often take several months to substantiate and require payment by the student, despite being subsidised by the government and universities. The amount of payment is not fixed and must be estimated by the adviser; it is not subject to financial aid provisions, and fees must be borne entirely by the student. While most institutions have designed graphically attractive home pages, navigation to important information for pre-enrolment is often difficult, since it is rarely designed from the user's perspective. On some sites, even the most fundamental design principles are ignored: back buttons do not work; pages of text are displayed with no exit or back-to-menu option; and vital information is buried several layers down, almost guaranteeing prospective students will abandon their search.

Post enrolment support

After the enrolment also there appears to be wide variations in the support services necessary to increase student satisfaction with the learning experience. Online enrolment should be possible and should immediately generate further information on subject content guides, suggested study schedule, learning resources required and recommended, contact names of teachers and tutors and their qualifications, and details of who developed the materials if the developers differ from the teacher. Orientation to the particular systems of the provider are essential at this point, and many institutions are now finding that at least one face-to-face session in information literacy skills and basic computer access is necessary for online learning.

For relatively confident users, a self-paced module to assist in accessing online resources should be provided, along with a module in independent learning skills and time management. Such skills are best learned in a subject specific context, and hence integrated in the subject materials, there are information retrieval skills which can be taught independent of particular knowledge domains. Library services are crucial to external students, and the mere provision of access to databases and catalogues often represents only a tantalising glimpse of what might be available if it were online. A reference librarian available in real time as a distance student is searching would constitute an excellent support service.

Continuous communication and contact between students, and between students and staff, is critical in all cultural contexts. The commercial vendors who tout the cost-effectiveness of virtual education for thousands at little marginal cost are deluded, at least until automated response systems are routine and affordable. Certainly the more serious online providers such as UoP and OLN, work on ratios of 9/10:1 to enable close attention to individual students and constant encouragement and feedback. UoP's pedagogical philosophy is predicated on collaborative learning and a Vygotskian principle of social group motivation, even in their on-campus courses. Hence classmates will progress through a programme together, and students are expected to "meet" once a week outside their online times to provide their own group learner support.

Frequently asked question (FAQ) pages, non-curricular and curricular chat rooms and class conferences provide essential support. Yet it is apparent that the teacher plays a critical role in explaining and demonstrating and that a virtual environment requires a different mindset for learning, one that does not always demand an "expert" teacher-answer to every question, in the same way as on-campus students explore concepts and clarify misunderstandings together.

The importance of this communicative aspect of the learning process may be reflected in the University of Southern

Queensland statistics which reveal that 70 per cent of their hits are for communication, not content pages. Obtaining texts and other resources was an issue of concern to Potter's survey group, as it is to all distance students. Current copyright laws limit access to many texts online, although many institutions such as Queensland University of Technology are developing limited digitised collections in some areas under licensing regulations. Other agencies have developed fee-based regimes to assist distance learners, such as UnCover, the Colorado Alliance which has a document delivery service. One further software development will ultimately prove of particular use in learner support: the learner management systems which are beginning to be fully integrated with information systems. There are two forms of these.

The first links student records with current subject study and assignments, allowing students to track their grades and learning activities, payment and loan records, and institutional administrative systems in a seamless interface between student learning and institutional systems.

The second and potentially more revolutionary system is in the form of a dossier of all an individual's learning activities over a lifetime, whether formal or informal. This has been termed a "knowledge management system," somewhat tangential to the notion as it is proposed by the Organisation for Economic Co-operation and Development. OECD conceives of knowledge management as a systematised approach to sharing knowledge in educational systems through using the potential of ICTs to enable networking within and without educational institutions, to "open" education to all organisations in the knowledge economy.

Such systems support the notion of lifelong learning, through recognising prior learning, and encourages a greater articulation into formal learning programmes. They encourage challenge tests to ensure knowledge and skill competencies, thus eliminating the need for lockstep cohorts and repetition of study. The promise of learner management systems is dynamic, interactive and personalised learning tailored to the individual's needs and, at best, to the individual's personal learning style.

Both e-business and e-commerce uses of new digital technologies in order to encourage graduates to contemplate continuing professional education and leisure learning with a particular institution, as well as donations to the institution. For distance students, the services could include employment links and opportunities, as well as continuing access to library resources and discounted ISP services.

Support to students with special needs

One of the emerging issues for online educators at all levels is the accommodation of different forms of disability. Countries vary significantly in their legislative provisions for disabled access, and even disabled facilities on campus are relatively new. The US government has only recently mandated that government web sites must be accessible to the blind and mobility impaired; for example, sites must allow keyboard navigation for those unable to manipulate a mouse, and read-aloud software must be installed for blind users. The UKOU also has a concerted equity programme: it provides captions on videos for hearing impaired students, transcripts of audio cassettes, and its learning centres are equipped with screen magnification devices on computers. However, there appears to be copyright difficulties associated with reproduction of some sites via assistance devices, as this constitutes re-digitisation of materials, a situation which must be addressed if disabled students are not to be disadvantaged. General web site design principles are useful. Test sites for evaluating usability are available. Other agencies have developed extensive guidelines specifically for educational institutions seeking to facilitate learning by the disabled and other equity groups.

Disability interest groups have made much progress in producing appropriate principles for access to online educational provision; these are comprehensively superior to most general guidelines on enhancing educational institutions' provisions for students with disabilities. Few institutions have made much progress in online support for personal counselling and health services, although Indira Gandhi National Open University (IGNOU) apparently offers a chat mode or e-mail service. Some have placed health and safety regulations and guidance online, and student guilds and unions often provide links to authoritative sites for generic guidance on sexuality, financial planning and cheap meal preparation. As an interesting aside, Arizona State University offers a distance education programme for the parents of its first year on-campus students, providing online lectures, weekly assignments and chat rooms to help parents help their student children adjust to living and studying away from home.

Even telephone counselling is challenging for distance providers because of the absence of visual clues to behaviour and state of mind. The economics of such a service are often prohibitive. Cost pressures in the last decade have forced UKOU to abandon its personal tutor-counsellor support for a call centre advisory service which relies on a student management database rather than personal knowledge of the student. Distance operations should forge links with community groups and health services within their students' localities. For all students, and in all course materials, there must be a clear and systematised recourse for complaints and problems — the online equivalent of the emergency button. It is too easy for students to slip through the increasing number of cracks in a system which has added technology to the education loop that is administration, teaching and resources.

Accessibility

Virtual education is predicated on access to a computer and having an online connection, and even in developed countries, this cannot be assumed. Even in the US, which has the highest rate of domestic connection, only 38 per cent of the population is home-connected, and that rate is strongly racially related, with

Hispanics and African-Americans far less likely to have home access. This statistic suggests that urgent government and business investment in public learning centres, as argued by Naidoo, and subsidised private ownership, are necessary. Examples of business investment to enhance the skills of their workforce as a learning organisation are few: in Finland, the practice is common, and in the U.S., Ford and the United Automobile Workers Union have forged a programme to provide every Ford American employee with a free personal computer and low-cost connectivity.

The World Bank has outlaid U.S.$20 million since 1997 to establish distance learning centres in developing countries; these have internet capability through landline connections where possible, or digital satellite equipment. They must be managed by local agencies to ensure some degree of "ownership" of the service, and, like the ICT Centre in Maseru, Lesotho, they are intended to be self-sustaining examples of private-public collaboration.

However, access to a basic computer and internet connection remains a major inhibiting factor for online distance education in most undeveloped economies. Online educational initiatives in the main appear to be confined to particular institutions and local projects, although the African Virtual University intends to cater to continent-wide distance education at all levels. Such embryonic projects suggest both potential structures and services, and the problems that must be overcome before distance learning via the internet becomes a reality. The Virtual Library Support Facility (VLSF), based in Nairobi, Kenya, channels resources from the African Virtual Library Initiative in an attempt to put all sub-Saharan African libraries online by 2010. It offers a hosting facility for library catalogues and digital publications.

India appears to be leading the non-Western countries in the development of software applications generally, and in relation to online education, following a determined national ICT policy with a heavy education emphasis. IGNOU is the major external higher education provider, and while 80 per cent of its materials are print-based, in 2000 it launched its first wholly online bachelor's course in ICT, along with an Advanced Diploma in ICT, and web-supported subjects in its M.B.A. and management continuing professional education courses. It is recognised that web-based delivery cannot yet replace print modes, but for those with the requisite skills and access, downloading course materials obviates chronic problems with late receipt of course packages.

Through the Virtual Campus Initiative (VSI), IGNOU is enhancing administration of its courses through online registration and payment options. Several subjects feature online assignment generation, assignment sub mission, online multiple-choice-question examinations, and automatic grading and record keeping, all conducted via study centres. Online orientation programmes assist students to learn in the new medium, and other computer-based tutorials are available in the study centres, often a rented space from major private ICT providers in major cities.

School sector developments

Because primary and secondary education is the basic vehicle for community and social learning, school sector distance education is a minuscule proportion of state education activity, even where, as in Australia, with its remote small populations, there are well-established, excellent distance programmes. State governments in Australia have instituted pilot programmes online to increase the subject range for smaller secondary schools in rural areas. They have also supplemented more traditional distance methods such as radio with internet communication, but the cost of long-distance telephony in Australia remains prohibitive for many families, and technical problems caused by sunspots disrupt service frequently.

Numerous government reports on the potential of the internet at school level suggest its usefulness be supplemental. Many state and regional education authorities have sponsored resource collections online, vetted to ensure their suitability for particular grade levels. Professional associations have vast databases of educational materials, and many individuals within educational institutions have combined their subject passion with the distributive power of the internet. Commercial sites are also useful, some blending free and fee-based services. Exploiting the full potential of such materials has thus far proved difficult for distance educators at the school level.

The greatest potential for online education is in the realm of lifelong or continuing education, most particularly work place-based education. Certainly that is the sector targeted by commercial providers and the training units of corporations, where the drive is as much budgetary as it is the competitive drive for speed of distribution. Many companies are reporting strong resistance to losing face-to-face training, for the same reason that online education has been resisted within school leaver populations at university: that the social process of company training is as important as the technical or performative knowledge gained.

A company intranet for education and training has become a standard feature of large professional consultancies. Policies and procedures are quickly shared across the globe; a query posted to a bulletin board elicits answers or suggestions or examples from a dozen different offices. This, of course, is informal learning in the main and may be termed distributed expertise. It reveals the power of the medium to stimulate collaborative social learning within a group: in this case a group ethic has already been developed, albeit one based on company and individual performance. But the learning process could well be applied in an educational situation if a community of learners has been formed.

In more formal training programmes, such as certifications in the ICT industries, online learner support appears of little concern, since the training is so focused. Although Microsoft's early venture into online training, Microsoft Online, was not a success, the company is now licensing a number of training providers to develop online educational programmes which incorporate Microsoft's own training materials, including e-mail tutor support, for certification programmes in proprietary software products.

Because the training is confined to the use of a product, there is little learner support offered; motivation is presumed to be intrinsic, the learning is narrow and instrumentalist and there is no reference needed to resources beyond the package. Large corporations have both the resources and the infrastructure to support their staff's training needs. They often encourage distance education as a mode of continuing professional education because it improves staff work performance, and it is generally conducted in the staff member's own time, rather than in company time.

Lifelong learning, frequently conceived as work-related skills training, is considered critical to the survival of small and medium enterprises (SMEs). "Distributed" learning, a form of distance education, and more particularly online learning, is the favoured medium for such learning Hence the UK's University for Industry (UfI) was established with a double mission to re-skill British workers for the knowledge age and to use ICTs to achieve this goal. Through learndirect, a network of over 700 learning centres equipped with computers, over 80 per cent of its courses are offered online; it promises that "help is at hand at your learndirect centre, or you can call the freephone learner service helpline." UfI contracted Marchmont Observatory, at the University of Exeter, to both facilitate and review the success of the operation. The result has been a series of workshops for practitioners and managers and SME employers and employees, as well as a listserv and an electronic news-letter-sharing experience on the programme.

On each of the themes that Marchmont has identified as critical to lifelong learning, the unit prepares a final research brief, a simple four-page summary and analysis of the main topics raised in each forum, and a brief reading list. It restates the guiding mission of the UfI planners that effective learner support is crucial to the success of the UfI learning model. This is supported by a joint survey of e-learners, providers and employers which reveals that 96 per cent of learners wanted support.

The technology itself is daunting to non-traditional learners with little experience in using computers. Free ICT lessons may be a necessary precursor to online education, along with learndirect centres, where employers and workers can access mentors, tutors and equipment, complemented with call centres staffed with expert advisers fully conversant with the range of available work-related and academic programmes. While the UfI concentrated on developing programmes of content, it overlooked the critical importance of supporting students through a programme and of acknowledging a maximum "shelf life" of 18 months for its industry programmes. Nor did its managers acknowledge the difference between supporting students who had close access to a learning centre, and those remote from such centres.

Controlling forces

The strength of drivers for innovation may overcome opposing factors, leading to adoption of the practice; equally, opposing forces, which may include resistance among staff or external factors such as costs, may prevail and prevent widespread adoption. If the drivers are visionary, and the constraints are financial and technical, we can generally assume that mainstreaming will be long delayed. In the case of virtual education, the drivers are clearly visionary. Policy-makers see the potential of the internet to relieve the escalating costs of physical infrastructure in education, particularly in developing economies with high populations, and the importance of "leap-frogging" the elitist stage of physical educational systems. Politicians see a dream to hold out to their constituencies.

Education managers see savings in staff costs, typically the largest component of an education system, if students become more independent learners and learning materials can be developed for reuse in multiple contexts and can be delivered virtually. They also cling to visions of larger, fee-paying markets. Some educators see the real attraction of speed of communication with distance learners and the potential for social learning among peers, previously unavailable via conventional distance methods. Among practising distance educators, the drivers for online learner support services are strong forces: the immediacy of communication is of obvious benefit in motivating students, allowing for the feedback which is a constant concern to distance learners.

A skilful facilitator can create a community of learners which can replicate the social learning atmosphere needed by most learners. The social factor that prevents students from considering distance education can be addressed, and constant frequent motivation supplied by both teacher and fellow students in a class situation can reduce the lack of support that leads to withdrawal. A world of resources outside the home institution can be accessed. Student record-keeping and administration can be made convenient and transparent for both teachers and students. However, the constraining forces appear to dominate at present, and cost, rather than technical difficulties, is the greatest of these.

Even where the infrastructure has been installed, the costs of quality learner support are substantial. Managers have often severely under-estimated the maintenance costs of intranet and internet systems, both in relation to the current instability of many applications and the integration of different platforms, and to the human resources needed to support students and teaching staff in a new technical and pedagogical environment. The authoritative literature now concedes that far from being a cheaper alternative in educational applications, virtual education has high development costs. The "help desk crisis," frequently reported in Steven Gilbert's AAHESGIT listserv is only another aspect of this. Teachers are also reporting greater demands from students, deluges of e-mail and more frequent recourse to technical assistants.

Extensive professional development is necessary before teachers can utilise internet-based communication modes to benefit their students and themselves, and as the guidelines canvassed above indicate, there are numerous considerations that most teachers have rarely considered. In countries without an extensive and stable telecommunications system, a low GDP and little personal disposable income for computers and connection charges, the cost constraints are staggering. One area amenable to cost reduction is sharing of distance library resources through joint buying power and licensing arrangements for databases.

Policy-making

Virtual education is not a panacea that can solve all educational problems, notwithstanding its undoubted promise. This is partly because of the immense costs involved, even if wireless applications and satellite links can replace landlinks in remote and rural areas, and where physical infrastructure is commercially unfeasible. It is also because of entrenched beliefs about education as a social and socialising experience which can never be satisfactorily replicated in a virtual environment. Although distance education is generally perceived as less costly than classroombased education, and organisations like the UKOU have demonstrated that with volume they can educate an adult for substantially less than an on-campus student costs and at significantly less cost to the student as a result of savings in travel and living expenses and the opportunity costs of full-time study, these savings are based on print and post-delivery modalities. Development costs of online materials and the systems to support them are considerable; ongoing institutional costs increase with the necessity of help desks for technical and academic learner support. Learner costs increase as download volumes increase, and the student bears the costs of printing.

The digital divide in current computer ownership and connection rates, even in developed economies, means that internet-based education denies one of the underlying principles of distance education: to cater for those disadvantaged by income and circumstance. We cannot exclude students because they lack the means and the skills to benefit from education at any level. Equally, we cannot exclude those whose circumstances include computer ownership and connectivity, but who lack the time or ability to learn on campus.

While there has been an encouraging increase in the number of general and education web sites emanating from non-Western sources, the high costs of creating original resources continues to reinforce the dominance of US web browsers and sites. This is not to denigrate the quality and usefulness of materials on the simplistic grounds of source or ideological opposition. However, most national governments are concerned about providing for their citizenry materials which reflect their cultural, social and economic contexts, and which contribute to national interests. Automated translation programmes might appear to provide a technical solution to support services in a home language, but language is not the only cultural consideration in learning.

Under the combined pressures of vocationally oriented education and training, web-based short courses, the promises of individually customised and modularised topics of study and the interests of educational institutions and commercial vendors in the continuing professional education and lifelong learning market, it would appear inevitable that evaluation and assessment of learning activities will become a significant component of the education sector. Many US companies have already established a niche in evaluation of certification programmes, such as those in the ICT industry.

ORGANISATIONAL ARRANGEMENTS

The trend towards partnerships and alliances in virtual education reflects a larger trend in society, especially in the business sector. Corporate partnerships and alliances dominated business news headlines at the end of the 20th century. The partnerships were often driven by the need to expand business by building new sources of customers, something referred to as increasing "market size." In order to support existing infrastructures and ever-increasing costs of doing business, corporations were driven to increase their revenues by increasing the size of their customer base. It was no different for institutions of higher education.

In many places, large percentages of the population live in isolated areas and cannot afford to leave those areas to pursue higher education. In Hong Kong, the world's second most densely populated urban centre, the issue is not distance but rather space to accommodate additional learners. More than 100,000 students have studied at the Open University of Hong Kong during its first 11 years of operation, about 10 per cent of them earning degrees so far. Those numbers are very attractive to US institutions looking to export their distance learning programmes to new student populations. In India Carnegie Mellon has set up a new distance education programme in conjunction with the internet service provider, Sterling Infotech Ltd. The programme will lead to a certificate in computer programming. Carnegie Mellon, with a total US enrolment of fewer than 8000 students, hopes to enrol 15,000 students in India in online courses in 2001, growing to 100,000 in a couple of years.

Size of the potential market for distance education is attracting large investments by businesses and venture capitalists. Many of the new distance education programmes are internet-based. Businesses see the internet as facilitating education opportunities for people who have not had access to such opportunities in the past. They have been willing to invest in that potential, at least until the stock market pull-back in the middle of 2000. Investment in online education companies is just a small part of the enormous investment made in internet-based companies in general in the late 1990s.

According to an annual study by Andrew Whinston of more than 3000 businesses that receive at least part of their income from the internet, the internet economy grew by 62 per cent from 1998 to 1999, producing $524 billion in revenue According to International Data Corporation, which follows more than 200 electronic-learning companies, the e-learning market will grow from $550 million in 1998 to $11.4 billion in 2003. Much of the new investment in virtual education involves the development of new institutions as well as the creation of new partnerships and alliances among existing institutions and companies.

Virtual Universities

Since the UK's Open University (UKOU) rolled out its successful model in 1970, most countries have opened at least one open and distance university. The mega-universities which are providing distance education include:

i) Anadolu University, Turkey, 578,000
ii) China TV University, China, 530,000
iii) Universities Terbuka, Indonesia, 353,000
iv) Indira Gandhi National Open University, India, 242,000
v) Sukhothai Thammathirat Open University, Thailand, 217,000
vi) Korean National Open University, Korea, 211,000
vii) National Centre for Distance Learning, France, 185,000
viii) The Open University, Britain, 157,000
ix) University of South Africa, South Africa, 130,000
x) Payame Noor University, Iran, 117,000
xi) National Centre for Distance Learning, Spain, 110,000

African Virtual University (AVU)

The most ambitious venture in recent years that uses information and communication technologies (ICTs) to deliver distance education has been the African Virtual University (AVU). Recognising the close tie between education and economic growth and prosperity, and with higher education in sub-Saharan Africa in a crisis, in mid-1997 the World Bank provided initial support to develop a prototype phase of the AVU, a "lifeline from cyberspace" for the sub-Saharan African countries. AVU would use satellite television, the internet and printed materials to help overcome the many financial and physical barriers that prevent students in the participating African countries from gaining access to quality higher education.

AVU was seen as particularly relevant in the emerging economies of African countries whose workforces lacked vital technical skills. Initial courses would focus on science, engineering and business. The plan was for AVU to evolve over a three- or four-year period and to be self-financing at the end of that period. Others joined the World Bank to provide start-up funds for AVU. The World Bank contributed several million US dollars. The Africa Region Development Fund provided $1.165 million; the Canadian Trust Fund donated Cdn.$1.5 million; the Irish Trust Fund contributed £200,000; the European Commission pledged ECU 1 million; and Portugal pledged funds to develop Portuguese language programmes.

Since July 2000, Kenyatta University in Kenya has been the host institution for the AVU headquarters. A pilot phase was launched in April 1998. Twelve universities in six English-speaking countries were connected through AVU to universities in the United States and Europe. Just a few months later, the pilot had grown to include 25 African universities, including some in the francophone countries of Benin, Burkina Faso, Cote d'Ivoire, Mauritania, Niger, Rwanda, Senegal and Togo. Supporting universities had grown to include the University of Massachusetts and the New Jersey Institute of Technology in the United States and the University College Galway in Ireland. During this pilot phase, there were no exclusive virtual university students; selected students enrolled in existing courses at participating universities, received instruction and took exams via the technology.

A second phase, begun in January 1999, offered complete curricula for full-fledged undergraduate degree programmes. By mid-2000, AVU had expanded to include 25 learning centres spread across eight anglophone and seven francophone countries. More than 5000 students had completed semester-long courses in the sciences and over 2000 had taken part in seminars on topics such as e-commerce. Over 30 academic institutions, including those from Africa, Europe, Ireland, Canada and the United States, provided course material.

There are difficulties inherent in education through the internet in Africa. While enrolments in secondary schools have increased in recent years increased poverty has reduced many individuals' ability pursue higher education. The potential barriers to the success of AVU can be summarised as follows:

i) The technological challenges.
ii) The lack of trained professionals to support the implementation of distance education.
iii) The absence of clearly defined national distance education policies.
iv) The lack of connectivity.
v) The high cost of tuition and internet services.
vi) The general poverty of the region.

The University of the Philippines Open University (UPOU)

The University of the Philippines Open University (UPOU) was established in 1995 to provide quality education to a growing population distributed over 7000 islands. It was seen as playing a critical strategic role in the country's economic, socio-cultural and political development and progress. UPOU is mandated to increase access to education, to sustain professional growth and to promote lifelong learning throughout the country. Collaborative arrangements and institutional agreements are built into UPOU's mandate. It uses print, audio, video and online resources to deliver course materials to distance learners and backs them up with once-a-month tutorials in learning centres. As of the 1999-2000 school year, UPOU had 1068 graduates and a current enrolment of 1209 students, which it expected to almost double the following year.

Taipei National Open University

The Taipei National Open University established in 1986 has received new recognition in Chinese Taipei. Distance education has been identified by the government as a key tool and a fundamental instrument for redeveloping vocational and technical skills throughout the country to keep the workforce competitive and to sustain economic development. Through 1996, the National Open University (NOU) had graduated 12,000 adult students and countless others had learned informally from the educational programmes broadcast by the university. The university's demographics are illustrative of how an open and distance learning institution can provide access to underserved populations: 70 per cent of the NOU students are female; 65 per cent are 25 to 39 years old.

Berean University and ICI University

In 1999, in US Berean University and ICI University merged to form the Global University of the Assemblies of God, a distance education institution that provides ministerial training, undergraduate and graduate education, and curriculum materials to the Christian community worldwide. Delivery systems include print, internet, CDROM and video-conferencing. The combined institutions have an enrolment of about 10,000 students pursuing undergraduate and graduate degrees and ministerial certification.

Open University Worldwide (OUWO)

The Open University in the UK established Open University Worldwide (OUWO), in 1996 to export its courses and services globally. By the end of 1999, OUWO had overseas enrolments of more than 20,000, and that number was growing. About the same time, the Monterrey Institute of Technology (ITESM) was expanding its distance education programmes beyond the borders of Mexico and into many of the Spanish-speaking countries of Latin America. Their system of one-way satellite and internet-based communications has 1302 receiving sites in Mexico and 127 in other countries in Latin America.

Indira Gandhi National Open University (IGNOU)

The Indira Gandhi National Open University (IGNOU) has for years used multimedia kits and broadcast radio programmes to deliver courses to students at a distance. In July 2000, IGNOU also began to use online delivery. The Virtual Campus Initiative started with courses in information technology management. Established in 1985, IGNOU offers an extensive array of print and multimedia-based courses and serves as a resource centre for nine other state open universities. IGNOU operates 700 study centres throughout the country and is one of the chief resources in India for those who wish to improve their qualifications and sharpen their academic skills. The Virtual Campus Initiative is only the most recent innovation in distance education that IGNOU has introduced to India. In 1998, IGNOU sought to remove "three types of tyrannies" that often confront distance education programmes: the tyrannies of space, time and a fixed curriculum. IGNOU's goal was to transform itself into a global virtual university serving "anyone, anytime, anywhere." The Virtual Campus Initiative is still in the early stages of development.

University Initiatives

The rapid expansion of the distance education offerings of some for-profit institutions has been dramatic over the past couple of years, and it is likely to remain that way for the foreseeable future assuming that the institutions are able to tap into new lucrative markets for continuing education of adults. In the late

1980s, cable television operator Glenn Jones created a for-profit subsidiary to offer college-level telecourses over cable. Mind Extension University not only broadcast the courses but also distributed textbooks, referred students to colleges that offered the courses for credit, and generally facilitated student learning.

By the late 1990s, Jones had expanded his ambitions in education. He embraced internet technologies as well as cable and created a freestanding virtual university, Jones International University. It became the first electronic university in the United States to receive accreditation, being so recognised in March 1999 by the North Central Association of Colleges and Schools. Jones International offers a bachelor's and master's degree in Business Communication, a master's of Education in e-learning, and a master's in Business Administration, with specialisations in e-commerce, information technology management, global enterprise management, entrepreneurship, conflict management and health care management. It also offers professional certificate programmes in Public Relations and Marketing, Global Communication, and Leadership.

The largest for-profit university in the United States, the University of Phoenix, have announced a new plan for foreign expansion. Already serving 75,000 students in the US, the Apollo Group announced its intention to develop, acquire or create partnerships with institutions in Brazil, China, India, Mexico and several other countries in Latin America and Europe. Within 10 years, the plan is to have the overseas operation the same size as the US institution.

Investors in the new company, Apollo International, include Kaplan Ventures, Chase Capital Partners and some of Apollo's executives. The company had raised $40 million for the venture and is expected to raise a similar amount in secondary funding. The Apollo Group is driven by their view of the size of potential markets — 2.1 million college students in Brazil today will grow to 5.1 million by 2008; in Mexico the number of college students is expected to grow from 1.8 million today to 4 million by the end of the decade; in China, 21 out of 22 high school students have no place to go for higher education. That market potential is also leading one of the University of Phoenix's competitors, Sylvan Learning, to expand its overseas operations.

Other competitors such as DeVry Inc., Harcourt Higher Education and the 30 colleges formerly owned by Quest Education, recently acquired by Kaplan, Inc., are expected to pursue overseas markets soon. By October 2000, the University of Phoenix had raised an additional $70 million on Wall Street by selling a tracking stock. In issuing the stock, the university noted that its online programme is growing twice as fast as the on-the-ground programme. Students in the online programme come from 25 countries, according to John Sperling, Chairman of the Apollo Group.

Virtual High schools

As early as 1968, Mexico introduced Telesecundaria as a tool to help classroom teachers improve the quality of education throughout the country. Telesecundaria's model has been to produce and broadcast 20-minute lessons. By 1993, the service was being used in 9000 schools throughout Mexico, serving 600,000 students. By 1999, the use had grown to more than 900,000 students. The lessons are correlated to Mexico's Study Plans and Programs curriculum. Since 1994, the programmes have been broadcast on six channels of EDUSAT. Telesecundaria's leaders credit its success to the involvement of four groups: educational content providers, video producers, broadcasters and the users.

The Open Learning Agency in Canada introduced a similar service, using a combination of broadcast and videos for some courses and totally online delivery for others. Open School promises "education anywhere anytime" by providing courses and resources that support educators of students in grades K-12 "in the Province of British Columbia, across Canada, and around the world." Open School provides a full range of course offerings that meet all the curriculum requirements of British Columbia. The resources can be used by teachers and home instructors in their entirety or can be adjusted to meet the needs and learning styles or other circumstances of the students. Parents are also encouraged to use the resources to encourage independent study and collaborative class work.

In India, a commercial venture, Infrastructure Leasing and Financial Services Ltd., plans to use ICTs to expand the reach of education, enhance the learning process, and catalyse continuing education through non-formal and vocational processes. Schoolnet India is developing learning programmes for grades K-10 to supplement the current educational system by aiding teachers in their pedagogy. Benchmarked to international standards and delivered over the internet, the learning programmes will consist of banks of lesson plans, multimedia resource kits, links to other educational resources and programmes of teacher training.

Schoolnet project is being explored in Africa where the digital divide is more severe than anywhere else on earth. In 1999, there were only about 100,000 dial-up internet accounts in all of Africa for a population of about 700 million. Schoolnet Africa hopes to lessen the divide and stop the marginalisation of the people of Africa in today's knowledge-based global society. The plan is to establish local Schoolnets in more than half of all African countries by 2005 and to connect all schools in Africa by 2020. The continent-wide initiative will complement the nascent efforts already underway in a few countries in Africa.

In the US, using the motto, "any time, any place; any path, any pace,", the Department of Education launched the Florida Online High School in 1997. The school provides students in grades 9 to 12 with high-quality technology-based educational opportunities. The school's courses are tied to Florida's "sunshine standards," the state's academic standards. They are provided free of charge to any high school-age Florida resident.

The student is responsible for the cost of a computer and internet access, but the school will lend the student the textbooks and any specialised software that might be required for the courses. Currently, students enrol in the Online High School through their local school districts and receive their diplomas from the local districts.

Towards the end of 1999, two US universities started diploma-granting virtual high schools. The University of Missouri and Indiana University had been offering correspondence courses to high school students for decades. Now, with accreditation from the North Central Association of Colleges and Schools, they serve students online who have not succeeded in traditional high schools, do not want to go to traditional high schools or who are being home-schooled. Financially independent of their founding universities, Indiana University High School and the University of Missouri at Columbia High School will support themselves through tuition. In launching these virtual high schools, Indiana and Missouri join the University of Nebraska, which formed a for-profit company, Class.com, to sell high school courses over the internet. Through Class.com high school students can take individual courses or work to complete a high school diploma. The fully accredited courses are offered through the Independent Study High School (ISHS). Almost 50 courses are offered online and another 130 through correspondence.

A nationwide consortium of US school districts, has developed the Virtual High School Project. VHS does not itself grant diplomas, relying on the participating schools for that. In exchange for contributing a small amount of teaching time, a high school in the collaborative can offer its students NetCourses from other participating schools. The courses range from advanced academic courses to technical and specialised courses. Each school can enrol up to 20 students for each course a teacher contributes. Quality of teaching is maintained by requiring each teacher to successfully complete *The Teachers Learning Conference*, a graduate-level NetCourse designed to give participants exposure to the best educational strategies and technologies for NetCourse teaching.

In the US, the Council for Adult and Experiential Learning (CAEL) has a highly regarded history of helping tertiary institutions establish procedures and policies that provide credit-equivalents for student prior learning. Through Prior Learning Assessment, CAEL provides a means for students to:

i) Validate the worth of learning they have achieved on their own.
ii) Understand what they need to learn in order to achieve their personal, career or academic goals.
iii) Shorten the time necessary to earn a college credential.
iv) Save money by reducing the number of courses they need to take.
v) Enhance their pride and self-esteem for what they have accomplished as learners. Become aware that learning is a lifelong process.

CAEL now offers an online certificate in Prior Learning Assessment in conjunction with DePaul University. In Canada, the Open Learning Agency provides a similar service to learners and also offers an online certification programme for Prior Learning Assessors. A variation on helping students obtain credit for their prior learning is the College Level Equivalent Program (CLEP). CLEP exams are recognised by almost 3000 of the 4000 tertiary institutions in the US They are particularly used by military members in the US to obtain university credit for learning they have obtained through military training programmes.

Virtual Institution Consortia

Many attempts to create consortia for distance education projects have ended in failure. In some cases, the non-equal status of the parties has been a problem. If one party is the "provider" and the other is the "beneficiary" of new services, it is difficult for the parties to form a consortium as equal participants. In other cases, it might be difficult for all the stakeholders to agree on the terms of the project since they approach the need from different points of views. Neverthless, there are examples of successful consortia of tertiary institutions for distance education. They might consist of two neighbouring institutions agreeing to cross-enrol students in distance education courses and then agreeing on which courses each would offer. Others might be "mature" arrangements that have existed for several years and no longer make the news, such as Going The Distance (GTD) Project offered by the Public Broadcasting Service (PBS). In that case, more than 200 community colleges have joined with 67 public television stations in 41 states to offer associate degree programmes through distance education telecourses. The project is aimed at expanding career opportunities for working adults who could not otherwise attend college, and increasing workforce competitiveness through adult education services.

The inter-institutional collaboration for distance education in can be see in the models of distance education developed by the Western Governors University (WGU) and the Southern Regional Education Board's (SREB) Electronic Campus. Both institutions span huge geographic regions but their approaches and records differ. Each evolved from existing groups of institutions and a regional organisation with years of history of encouraging co-operation among the institutions.

The WGU evolved from the Western Interstate Commission on Higher Education (WICHE) an organisation founded in 1953 to facilitate policy development and co-operation among the tertiary institutions in 15 states in western US. The SREB, founded in 1948, facilitates policy development and co-operation among the tertiary institutions in 16 states in southern US. WGU draws heavily from the course offerings of its participating universities. It has promised to introduce systemic change in higher education by offering degrees and certificates "based completely on competencies," for which the university has developed a new competency-based testing system.

The SREB aims to give students easy access to online courses offered by its participating colleges through its Electronic Campus. Through the Electronic Campus, more than 300 colleges are offering over 3500 courses per year, leading to about 150 degree programmes. Online library services are provided by Georgia Library Learning Online (GALILEO). The Electronic Campus has started an Academic Common Market Initiative to establish a single tuition rate for students no matter where they take their online courses within the Electronic Campus.

Twenty-four of the 28 Jesuit institutions in the US had joined forces to offer online courses through a new network, Jesuit-NET. They planned to translate the Jesuit-style of education, which emphasises personal instruction and attention to ethical issues, to cyberspace. The network would not offer courses itself, but would act as a "portal" for participating colleges to market their online programmes.

In the United Kingdom, a very ambitious multi-university distance education venture has been launched. The Higher Education Funding Council for England (HEFCE) commissioned the consulting firm of PricewaterhouseCoopers to design a model that would allow all the universities in the UK, in partnership with the private sector, to create a repository of quality distance education courses and course components. The "e-University" will be owned by the higher education sector and will draw content and services from existing higher education institutions (HEIs). An operating company will be formed to run the e-University. Initial response from the HEIs was strong, with three-quarters expressing their general support for the model. Response from the private sector was equally strong, with 91 companies responding to an initial advertisement for partners. Another distance education venture in the UK was launched to meet the needs of a more narrowly targeted audience. The University for

Industry will provide workforce training in targeted skills areas and for particular industries. Aimed at secondary school graduates who finished school least well equipped for the workforce, learndirect will deliver most of its services online. However, since most of its target audience has neither computers nor internet connections at home, learndirect will create many hundreds of computer-equipped learning centres in friendly places such as pubs and shopping centres.

Commercial Initiatives

Distance education has suddenly become an attractive area financially. The expectation is that distance education programmes can be not only self-supporting but can generate additional funds to support other departments at a traditional institution or can generate a profit for a commercial company. Recent years have seen several companies create corporate universities, mainly to educate their own workers Other commercial companies have developed distance education ventures. Some provide services to support distance education and training programmes operated by traditional institutions. Others form partnerships and alliances with traditional universities.

Corporate universities

Many multinational corporations have created their own universities. These corporate universities are sometimes larger and better funded than traditional universities. There is little doubt that some corporate universities are becoming competition to traditional higher education institutions, siphoning off students who might otherwise take college courses in management, production techniques, finance, marketing and other business-related subjects. Often, the students choose the "convenience" of the corporate courses over the "brand prestige" of the traditional university courses. This is causing some traditional institutions to reassess how they organise, deliver and market their courses.

Sometimes the reassessment reaches to the very core of the university, raising questions of the institution's goals, the institution's governance and the role of the faculty. Most of the corporate universities use a combination of pedagogical approaches. Face-to-face instruction remains an important component, although it is increasingly accompanied by ICT-enhanced instruction, especially in the case of corporations that have staff scattered throughout the world. Face-to-face instruction is especially used for courses that require "team" activities such as management courses designed to encourage collaboration among managers.

None of the corporate universities uses ICT-delivered instruction alone. Printed workbooks, audiotapes and video remain the primary means for non-instructor-led training in most corporate universities. Many corporations are turning to ICT enhancement of their courses as a vehicle for saving money. Although they spend substantial amounts to create ICT course materials, for example ranging from $100,000 for an eight-hour course at Michigan Virtual University to $4 million for a 45-hour course at Arthur Anderson Professional Learning, the amount saved in travel and "lost opportunity costs" more than offsets the cost of developing the materials.

University-Business allainces

Today, it has been common for higher education institutions and businesses to form alliances to develop and deliver distance education courses. This trend is expected to continue into the future. In some cases, this involves new relationships between an existing institution and an existing business. In other cases, it involves the development of new companies. One of the biggest example of distance education partnerships worldwide has been a venture of Universities 21, a network of 18 prestigious universities in 10 countries.

In June 2000, the Universities 21 group announced that it was joining forces with Rupert Murdoch's News Corporation to capture a major share of the growing global market for online higher education. Aimed at college graduates, the online courses would lead to advanced degrees awarded by the Universities 21 institutions. The institutions would provide quality assurance, assess student performance and award degrees. Towards the end of 2000, that agreement fell apart and the Universities 21 group announced that it would be working with Thomson Learning to develop online learning materials. The publisher would be responsible for course design, testing, student assessment and student database management. The universities would award the degrees.

However, within days of that announcement, the University of Toronto, one of the Universities 21 participating members, began to distance itself from the joint venture. By early 2001, the path for Universitas 21 had become even rockier. Five faculty unions from around the world had called on the universities in Universitas 21 to hold off establishing the arrangement with Thomson until all academic and employment issues were resolved.

A week later, the *Chronicle of Higher Education* reported that students at Australian colleges had attacked the plan to create Universitas 21, charging that the reputations of the participating universities involved would be threatened. The National Union of Students backed protesters who demonstrated outside Queensland University's governing-council. Nevertheless, a couple of weeks later the participating institutions were preparing to make substantial financial commitments to the new consortium.

Whatever the outcome of the Universities 21 partnership agreements, they reflect the condition of distance education at the tertiary level at the start of the 21st century. Institutions are anxious to form new partnerships to reach new populations. Businesses see the universities as sources of intellectual assets needed to develop distance education offerings.

Universities recognise that the businesses are experienced in developing, distributing and marketing products to mass markets. Both sides are struggling to devise relationships that would draw on the strengths of each to create and deliver new products to meet the perceived needs of vast populations of adult learners.

Some commercial distance education ventures undertaken by HE institutions have been narrowly targeted at specific populations. For example, Pace University joined with the National Advisory Coalition for Telecommunications Education and Learning (NACTEL) to create and offer an associate degree in Telecommunications aimed at workers who want to fill Network Technician jobs in industry.

The courses are offered exclusively via the internet from Pace University. The specially designed curriculum meets academic standards and reflects state-of-the-art practices in the industry. NACTEL is a consortium of four communications companies and two communications unions that together have over 350,000 telecommunications workers.

Another example of a university-business partnership that is narrowly focused is the OpenTech project of the Open Learning Agency in Canada. With sponsorship from Oracle Corporation, Cisco, Microsoft and others, OpenTech offers students a combination information technology certificate plus college credit.

For profit university subsidiaries

There are commercial ventures undertaken by tertiary institutions originate and remain within the universities themselves. Administrators at Cornell University, for example, saw a sizeable market for high-level courses taught at a distance through e-mail, discussion boards and CDROMS. The university formed a for-profit entity named e-Cornell. Taking a cue from the business world, Cornell decided to motivate e-Cornell's leadership to capture the market by giving them a share in the profits of the company. The example of e-Cornell, however, illustrates a difficulty of grafting new e-commerce onto the academic trunk of an existing tertiary institution. One catch in the e-Cornell planning was that the university's administration created the new company without consulting the faculty. When they learned of the new company and the plans for it, some of the faculty rebelled. They claimed that they were not against distance education but they wanted to discuss how it could fit into Cornell's academic culture. Citing competition from peer institutions and private businesses, the administration pressed forward in spite of faculty objections. Most of the faculty seem resigned to coexist with the new company, sharing the common belief that if it is not e-Cornell, some distance education programme will be started soon by the university.

In December 1999, Temple University created Virtual Temple to market online courses to reach more rapidly and efficiently the adult market. Virtual Temple would contract with faculty from Temple University and other universities to use their courses. This follows a pattern set months earlier by New York University and Columbia University. Interestingly, as with e-Cornell, some faculty members at Temple complained that the university's administration had failed to consult with the faculty in developing the plan for Virtual Temple. The University of Maryland University College (UMUC) also created a wholly owned for-profit arm to market its online courses. UMUC already offers 430 online courses, serving more than 20,000 students.

Until recently, the education process within the university was a self-contained process, with the faculty member responsible for most of the process. Curriculum development, creation of course materials, delivery of instruction, student advising, testing, grading and accreditation would be done by the faculty member on behalf of the university. Other university personnel handled the rest of the process, including functions such as registration, bookstore, library, counselling, housing, food services, etc. But some years ago, traditional higher education institutions began to unbundle and outsource some peripheral components such as food services and bookstore functions.

The advent of distance education has led some institutions to question whether other components of the educational process could be unbundled. This opened up opportunities for businesses to provide some of those services, theoretically more efficiently and economically than the university could. It was not long before businesses started to provide library and bookstore services for distance learners.

Companies such as Real Education soon offered to develop courses online and deliver the core parts of the courses to distance learners. Others, such as Prometric, began to market testing services. Yet other companies, such as Blackboard and WebCT, began to develop and market integrated educational packages that brought together almost all of the components of the educational process into a single platform.

Government-education alliances

Today, the governments are becoming a major potential player in distance education. Educational opportunities are seen as a key incentive for attracting and retaining recruits to voluntary military service. While the US military has for years funded access for its members to traditional and non-traditional education opportunities, in 2000 several new programmes were launched by the Department of Defence and one or more of the branches of the armed services. US service members have the option of choosing from many forms of education. Tuition is paid by the US government. One concern of the Pentagon is that various colleges and universities use different software applications and technology platforms for their online courses.

With funding from the Defence Department's Advanced Distributed Learning Initiative, several public universities in Wisconsin are compiling a set of voluntary technical standards for companies that make and sell software and platforms for online courses. The goal of this project is to make it easier to migrate courses from one platform to another. In August 2000, the US Army announced what might be the largest distance education programme ever undertaken, planning to spend $600 million over six years to enable any interested service member to take courses on the internet, at little or no cost, wherever they are stationed. Through a Request For Proposals (RFP), the army would contract with a single "integrator" who would set up the technology to deliver the courses and would subcontract with colleges and universities that agree to use the system to offer their courses to service members.

The US Navy had announced a programme to provide distance education college courses to its service members all over the world, again as a way to recruit and retain sailors. Unlike the army's RFP, the navy's did not require a single integrator. Instead, the navy chose 16 colleges and universities and plans to work closely with each, more like a partner than a contractor. Fifty-two institutions had applied to participate in the programme. The navy programme is significant in at least two ways. First, only colleges offering complete degree programmes at a distance were eligible for consideration. Second, because many sailors are isolated on ships, the courses had to be available without internet access; the navy was not interested in programmes that offer only online courses.

Forces which control the organisational arrangements include:

i) *Societal and Institutional needs*: Many of the new virtual education organisational arrangements reflect strongly felt needs in a society or an institution. For example, the African Virtual University is being developed to address the lack of adequate tertiary opportunities in the participating countries. NYU Online is being developed to capitalise on the human resources of the institution, using the technologies to reach and teach additional students. Often, the identified needs can best be met through partnerships or affiliations of two or more institutions.

ii) *Learner needs*: Learner needs is playing a major role in creating and molding new organisational arrangements.

In developing countries, although the term 'distance education 'is used often, many of the students live no more than 30 kilometres from a tertiary institution. In their cases, 'convenience' is a more important consideration than 'distance'. Learner needs are also affecting the nature of the courses provided. Because many of the learners are adults who are in the workforce, they are demanding that the courses be practical and contain information and skills that they can put to work immediately in their jobs.

iii) *Available academic resources*: Presence of academic resources might drive the development of a new institution or programme, absence of such resources might constrain development.

iv) *Available technology infrastructures*: The virtual organisation will not be in a position to develop the technology infrastructure. It must ride on whatever exists. A strong infrastructure might drive new virtual education organisational arrangements, especially if there is unused capacity within the infrastructure. A weak infrastructure might constrain new virtual education programmes, even if the need is great.

v) *Unbunding the educational process*: In recent years, institutions have begun to "unbundle" the package of services they offer and contract some to outside vendors. Any virtual institution created today must determine which services it will offer directly and which others might provide more efficiently or effectively. The ability to contract some services to outside vendors might drive the creation of new organisational arrangements for virtual education.

vii) *Targets and opportunities*: Sometimes new virtual education arrangements will lead to special targets of opportunity, providing occasions for developing new programmes or serving new populations. Such targets of opportunity can drive further development of the new organisation.

QUALITY ISSUES

Establishing and maintaining qualitative integrity is critical to all the stakeholders of a new virtual education organisation: the funders, the administrators, the faculty, the students, and the regulators. Open and Distance Learning (ODL) systems have generally been introduced to meet the increased demand for educational opportunities at all levels by supplementing face-to-face provision while striving to balance the access-cost equation by reducing infrastructure and full-time faculty costs. The very features of flexibility and accessibility which make ODL an attractive option to the part-time adult learner, also mean that it has frequently been viewed with suspicion by conventional institutions and the public, who are more comfortable with the traditional face-to-face world of the institutional classroom. In such an environment, quality may be assumed to have been to a large extent assured by the qualifications of the full-time tenured faculty member, who has total control of the pedagogical process, and by the qualifications of the students at entry.

The best single-mode ODL providers have been acutely conscious of the need to devise processes that can assure the quality of learning outcomes and thereby defend the legitimacy of their programmes and awards. Dual-mode institutions, for their part, have been required to develop quality assurance protocols that demonstrate that their open and distance offerings are of equal quality to these offered in parallel by traditional classroom-based methods. To provide their stakeholders with the necessary reassurance, quality assurance protocols in ODL tend to focus on output measures which are able to demonstrate the value to the student by participation in the process.

Large-scale, mature open universities such as the Open University in the UK (UKOU), Indira Gandhi National Open University in India (IGNOU) and the Open University of Hong Kong (OUHK), are systems-driven organisations. From their establishment, in order to gain acceptance in the higher education community, they consciously adopted and adapted quality assurance measures from the conventional sector and sought to demonstrate the rigour and dependability of the systems which underpinned the key educational processes: programme planning, course design, course development, course delivery and student assessment and award.

The rapid development and use of instructional technologies in both distance and face-to-face institutions since the late 1990s has resulted in a three-way convergence of distance and face-to- face education and electronic technologies. In this new, flexible learning environment, the instructor or teacher is no longer the sole source of knowledge, but plays the role of facilitator, supporting active technology-mediated student learning. In cyberspace, the physical proximity of teacher and student is irrelevant, and group, one-to-one, and one-to-many interactions between student and student and students and teachers are freed from the tyranny of the fixed timetable by the capacity of internet-based technology to provide opportunities for both synchronous and asynchronous communications. The emergence of the new instructional paradigm means that all institutions that use information and communications technologies (ICTs) to facilitate the interaction of students with content sources, faculty support, information resources or other students, need to review and revise their quality assurance protocols to ensure that they are focusing on appropriate inputs, processes and outcomes.

In an internet-enabled environment, the traditional measures of the size of institutional library holdings and access to databases need to be replaced by measures relating to the mechanisms for information provision and support for student's research work. Similarly, in a disaggregated environment where the instructional design process and the provision of technical support and tutorial services may have been contracted out by the institution to commercial providers, it is no longer appropriate to rely solely upon the procedures for full-time faculty appointment, development and promotion to provide reliable indicators of overall academic quality. Instead, one is looking for evidence of mechanisms put in place by the institution to ensure that its staff at any time are competent for all the tasks required of them and that the procedures for contracting out services are informed by an understanding of best practice in each domain.

Technological developments that have led to the convergence of face-to-face and distance learning, and the emergence of a new flexible learning environment for on- and off-campus students of single- and dual-mode institutions, have also facilitated the emergence of providers of educational services that are dedicated to online learning: virtual schools, colleges and universities that offer the opportunity to study anything, anytime, anywhere. In order to flourish against global competition, both the public and privately funded e-learning institutions need to establish their credentials within their niche in the new global education marketplace.

Potential students need reliable indicators of quality to enable them to navigate the increasingly bewildering array of courses and programmes on offer, without falling victim to unlicensed "web-cowboy" operators, who like their disreputable precursors, the "diploma- mills" of the age of correspondence courses, may fail to live up to the promises they make and bring the whole new world of technology-mediated distance learning into disrepute.

Application of new technologies in the learning environment is not only removing the distinction between conventional and distance education, it is also eroding political and geographical barriers to the movement of knowledge. Whereas within frontiers at the state, national or regional level, structures exist for the regulation or self-regulation of educational activities, there has traditionally been less regulation across frontiers and there is certainly less still in cyberspace.

The growth of the export trade in educational products during the last 10 to 15 years has alerted countries which are net recipients of such products that there is a need to erect barriers in order to safeguard their citizens and institutions against the worst excesses of some entrepreneurial providers, whose major concern is the financial bottom line rather than the educational experience of the students on the course. While protecting local institutions from the threat posed by the global ambitions of entrepreneurial offshore institutions, such legislation may, paradoxically, increase the risk to the unwary individual student that the credentials earned through participation in an online course may not be recognised for further study or employment in the participant's country, even though the institution which offers the course may be accredited in its own home jurisdiction.

The increasingly global nature of educational provision therefore brings with it a need and a market for consumer advice about what to avoid and what to choose in terms of technology-mediated learning opportunities to make sure that they live up to the claims of convenience, relevance and interactivity that are often made for them. In response to the need for guidance on how to select reputable and appropriately accredited online courses, a number of distance learning hub sites have been developed which offer advice on how to avoid falling victim to diploma mills and fly-by-night "institutions" offering cheap degrees. The advice includes treating as suspicious any institutions with unfamiliar accreditation credentials, institutions with "international," "global" or "world" in their titles, and "sound alikes," which are schools that incorporate the names of legitimate institutions into their own names.

As lifelong learning becomes an imperative for active, full-time participants in the labour market, part-time adult distance learners will increasingly seek the convenience offered by technology-mediated learning to meet their professional and technical updating requirements. Such students are more likely to pay their own fees and, as consumers, will expect high-cost efficiency and effectiveness from their chosen providers. They will demand flexibility which extends beyond the curricula to include entry and exit points, access and accreditation of prior learning, study periods and modes of delivery. Prospective students will want to take the following steps to ensure that the course for which they register can meet their requirements:

i) Check the accreditation and determine whether it passes muster. It appears that accrediting agencies exist which are prepared to rubber stamp colleges for a fee.

ii) Grade the school by checking out the courses, teachers and credit accumulation and transfer policies and procedures.

iii) Tour the campus by looking at the institution's web site to see if it's up-to-date and well designed.

iv) Use sample courses and sit in on or a virtual class to determine whether the online format is what they want and to discover whether their computer meets a course's technical requirements.

v) Crunch the numbers and read the fine print to check that it is what they expect from an online course and that they will not need to visit the campus to register, take exams or participate in classroom discussions.

Many governments have made effort to protect the reputation and market share of higher education institutions in the global education marketplace. For example, the Canadian government has funded the development of a consumers' guide, based upon extensive research into the literature relating to quality in technology-assisted distance learning. The project, which is being prepared for the Community Association for Community Education (CASE) and the Office of Learning Technologies (OLT) of Human Resources Development Canada (HRDC) by Dr. Kathryn Barker of FuturEd Consulting Education Futurists (FuturEd) aims to produce Consumer-Based Quality Guidelines for Learning Technologies and Distance Education.

The guide is designed to be applied to education and training products at any level which are delivered by "technology-assisted distance learning," which is defined in the guidelines as "where the learner is in one location and the provider of the learning is in another and technology is used to make the link." In this context, the quality of the education and training products and services is defined in terms of what makes them effective and efficient. Underpinning the guidelines is the belief that all learning products are a combination or system of inputs and resources, processes and practices, and outputs and outcomes. While all are important, "from the consumer's point of view, the outcomes are the most important, then processes and practices and finally inputs and resources that have gone into the design, production and delivery of the learning product/service." The guidelines list the desirable features of a high-quality course or programme and are structured to reflect the hierarchy of concerns, starting with quality outcomes:

i) *Acquired content skills and knowledge should be*:
   a) Relevant.
   b) Transferable.
   c) Specific for the purpose.
   d) Blend traditional education and applied technology skills.

ii) *Necessary learning skills are acquired for*:
   a) Course/programme completion and success.
   b) Lifelong learning.
   c) Self-directed learning management.

iii) *Completion takes the form of credit or credentials that are*:
   a) Recognised by professional accreditation bodies and employers.
   b) Recognised by other educational institutions.
   c) Of the same value whether acquired through on-site or distance learning.
   d) Transferable within programmes and institutions, locally, nationally and internationally.

iv) *Return on investment of the learner's time, finances and energy meets expectations for*:

a) Accessibility as needed and when needed.

b) Objective benefits and utility.

c) *Effectiveness*: subjective achievement of personal goals.

d) *Efficiency*: best use of resources.

e) Customer satisfaction with all course/ programme elements.

The guidelines define the attributes of good teaching processes, good assessment practices, appropriate use of technologies and communications facilities and include the need for effective human resource management practices and an inclusive programme management system.

Governments in many of the advanced industrial economies have not been slow to embrace e-learning, recognising the potential presented by the global market for education to secure new revenue to offset high infrastructure and development costs and at the same time to further their ambitions to trade in other economic sectors. The advantages presented to learners in developing countries by the opportunity to access scarce, top-quality expertise anywhere in the world and to gain access to curricula that embrace a broader spectrum of knowledge than any one institution might accomplish, must be offset by the danger of the emergence of a new cultural imperialism. The globalisation of content facilitated by the new communications technologies leads to a potential loss of cultural diversity and richness. In the domain of quality assurance, global access makes the application of standards and performance measures even more problematic. If standards are relative to the context, to the needs of the students and to their approach to learning, they will be disparate.

In many countries quality assurance agencies have published guidelines to meet the needs of their constituent institutions which are engaged in the delivery of open and distance learning. Examples include those produced by the Quality Assurance Agency of the UK in 1999, which are based upon generic guidelines on quality assurance procedures originally developed for programmes delivered face to face, published in 1996, and the NZAAU's guide to "External Quality Assurance for the Virtual Institution" referred to earlier. In Australia, where open and distance learning at university level is provided on a very wide scale through dual-mode institutions, and where the development of technology-mediated flexible learning resulting from the convergence between distance and face-to-face modes of delivery is well advanced, all institutions and programmes are audited according to a single set of benchmark standards irrespective of the mode of delivery.

The approach of these agencies is influenced primarily by their mandate to assure the accountability of institutions in their sector for the expenditure of public funds and to maintain the credibility system by ensuring comparability of standards at the national and international level. In the US, there is no national academic audit agency, and accreditation is a voluntary activity undertaken usually at the regional level among groups of institutions. In the global virtual education market, students continue to seek assurance that the programme they are studying is accredited by a reliable agency or that it bears the insignia of an institution or group of institutions, whose names are synonymous with excellence.

The development of consortium arrangements for the delivery of online courses and programmes is mirrored by greater collaboration in policy development across accrediting regions and states. For example, the Guide to Best Practice for Electronically Offered Degree and Certificate Programs has been developed by the Western Cooperative for Educational Telecommunications, an arm of the Western Interstate Commission for Higher Education (WICHE) spanning 15 western states in the US. This project takes as its starting point the fact that well-established essentials of institutional quality found in regional accreditation standards are applicable to the emergent forms of learning.

The set of quality benchmarks for internet-based distance learning published by the US Institute for Higher Education Policy (IHEP) in April 2000 under the title "Quality on the Line" is based upon a study which identifies first-hand practical strategies to achieve quality learning being used in US colleges which are acknowledged to be leaders in online distance education. As the press release which accompanied the launch of the study stated: "Many (of the benchmarks) are common sense, but the study validates their importance." The key areas affecting the quality of technology-mediated learning are common to all of the published benchmarks and guidelines and relate to:

i) *Institutional support*: Reliable secure technology; established systems for development and delivery of distance education.

ii) *Course development*: Learning outcomes driven; regular review and updating; "designed in" learning activities.

iii) *Teaching / learning*: Required and facilitated student/ faculty interaction; constructive and timely feedback; instruction in effective research methodology.

iv) *Course structure*: Pre-registration consultation; clear information on course objectives and learning outcomes; access to library resources; clear expectations on assignments and timelines.

v) *Student support*: Full information on requirements and support services; hands-on training; access to technical assistance; transparent advisory and complaints structure.

vi) *Faculty support*: Technical assistance; initial training and assessment in online instruction; on-going support and mentoring; written resources.

vii) *Evaluation and assessment*: Evaluation of educational effectiveness and teaching/learning process by multiple methods using specific standards; use of quantitative data to evaluate effectiveness; regular review of learning outcomes to ensure clarity, utility and appropriateness.

As external accreditation agencies and educational policy-makers are seeking to realign their quality criteria to meet the needs of institutions and students for appropriate benchmark standards in technology-assisted learning, the role of the media is driving an increased emphasis on internal quality review and the publication of performance indicators.

As education becomes more competitive, there is an increased consumer and stakeholder demand for market information. Publications already exist to meet this demand for rankings in relation to face-to-face institutions. External awards and media rankings alone cannot satisfy consumer needs for information on the quality of the education offered by virtual providers. Higher education institutions competing in the worldwide virtual education market may find themselves having to develop and disseminate information on the quality of their services on a continuous basis and to make it available to potential "clients" in readily accessible forms. In this regard, student and employer satisfaction surveys are already rapidly becoming key evaluation mechanisms which demonstrate responsiveness to market.

Technology-assisted delivery provides new opportunities to access data for the feedback-evaluation-quality improvement loop, which is an essential element of an effective quality assurance system. Policy-makers opting for technology-mediated learning solutions must factor in the cost of designing quality management systems which use the data collected as part of a constant quality improvement process. In addition to formal evaluation tools administered by the individual institutions providing technology-assisted distance learning, a number of the sites which act as brokers of online courses and programmes provide an opportunity for learners to review the offering and post it for consideration by prospective users. While this public scrutiny contributes significantly to the transparency of internal quality assurance mechanisms, and while learner feedback is an essential component of a fully developed quality assurance system for any institution, these measures are not of themselves a sufficient guarantor of quality in a global market in which technology-mediated education is growing exponentially.

To achieve the prescribed benchmark standards of the relevant accrediting agencies and meet the demand for transparency in educational processes, virtual institutions must be actively engaged in educational quality work (EQW) in the context of technology-mediated learning. Like much work in quality assurance in education, EQW has its roots in the ideas of Deming, Baldridge and ISO 9000, but is grounded in the context of academic operations. The framework for quality management based upon EQW should empower and stimulate faculty to continuously improve teaching and learning. The five key domains of EQW are familiar from the current literature:

i) The determination of learning outcomes.
ii) The design of curricula to meet the learning outcomes.
iii) The design of teaching and learning processes.
iv) The design and use of student assessment measures.
v) The implementation of quality assurance.

In this methodology, institutions and departments exemplifying best practice should be able to demonstrate that they:

i) Define educational quality in terms of learning outcomes.
ii) Focus on the process of teaching and learning to strive for coherence in curricula and educational processes.
iv) Work collaboratively to achieve mutual involvement and support.
v) Base decisions on facts wherever possible
vi) Minimise controllable quality variation.
vii) Make continuous improvement a top priority.

The basic aspects in which appropriate quality assurance systems for technology-assisted learning differ from those designed for conventional face-to-face delivery are in their concern for the appropriate choice and effective management of the technology to meet the expectations of all of the stakeholders and in the emphasis they place on the need for faculty and student training and support systems to enable them to operate effectively in the new learning environment.

In US a 1997-98 federal survey of distance education estimated that 1.4 million students were enrolled in for-credit college level courses. New estimates are that about 75 per cent of established colleges and universities have some online presence including the requirement that students in conventional face-to-face institutions take at least one online course each semester, which means that virtual education is a reality for over one million students. According to IDC, a technology research firm, approximately 85 per cent of established colleges and universities will rely on some form of distance education by 2002. If one takes into account the accredited for-profit universities, the institutions formed by alliances of institutions and the prestigious face-to-face institutions proposing to provide global access to some of their courses by e-learning through links with educational technology companies, one might be forgiven for assuming that virtual education provides worldwide access to educational opportunities in quantity and quality unparalleled in the history of open and distance learning.

Technology-assisted learning holds out the promise of enhancing distance education by:

i) Enabling the active engagement of the learner in the construction of knowledge.
ii) Making available real-world problems and situations.
iii) Providing representations in multiple modalities.
iv) Drilling students in basic concepts to reach mastery.
v) Facilitating collaborative activity among a diverse student group.

vi) Requiring students to learn the tools of scholarship.

vii) Simulating laboratory work.

viii) Providing continuous opportunities for self-assessment.

Despite the potential of technology to deliver convenient "any time any place" education, the primary demotivating factors for the virtual e-learner continue to echo the long-running complaints of the distance learner, which stem from a sense of isolation from a learning community:

i) Lack of access to student support.

ii) Unavailability of financial aid.

iii) Lack of timely feedback.

iv) Technical problems with delivery techniques.

In all of the hyperbole surrounding the marketing of e-learning as the golden key with which worldwide learning opportunities will be unlocked, it is easy to lose sight of a number of barriers which continue to affect the achievement of quality goals in technology-assisted learning. The first and most significant of these relates to inequality of access to the technology itself: the so-called digital divide. Even in the US where the penetration of the internet is reaching 43 per cent and where online education is most prevalent, most Americans do not have a computer at home hooked up to the internet, and those that do are using a 28.8K modem which effectively limits the ability of faculty and instructional designers to develop truly effective and appealing online courses. Moreover, if one takes into account the fact that in China, penetration is only 2 per cent and in India 3 per cent and even less in other jurisdictions, those without access to the hardware, connections and skills to use the ICTs will be effectively disenfranchised, unless providers recognise that the provision of access to lifelong learning opportunities tailored to meet the learners' needs is part of their mission as educators. The accusation that a global, technology-mediated education is "inherently immoral, consumerist, and substandard" is one element of the vociferous opposition to virtual learning, expressed by traditional universities.

Rapid development of ICTs and the resulting emergence of a common technology-mediated flexible learning paradigm in both face-to-face and distance teaching has necessitated a change in the role of faculty "from being mainly a content expert, to a combination of content expert, learning process design expert and process implementation manager", which, at the very least demands that they undertake a serious reappraisal of their function, competencies and mode of interacting with students. It is evident that e-learning will require the acquisition of new technological skills and knowledge, and that it has the potential to undermine faculty status prerogatives, may lead to the loss of faculty jobs, threaten ownership of intellectual property and decrease personal contact with students, while at the same time requiring them to provide 24-hour access by e-mail and to give prompt and clear responses to all queries.

The resistance from academics is to some extent motivated by self-interest but indicates that many are troubled by the prospect that a combination of market forces and internet technology will produce 'digital diploma mills,' undermine the fundamental faculty prerogative of tenure and accelerate the growth of an instructional underclass while at the same time, necessitating greater administrative control of academic activity; the potential for administrative scrutiny, supervision, regimentation, discipline and even censorship increase dramatically.

Governments in the developed world have recognised both the potential of e-learning for meeting the needs of their citizens, and the danger inherent in being left behind. For example, the Canadian Advisory Committee on OnLine Learning, in its March 2001 report to the government, points out that if Canada does nothing, online learning will still come to post-secondary education in Canada, but it will increasingly be provided to Canadian learners by offshore institutions and corporations that will be responsive only to global market forces and their own domestic exigencies. The requirements of Canadian learners, communities and employers will not be of much concern in most cases.

In Finland the policy discussion paper which marked the first steps towards the establishment of a National Virtual University for Finland the researchers were given the task of designing a structure which could maximise the benefits of the use of new technologies to higher education in the most cost-efficient way. After comparing the results of the California Virtual University and the Western Governors University, the team concluded that "The opportunities presented by a NVU will be best exploited if it covers a full range of university features including [not only] teaching, [but also] research, technology transfer, careers advice, and if it links to local/ regional learning communities."

In December 2000, the Web-based Education Commission to the President and Congress of the United States submitted its report entitled "The Power of the internet for Learning: moving from promise to practice." It identified the promise of the internet:

i) To centre learning around the student instead of the classroom.
ii) To focus on the strengths and needs of individual learners.
iii) To make lifelong learning a practical reality.

The report identified the existing barriers to realising the potential of the technology for enhancing learning and made a series of key recommendations on how to remove them.

Technology-mediated learning has the potential to enable more learners to achieve quality learning outcomes. In order to meet the needs and aspirations of the learners, appropriate, culturally sensitive quality assurance mechanisms must be designed, keeping in mind all of the processes contributing to the educational programme.

REFERENCES

Allen, M., "Don't be a troll! Using the Internet for successful higher education", *Paper presented at Queensland University of Technology*, Brisbane, Australia, January, 2000.

American Council on Education, *Developing a Distance Education Policy for 21st Century Learning,* Washington, D.C.: American Council on Education, 2000.

Barker, K., "Consumer-Based Quality Guidelines for Learning Technologies and Distance Education." *FuturEd,* February 2001.

Belawati, T., "Increasing Student Persistence in Indonesian Post-Secondary Distance Education", *Distance Education* 19 (1) 81–108, 1998.

Besser, H. and S Donahue., "Introduction and Overview: Perspectives on Distance Independent Education", *Journal of the American Society for Information Science* 47(11) 801–804, 1996.

Bester, G., "Guidelines for Structuring and Managing Multi-purpose Community Learning Centres," *Unpublished Master's Thesis*, 2001.

Brown, K., "The Role of Internal and External Factors in The Discontinuation of Off-Campus Students", *Distance Education* 17 (1), 44–71, 1996.

Butterfield, S, et. al., "External Quality Assurance for the Virtual Institution", *AAU series on Quality* Number 4, Wellington: New Zealand Universities Academic Audit Unit, 1999.

Carr, S., "Two More Universities Start Diploma-Granting Virtual High Schools," *The Chronicle of Higher Education*, Dec. 10, 1999.

Darkwa, O., and F., Mazibuko, "Creating Virtual Learning Communities in Africa: Challenges and Prospects", *First Monday* 5, no. 5, 2000.

Dewey, J., *Democracy and Education: An Introduction to The Philosophy of Education,* New York: Free Press, 1997.

Dirr, Peter, "Distance and Virtual Learning in the United States", In *The Development of Virtual Education: A Global Perspective*, Vancouver: The Commonwealth of Learning, 1999.

Dhanarajan, G., "On-Line Learning — A Social Good or Another Social Divide?" *Keynote address presented at the International Conference on Learning and Teaching Online*, South China National University, Guangzhou, China, January 2001.

Erhmann, Stephen, C., *Ivory Tower, Silicon Basement: Transforming the College*, Washington D.C.: The Learning Technologies Group, 2000.

Farrell, Glen M., (ed.), *The Development of Virtual Education: A Global Perspective*, Vancouver: The Commonwealth of Learning, 1999.

_______________, *The Changing Faces of Virtual Education*, Commonwealth of Learning, Vancouver, Canada, 2001.

Johnston, David et al., "The e-learning evolution in colleges and universities: A Pan-Canadian Challenge", Ottawa: Industry Canada, 2001.

Galagan, Patricia A., "The E-Learning Revolution," *Training & Development Magazine,* December, 2000.

Kenniston, K. and D. Kumar.,*Bridging the Digital Divide: Lesson from India*, India: National Institute of Advanced Sciences, Indian Institute of Science, 2001.

OECD Report, "New Technology and Its Impact on Educational Buildings," Paris: Organization for Economic Co-operation and Development, 1994.

Porter, David, *Learning in a Wired World: Moving Beyond the Course as the Unit of Learning*, Vancouver: Open Learning Agency, 2000.

Smith, R., "E-learning — it's the new rage in distributive training, but is there a downside?" *E-learning Magazine,* October, 2000.

Tapsall, S. and Yoni Ryan, "Virtual Education Institutions in Australia: Between the Idea and Reality." In *The Development of Virtual Education: A Global Perspective*, Vancouver: The Commonwealth of Learning, 1999.

Taylor, James C., "Distance Education: The Fifth Generation", *Paper presented at the 19th ICDE World Conference on Learning and Distance Education*, Vienna, June 20–24, 1999.

UNESCO, *Higher Education in the Twenty-First Century: Vision and Action*, World Conference on Higher Education in the Twenty-First Century, 1998.

6

Information Services in Distance Education

Today, a large segment of the population is pursuing its studies through distance education systems. Obviously library services are important for distance learners, if they are to succeed in their studies. There are a number of reasons for library support to distance learners. These include:

i) curriculum requirements,

ii) student and faculty research needs,

iii) library standards for equity of student support,

iv) accreditation criteria, and

v) the importance of information literacy

In addition to library and university accreditation, individual academic programmes may have their own accrediting organisations which evaluate library services offered. Librarians must be aware of changing trends in education and the impact these trends have on the delivery of library service. In any academic community, the library plays a central support role in the educational programme and must be responsive to curriculum development, to group and individual learning needs, and to changes in teaching methods.

Current education theories are influencing the way education is delivered and consequently the way library services are delivered. The major principles of adult learning theory are: active rather than passive learning, the teacher's role as facilitator of the learning process, and the development of learning skills as opposed to factual knowledge. Librarians have an crucial role to play in assisting students to become critical thinkers by helping them to develop their research skills and the ability to critically analyse information they retrieve.

Distance learners may have been disadvantaged in regards to prior schooling and many not have had exposure to libraries in any substantial way. Because of this lack of library experience, librarians should make assumptions about the abilities of the distance learner in regards to even the most basic library concepts. Students will inevitably have a wide variety of prior library experience and this must be taken into account by librarians when they are preparing bibliographic instruction tools.

Organisational structure of the distance education library may vary depending on the educational institution which houses it. In Indian educational institutions, there is a core library located at the main institution. This core library administers other smaller libraries located at regional centres. The University of Athabasca provides a local example of this sort of structure. The institute's headquarters are in Athabasca, Alberta. The institute also has regional centres in Calgary and Edmonton. Such institutes primarily serve distance learners. Other institutes which provide courses through distance education may operate mainly as a traditional university. The University of Calgary and the University of Alberta primarily serve on-campus students, but they also offers individual courses and complete degrees through distance education.

Because the success of the distance learner is so dependent on course materials, library service to this group is crucial. Students do not have classroom lectures, seminar discussions or the informal learning experiences of the traditional student. Requirements of distance learners can be grouped into three categories: the need for materials and facilities, the need for information services, and the need for user services. Materials and facilities include traditional resources such as reference materials and textbooks, but non-traditional resources are needed as well. These include such things as audio-video equipment, computer equipment and photocopiers. The need for information services includes: bibliographic information about reference sources, books, journals, and non-print materials available at their own library or through inter-library loan, information on other organisations offering distance education courses, and information on regional study centres or libraries and the services they offer. The need for user services includes guidance from library staff regarding how to use the library collection and equipment available at the library, choosing reading material, planning their learning and using study skills for independent learning.

Librarians must also provide materials for bibliographic instruction either through written materials, instructional videos or electronically via CDROM tutorials or the WWW. The manner in which library services are delivered to distance learners will depend on whether the students is able to visit a library in person. For example, locally networked CDROMs can be an option for students able to visit a library whereas library information may have to be delivered to the student via the WWW or the mail if the student can not physically access a library.

The provision of a good collection does not necessarily make for good library service. Collections are passive resources dependent on good staff to enliven them, to provide access and research support. In endeavouring to fulfil the library needs of the distance learner, librarians face several problems.

In the matter of document delivery, the librarians faces the following problems:

i) lack of infrastructure facilities at resource centres,

ii) staff shortages,

iii) limited finances,

iv) the proliferation of literature,

v) increased costs and the complexity of demands from users.

These problems in turn impact on document delivery and access to materials.

In the past, librarians relied heavily on delivering library materials to distance learners via the postal service. Photocopies were made for each student requiring a document or the entire book was mailed to the student. This was very costly and slow. Timeliness is crucial in document delivery to distance learners. The central problem of library service to large numbers of distant students who face fixed due dates in their work programmes is that of time. The problem in part arises due to the fact that an assignment will be due for all the students of a particular course at the same time. Today, the effectiveness of electronic resources in addressing such issues becomes glaringly obvious. By putting a needed document on the World Wide Web, all students, provided they have the necessary equipment, can view the document at the same time. This ensures the student gets what s/he needs, the library only has to deliver the document once, and money is saved by not having to send books through the post or order multiple copies.

In developing countries where modern sophisticated gadgets like the TV, VCR, tape recorder, radio, telephone, computer, etc., are not equally and adequately accessible to all the distance learners, library facilities have to remain one the basic student support services to learners. Although technologies such as the WWW can solve many document delivery issues, it simply will not work if students do not have access to a computer. The cost of providing library services to distance learners appears to be an unresolved issue in the literature.

The mission statement for the University of Calgary Library's Distance Education library service, Library Connection, provides an example of the ideal librarians should strive for: "To provide library services to all individuals directly involved with academic courses offered away from the traditional academic campus equivalent to library services available to individuals directly involved with academic courses on the campus." The essence of this mission statement has never been fulfilled, primarily due to lack of money, lack of library staff and lack of institutional will.

Because the electronic library services to distance learners are relatively recent, no thorough cost assessments can really be done. Presumably, this could only be accomplished in the future. Only by comparing the costs of services after a number of years could it be determined if extensive electronic services to distance learners are actually costing libraries more or less. The specific services to be compared is an important issue to consider as well.

There is a great crossover in regards to who uses the services. For example, not only distance learners would access the library's catalogue remotely. Students who attend classes on-campus may use remote library services just as much as distance learners. As well, comparisons would be impossible to do for new courses. For example, the internet course EdPsych 597 offered at the University of Alberta could not be compared to an internet course offered through the mail. The comparison would likely be to the class taught by on campus through the School of Library and Information Studies.

Possible solutions to the challenges presented by document delivery, cost and access issues include resource sharing, partnerships with educators, and the new technologies.

NETWORKED RESOURCE SHARING

Resource sharing is the only means to cope with the present situation and to meet the demands of library users by ensuring access to a wide range of resources available at various libraries, viz., academic, special and public. For example, in some countries, public libraries may serve distance learners who do not have access to university libraries or affiliated learning centres. Networks of libraries or consortiums are becoming a viable option to expand the resources of individual libraries. This sort of sharing is occurring all over the world.

Automation of library operations and networking of all types of libraries can facilitate extending the library and information services to distance learners. The development and the cooperative sharing of staff expertise across campuses and libraries. In a tight budgetary environment, sharing experiences and expertise in this way will allow libraries to make the most effective use of their limited resources.

The Electronic Library Network of B.C., provides a Canadian example of a large library network already operating. ELN's objectives are to extend the collective resources of the province's post-secondary libraries, to make these resources available to students and researchers regardless of their location in the province, and to enhance resource sharing among libraries through the innovative application of technology. At the end of 1995, ELN served 28 member libraries, 25 of which are provincially supported universities, colleges and institutes. ELN offered the following services to its members:

i) *Three union databases*, updated annually, containing over 2 million catalogue records from almost 60 libraries. These three databases include serials, videos, films and records for the collections of 53 BC libraries.

ii) *Consortium access to reference databases:* This consortia approach means that, together, libraries are able to offer more resources to their users than they ever could alone. As well, costs can be reduced in regards to overall costs for licenses, data and storage and system/contract administration.

iii) *Online Journal Access (OJAC) Service*: A journal request and delivery service that allows users to search databases, retrieve citations and order documents all in one online session. This saves the time of both the user and library staff and is a more economical approach to inter-library loans.

iv) *Training programmes:* These include internet training programmes to staff in member libraries, who in turn can train their own users. ELN has published two internet training manuals, which will be available on the WWW in the future.

v) *Development of new resource sharing models*: In 1992, ELN commissioned a major study that resulted in 15 recommendations. Following the study, ELN formed a task force to further resource sharing among post-secondary libraries. One of the goals of ELN is to provide access to all member libraries through one seamless interface.

ELN works to ensure that member libraries with the most basic equipment can fully participate in services.

It is not just tangible resources that should be shared, but expertise as well . For example, librarians need to act as members of the "education team". They need to be aware of the policies and objectives of their institutions concerning distance education so that they may define their own roles in the process.

The basic philosophy of the academic library is the encouragement of learning; it is a reflection of the philosophy and aims of the institution by reason of its support for the teaching programmes. By becoming part of an education team librarians broaden the scope of their role in the learning process. Academic librarians who continue to concentrate on their custodial and service roles will find themselves increasingly marginalised from the teaching and learning process.

If librarians make the education function the central focus of its services, the library will move from its usual position on the periphery of the institution to a more prominent position on campus. There is also an overlap between the roles of teachers and librarians in distance education. So many of the issues facing educators also face librarians as they are becoming teachers as well. Perhaps they have always been teachers, but now more than ever bibliographic instruction or information literacy is a vital part of the academic librarians job, considering the changing philosophy of education as a whole.

The new technologies available to librarians today are changing the way library services to distance learners are delivered, as well as providing opportunities for services never before possible. V. Wilson points out that, "technology is making the physical location of resources irrelevant and is placing the responsibility for locating and manipulating information sources firmly in the hands of the user." Technology has provided options for library services to distance learners in a number of areas including document delivery, bibliographic instruction and reference assistance.

There are many practical considerations for the setting up of electronic library services to distance learners. A pilot project in place at the University of Buffalo (UB) Libraries used the WWW to provide access to course related materials, electronic library services and resources on the internet. Students accessed the programme either through a link on their department's homepage or through the library's homepage. Materials placed online included syllabi, class schedules, lecture notes, handouts, and homework assignments. Initially, only these non-copyrighted materials were to be included, although it was stated on the web pages that these materials were the intellectual property of the instructors who created them. Thus, reproductions could be made only for research or instructional purposes as stated under the fair use guidelines of the US copyright law.

At the outset of the project anyone could access these materials. It is assumed that in the future students will be assigned passwords to access the materials, especially if copyrighted materials such as journal articles and excerpts from books are to be included. In this particular case, librarians were responsible for a great deal of the project, perhaps more so than would be the case in many institutions. Faculty members provided the librarians with all the course materials that were to appear on the site. This created new challenges for the librarians.

Many documents were submitted to the librarians as handwritten or typed photocopies which had to be scanned in and then formatted in HTML. Much of the material received contained mathematical notation which HTML does not handle well. Therefore, these items had to be scanned and put on the web as either GIFs or JPEGs. Adobe Acrobat PDF was used as an alternative to GIFs, JPEGs and HTML. Adobe Acrobat preserves the original page layout of a document including such things as mathematical notations. As well, Adobe saves images as dynamic rather than static images. GIFs and JPEGs cannot be manipulated whereas a PDF file can be enhanced to include hypertext links. Hardware and software required for this particular project was as follows:

i) HP ScanJet 4c scanner
ii) OmniPage OCR software to scantext
iii) HP DeskScan II software for scanning images
iv) Adobe's Photoshop software was used for fine line drawings that required special handling.
v) HTML Assistant Pro 2 was used to automate as much as possible the HTML formatting of text files.

The project team anticipated the issue of student access to computers and software. They were sensitive to the fact than not all their students would have access to a graphical browser such as Netscape. In response the this situation, the focus was on text-based materials and the web pages concentrated on content rather than design. However, the content of the course materials made the web sites much more graphical than anticipated. The nature of the engineering programme was such that a large amount of graphs, charts and mathematical notions were included in the web sites. Eventually a note was placed on the pages to alert users that they would not be able to view the many image files with Lynx.

Technology solves many of the problems of delivery library services to distance learners. Those students who are the most disadvantaged in terms of library services because they cannot access any alternate services will likely benefit the most from library services delivered electronically. However, the technological tools required may not be accessible to all students. Students' access to personal computers has risen dramatically in the past decade.

In a 1996 survey of off-campus students at State University of West Georgia, 59 per cent had a computer and modem. She also found that many students who do not have access to the technology required to access electronic library services cannot afford to purchase the equipment or are reluctant to do so because they are not confident in their technological abilities. This issue may be resolved in part by providing equipment at regional libraries that are part of the larger institutions or by partnerships with other libraries.

For those who chose to study at home however, the issue is more complicated. Some institutions are offering equipment leasing options. Other students may find that purchasing a computer and the necessary software is actually cheaper in the long run when compared to the costs incurred by quitting full-time employment to return to school, or commuting to the campus.

Internet is useful for distance learners not only to access course materials and library services but also for accessing information on related topics. Students accessing the course web pages in the UB project discussed above were also directed to other internet-based resources, which were selected by the appropriate subject librarian. The University of Manitoba's library web page also provides a good example of this.

Essentially students accessing the system can receive virtually all the services they might if they were to visit the library in person. This includes asking a reference question, renewing a book, requesting a journal article through interlibrary loan or searching the online library catalogues available through the university. Another problem addressed by the use of the WWW is limited library hours. One of the reasons students choose to learn off-campus is that they have time limitations due to employment or family responsibilities.

Since the web and the internet has such an integral role to play in the delivery of library services to distance learners, the technology warrants some scrutiny. Michael J. Albright provides a concise list of the advantages and disadvantages of internet-based teaching. He lists the following as advantages:

i) With the proper software, the resources on the internet are universally available to any connected computer in the world.

ii) No space or time restrictions are present in a virtual course.

iii) WWW based materials are available across a variety of platforms.

iv) With proper training, the technology is relatively easy to use.

v) Web-based materials are easy to update, providing students with current information.

vi) The internet provides a student-centered learning environment.

v) Courses can be designed to accommodate different learning styles.

vi) Students become skilled at using internet resources.

vii) Another advantage of the internet cited by Orr et. al is that students have their own terminal to work on. Often in library tours and demonstrations, one terminal is used for a group session and not all the students can really see what is going on.

Michael J. Albright lists the following as disadvantages to using internet-based teaching:

i) Access speed can be a problem during peak usage periods. Students with slow modems can have a particularly frustrating experience.

ii) Several web-based courses can overwhelm the computing resources of an institution.

iii) Courses may focus on the technology rather than the content.

iv) Web-based course materials may be time consuming for the professor/librarian to develop.

v) Although students and faculty are more technologically literate than ever before, many still find the internet confusing and intimidating.

vi) The active learning required by internet-based courses may be difficult for students conditioned to be more passive learners.

vii) Lack of access will put some in a disadvantaged position.

viii) Courses on the internet often attract non-students participants.

ix) Copyright issues have not been entirely sorted out.

xi) An active campus support system is essential.

FACULTY PARTNERSHIP FOR DISTANCE EDUCATION

Library resources are very important to distance students as the majority of them indicated that success in the course required access to library materials. Active partnership between course instructors and librarians creates real opportunities to enhance the academic experience for distance learning students by combining the commitment and expertise of these two critical academic groups. Research literature clearly points to the importance of integrating on-campus library services with distance education programmes.

Driving forces behind the integration of library support include curriculum requirements, student and faculty research needs, library standards for equity of student support, accreditation criteria, and the importance of information literacy. Integration and partnership efforts are constrained by the forces of budget restrictions, technological limitations and network incompatibilities, librarian and faculty workload/ inertia, and the sheer magnitude of accessible information. The flexibility of distance learning programmes in terms of class sites and meeting times is very attractive to students. This means that they may be attending classes at local colleges, high schools, or community centres, during the evenings and on weekends.

As a result many distance students have no access to an academic library or have access to a collection that cannot support their research requirements. Some of these students start their coursework with a clear disadvantage compared to their on-campus peers. Moreover, variations among distance site library resources could result in clear inequity of access to essential sources that rivals the potential inequity between on and off-campus students. Individual academic programmes may have additional accrediting organisations that also look at library services. An active partnership between teaching faculty and librarians can help ensure continued accreditation by focusing attention on the provision of rich library resources, information literacy for students, and resource utilisation in course curricula.

Let us look at the model of the distance digital library service provided by The State University of New York at Plattsburgh. It began its Telenursing Distance Education Programme in 1994 with a five-year, one million dollar grant from the US Department of Health and Human Services. The programme currently offers a full RN to BSN programme, designed for part-time adult returning students. Plattsburgh nursing and library faculty teach from an on-campus studio over a live, two-way interactive, compressed audio/video teleconferencing system. The programme has graduated 42 students and has a projected Fall 1996 enrolment of 156 students, many taking two or more classes. Students progress through the programme along with their on-campus peers, have the same instructors, and the same course requirements.

Between four and six courses are offered each semester at the five distance site classrooms, all located at other SUNY two or four year colleges within this rural area of upstate New York. SUNY Plattsburgh Deans Virginia Barker (Professional Studies) and Cerise Oberman (Library and Information Services) worked together on the grant proposal with other key faculty, staff, and college administrators. Both envisioned a working partnership between their divisions that would ensure equity of academic richness and academic rigor for distance education students.

A library services component for the telenursing programme was built into the grant proposal and funding was provided for a part-time outreach librarian who would establish connections with librarians at each distance site. These site librarians played a significant role in shaping the library services component by agreeing to act as "first responders" to information requests and to work collaboratively with the Plattsburgh Outreach Informational Services Librarian to provide electronic access to additional resources. Grant funds were also provided for core nursing book collections at each distance site library, electronic access to the Nursing and Allied Health (CINAHL) database, and delivery of research materials not available at the site library collections.

Library support for distance education students is distributed throughout the Feinberg Library group organisational structure, although primary coordination and service responsibility rest with the part-time Outreach Information Services Librarian. In this distributed model, distance student interlibrary loan requests are handled by the interlibrary loan/document delivery staff; core collection acquisitions are handled by library acquisitions staff; circulation and course reserves are handled by patron services staff; and instructional and reference services are handled by the appropriate library faculty.

The Outreach Librarian has both guidance and assistance from the entire Division of Library and Information Services, which includes instructional engineering, systems operations, programming services, network management, and computing support services. Feinberg Library at SUNY Plattsburgh has a long history of wide-ranging support for the programmes offered by the college. Library faculty and staff work to enhance the academic experience in three main areas: curriculum enrichment, research instruction, and direct student services. Each of these requires different partnership strategies because of their different users and different objectives.

Librarians can provide research assistance to faculty as they develop their courses and create their reading and reserve lists. Some simple strategies employed at Plattsburgh are:

i) meeting regularly with faculty to discuss the courses and library involvement;
ii) reading copies of course syllabi and offering ideas;
iii) attending classes to get a real sense of the courses; and
iv) consulting regularly with faculty for input on library acquisitions.

Librarians have identified internet resources for faculty as part of internet demonstrations and teaching sessions, and have created web pages with links to important web sites. Librarians have also provided faculty with student handouts on copyright, subject bibliographies, citation style, and the research process. This partnership for curriculum enrichment works both ways.

Librarians consult with faculty to get suggestions for making library courses and instructional sessions more relevant to students. Faculty have been guest lecturers on research strategies and the publication process. Many academic libraries have a departmental liaison librarian programme or subject bibliographers who regularly consult with faculty about book orders and journal subscriptions. This liaison role can be developed into a more active partnership where faculty and librarians work together to enhance courses.

The difference between the traditional librarian supportive role and an active partnership role is one of both substance and timing. In a partnership, faculty and librarians work collaboratively to enhance a course. In such a relationship the contributions by the librarian are more easily identified as significant to student academic success. Librarians can also act as collegial instructors for faculty suddenly faced with new technology such as online catalogues, the internet, and electronic mail (e-mail).

Libraries are changing so quickly that even experienced faculty researchers need updates. Most campus librarians are proficient in distance communication and research technologies, even if they are not yet involved with a distance education programme. Librarians can provide faculty guidance on many issues relating to information and its use, including copyright issues. This is especially valuable in areas where legal compliance is critical, such as broadcasting a videotape to multiple distance sites.

Librarians have traditionally offered tours, training sessions, and research instruction to assist students with locating and using library resources. Distance learning programmes are designed and heavily marketed for adult and returning students. These students frequently lack library research skills, may never have used an academic library, or may never have used computerised research databases. Yet these same students must produce college level papers and research projects. Clearly some efforts to provide instruction and research technology training are critical.

Library research database instruction resulted in increased student database use and that students used a wider variety of resources. This would indicate that some basic library instruction is a minimal requirement.

Students at Plattsburgh have access to the book collection of more than 300,000 volumes, over 1,400 periodical subscriptions, and a significant collection of US Federal, N.Y. State, and Canadian government documents. The library provides electronic access to the collections via the campus computer network and the internet, and participates in regional and national resource sharing agreements.

Feinberg Library offers every distance student equivalent access to library services, as outlined by ACRL guidelines. Students generally use their distance site libraries first and then electronically connect to Feinberg Library for further research or additional reference assistance. Site library book collections were augmented by the Telenursing core nursing collection and a computer and printer were placed in each library for internet access to Plattsburgh and beyond. Journal articles and books are mailed directly to student homes with prepaid return envelopes provided for books. The Outreach Librarian is responsible for ensuring that students are aware of the library services, are successfully using them, and receive all the assistance they require.

The procedures by which resources are identified and delivered are different for off-campus students and on-campus students. Staff rely very heavily on fax and internet connections to provide distance students with access to the book catalogue, journal indexes, interlibrary loan request forms, and reference assistance. The Outreach Librarian teaches the library research course by interactive teleconferencing with E-mail office hours, and demonstrates computerised database searching by connecting a computer to the teleconferencing system. A software programme that shares computer display screens across the internet will soon be installed at the distance site libraries. This will make it easier for a librarian to guide a student through a search of the catalogue, databases, or in submitting an interlibrary loan request.

Librarians with existing departmental liaison responsibilities can expand their role by introducing teaching faculty to other library and instructional issues. Meetings previously scheduled to review new book selections can be broadened to include discussions of course syllabi and information research assignments. Departmental liaison librarians can build on the mutual respect that already exists, by using an incremental approach to partnership projects. If the librarian regularly distributes a bibliography to faculty; the next small step could be to offer to create a bibliography for students.

CONVERGING VISION OF INFORMATION SERVICES

Distance education is a growth industry for higher education institutions, as well as for commercial providers. Some have predicted that within ten years, 50 per cent of students enrolled in higher education will be distance learners or will be studying in a distance learning environment. A second assumption is that off-campus students are at a disadvantage compared to their on-campus counterparts, in part, because of the lack of personal contact with faculty and other students and because of problems in gaining access to library staff and resources. A third assumption is that powerful and pervasive interactive technologies will continue to improve the delivery of education and library support at a distance. Whether we agree or disagree with these assumptions, we cannot ignore their impact on each of the stakeholders in the educational process: administrators, students, faculty, accrediting bodies, and librarians. For administrators, the problem is clearly one of economics.

Libraries are expensive, and resources are not easily duplicated at satellite sites. In the past, administrators have been unable to fund equally and staff off-campus facilities at desired levels. In the future, technology may help to alleviate the problem as electronic access can be provided to many more resources than libraries are able to purchase with diminishing budgets. For students with job and family constraints, the need for pursuing an education at a distance may mean the difference between having an education or not having one at all, making any disadvantages in terms of academic isolation an acceptable tradeoff.

In the future, technology can help to reduce the isolation by providing many options for human interaction through electronic communication. For faculty, it is important that academic standards apply equally to off-campus classes. They need to be able to make library assignments knowing that distance students are able to access the library to complete them. In the future, technology will help to bridge the gap between the distant learner and the library. For accrediting bodies, standards and the review process can bring about the measure of quality assurance needed to bring off-campus programmes into the higher education mainstream.

In the future, technology will enhance delivery of education and access to libraries making it important to re-examine the standards to insure their relevance to an evolving academic setting. For libraries, the potential for user-centered, rather than library-centered, service will be enhanced, as less emphasis is placed on building collections and more on providing access to resources.

In the future, technology will enable libraries to serve distant learners better through networked access and web connectivity. Library schools will need to take the lead here in educating the next generation of librarians, who must be computer literate and sensitised to the special needs of off-campus/distant learners. The curriculum of tomorrow's Library schools will need to reflect a new philosophy of service that is user-oriented rather that library-oriented. Libraries and librarians will have to build new paradigms to serve the many invisible users remotely accessing library catalogues and online databases. The extended campus will be a part of every library's future for two reasons.

i) as more emphasis is placed on providing access to information, and less on building collections, the philosophy of library service that required users to come to the library for help and resources will no longer be dominant. Along with the paradigm shift to the electronic library will come the need for a new client-centered philosophy that encompasses remote users and distance learners. Service to the extended campus will become more the norm rather than the exception, and the client-centered service models developed for distant learners will move library service to off-campus and distance education into the forefront.

ii) as technology is used to further library connectivity, we can anticipate significant advances in the delivery of library support to off-campus/distant learners, minimising the physical disadvantages previously encountered. With more and more academic libraries forming consortia on a statewide basis to provide common access to electronic records, there will be a kaleidoscope of options for distant learners to choose from in terms of internet and web access, full-text retrieval, seamless document delivery from publisher to workstation, online reference service, and electronic communication. While geographic isolation and social disadvantage cannot be wholly eliminated for the distant learner, improvements can be anticipated in this area with existing technological advances.

In the present multimedia, interactive, electronic environment, access to instruction and resources is greatly facilitated. Socialisation of students can be accomplished through the use of e-mail, and electronic mentoring can help to compensate for the lack of faculty and student face-to-face contact. Electronic chat rooms can further enhance communications among distant learners. With the aid of powerful interactive technologies and the forging of statewide and regional alliances, education and library support will produce new synergies for cooperation in the absence of walls and institutions. Home librarians, not just off-campus librarians, will serve remote users and distant learners.

Libraries using webpacs will be able to reach out beyond the walls of the institution, expanding exponentially their collections, electronic resources, and expertise. Collectively, libraries will have access to a much larger body of resources than they would have been able to afford and acquire individually. This potential will be more fully realised in the extended campus environment in the next five years. Two areas that may not change in the next five years are attitudes toward distant learners and mindsets of librarians trained in a non-electronic environment. Some librarians are not prepared to make the leap of the imagination necessary to harness these powerful interactive technologies in creating new service models that capitalise on the new technology, rather than modifying old service models that merely accommodate it.

Although the passage of time will bring some changes in the way in which we deliver higher education and library services, to a great degree, the direction which library services for distance education takes will depend upon the route taken by higher education in general, as well as the path our own individual institutions take. We read constantly about various institutions experiencing budget problems, the rising costs of technology, and non-replacement of faculty and staff.

Concurrently, or perhaps because of this, we also hear about the need to increase enrolment via distance technology, the need to provide better services to our students, and the need to see our students as customers to whom we must deliver quality education at their convenience. As budgets become more restrictive, institutions are being forced to examine their academic programmes, not only in terms of the way in which they deliver courses both on and off-campus, but the way in which they provide support services to their extended degree/distance students.

The ACRL Guidelines for Extended Campus Library Services states that the parent institution should be responsible for providing library services to its constituency. It also suggests the levels of support that should be available to distance students. The latest draft of the Guidelines (*Guidelines for Extended Academic Library Services: A Draft*) is more explicit about both these areas and yet, at the same time, appears to be futuristic and broad, allowing for all contingencies, regardless of how technology and attitudes change.

As now, there will be at least two philosophies governing the way in which these services are provided. Both will be customer oriented. One, however, is more service oriented — the "give 'em what they want" school — whereas the other places greater emphasis upon student self-sufficiency — the "teach a man to fish" school. Both are valid approaches, particularly if we recognise the difficulties which distant students often encounter when using the library.

Although the student population is becoming more computer literate, it does not necessarily follow that they are information literate, nor does it follow that they will have the necessary access to technology. Therefore, it will still be essential to provide instruction and assistance in the use of library and information resources. This will be provided via print and electronic means, on web sites and via e-mail, as well as by telephone, video, audiotape and even face-to-face. When developing library services for extended campus students, some institutions will grapple with the question of whether these services should be handled independently or whether they should be transparently integrated into existing library departments.

The decision an institution makes will be based on finances and philosophy. Some institutions may be able to make a philosophical commitment to serve off-campus students but may not be able to make the budgetary commitment to create a new position or to provide the fullest of services. Some institutions may elect to employ a person whose responsibility is to oversee, coordinate, and manage all library support services provided to distance education students, either on a full-time or part-time basis. Other institutions may choose to integrate all services into existing units so that reference requests are handled by whomever is at the reference desk, instruction by a subject specialist or an instruction librarian, and document delivery by ILL or by a central document delivery unit.

Economy of finances and space will cause some libraries to combine all document delivery functions within one unit in the library. This unit will provide delivery of library-owned materials to off-campus patrons, as well as interlibrary loan to both on- and off-campus constituencies. Although separate statistics may be maintained for budgetary and administrative purposes, this arrangement will facilitate cross-training of staff and will also enable all necessary equipment and supplies to be housed in one common area. This plan is suggested by Bazillion and Braun in *Academic Libraries as High-Tech Gateways: a Guide to Design and Space Decisions* as a practical and cost-effective means of utilising staff, space and materials, in addition to its elimination of duplicate service points within the library. As more institutions perfect their use of interactive video and/or electronic classrooms, librarians will take a more pro-active role in the classroom and will work more collaboratively with the teaching faculty to develop assignments that are feasible in the off-campus/distant environment.

As involvement in developing strong courses for distance delivery increases, the relationship between teaching faculty and librarians will be strengthened. Even now, there are institutions whose contracts for teaching faculty state that they will be expected to teach in both on- and off-campus environments as well as via distance education technologies. As this occurs with more frequency, librarians will become more openly involved with the educational process.

REFERENCES

Goodson, Carol., "A Continuing Challenge for Librarians: Meeting the Needs of Distance Education Students", *MC Journal: The Journal of Academic Media Librarianship* 4.1, Summer 1996.

Heller-Ross, Holly, "Librarian and Faculty Partnerships for Distance Education", *MC Journal: The Journal of Academic Media Librarianship,* 4.1, Summer 1996.

Jagannathan, Neela, "Library and Information Services for Distance Learners", *Resource sharing and Information Networks,* 11.1-2 159-170, 1996.

Kascus, Marie A, "Library Support to Distant Students as a Library Education and Continuing Education Issue", *Journal of Education for Library and Information Science* 35, 344-347, Fall 1994.

Orr, Debbie, Trish Andrews, Margaret Appleton, "The Creation and Delivery of a Residential School Program for Geographically Dispersed Students", *MC Journal: The Journal of Academic Media Librarianship* 4.1, Summer 1996.

Unwin, L., Bolton, N. and Stephens, K., *The Role of the Library in Distance Learning*, Final Report, London: British Library, 1997.

Wilson, Alane, "Library Connection: Education From a Distance", *PNLA Quarterly* 59, Winter/Spring, 1995.

7

Opportunities in Distance Education

Distance education technologies are expanding at an extremely rapid rate. Too often, instructional designers and curriculum developers have become enamoured of the latest technologies without dealing with the underlying issues of learner characteristics and needs, the influence of media upon the instructional process, equity of access to interactive delivery systems, and the new roles of teacher, site facilitator, and student in the distance learning process.

Distance learning is a subset of distributed learning, focusing on students who may be separated in time and space from their peers and the instructor. Distributed learning can occur either on or off campus, providing students with greater flexibility and eliminating time as a barrier to learning. A common feature of both distance and distributed learning is technology. Regardless of whether students are on campus or online, there are many implications of integrating technology into education, i.e., in making learning distributed.

Distance education and on-campus instruction are converging, with online delivery systems and approaches being employed for distant, commuting, and residential students. This convergence of "clicks and mortar" in the form of technology-mediated education is distributed learning. Distributed learning is much more than an online substitute for lectures. Distributed learning extends the opportunities for interaction between faculty and student, incorporating simulations and visualisations, as well as collaborative learning. In fact, the "anytime, anyplace" nature of this new set of electronic educational opportunities may well have its greatest impact on residential education. Not only does distributed learning occur anywhere and at any time, but these conditions can be modified along a number of dimensions.

Distributed learning environments may augment traditional instruction through reinforcement by providing the opportunity to explore a subject in much greater depth, allowing learners to study the material on their own time, or to gain additional experience outside of the defined classroom times or homework assignments. In distributed learning, the learning experience is no longer bounded by the length of the class session.

Distributed learning, rather than distance education, will become the dominant paradigm for higher education -although, in the short term, institutions are confronted with a multitude of challenges associated with the "distance" component.

The future of distributed learning — and of higher education — will not be a one-size-fits-all approach. Far from spelling the demise of traditional classroom education, online learning (i.e., learning environments that use the internet and/ or the web) allows for differentiation of institutions, learning styles, and pedagogy. The variations provided by online learning environments will not only rival, but are likely to surpass the diversity of types of institutions that currently characterises American higher education.

Educators can now construct learning environments that enable students to become engaged in learning any way the student chooses. The anytime, anyplace nature of the web allows students to spend as much time as they need searching for information, running simulations, or collaborating with peers. Beyond the fundamentally different characteristics of the web, those who have grown up "digital" actually work and think differently. It is no longer safe to assume that they learn as we do.

For instance, today's young people multiprocess -they do several things simultaneously. Adults tend to think that young people who are multiprocessing must not be concentrating. This may not be true. The attention span of teens often is between 30 seconds and five minutes -a figure that parallels that of top managers who operate in a world of tight deadlines, executive summaries, and rapid decisions.

Today's literacy involves not only text but also image and screen literacy. This new literacy is one of information navigation. Students today navigate the internet, assembling knowledge from fragments of information as opposed to visiting a library. This new form of information retrieval enables students to be their own personal reference librarians who know how to navigate through confusing, complex information spaces and feel comfortable doing so. Information navigation may be the main form of literacy for the 21st century. However, students need guidance in developing taste and discrimination in the selection of information on the internet.

Formal learning in an authority-based, lecture-oriented environment. Now, with incredible amounts of information available on the web, learning through discovery is becoming preeminent. Our generation tends not to want to try things unless we know how to use them. Today's learners want to "turn the thing on, get in there, muck around, and see what works. Today's kids get on the web and link, lurk, and then try it themselves." The web holds a number of implications for learning environments as well as for the type of students we are educating.

i) *Exploration*: E-learners use the web as an exploratory tool to access a plethora of information and resources. Experience: The web offers e-learners a comprehensive learning experience, from synchronous learning to threaded discussions to self-paced study.

ii) *Engagement*: The web captivates learners by enabling creative approaches to learning that foster collaboration and a sense of community.

iii) *Ease of use*: The web is easy to use not only for learners, but for learning providers as well. Content can be made immediately available to learners across all technical platforms.

iv) *Empowerment*: The web puts learners in the drivers's seat with a set of tools that enables personalisation of content and allows learners to choose the way in which they best learn.

v) *Effectiveness*: There is a growing body of evidence that, owing to the ability to create customised learning environments on the web, distributed education is more effective than the classroom lecture and the traditional relationship between student and faculty member.

Distributed learning support a specific strategic goal for the institution or is the rationale muddled. To gain the commitment of all those who must support a major initiative (board, executive cabinet, faculty, staff, etc.) it is important to articulate clearly the strategic goals behind the institution's interest in distributed learning.

An institution may have multiple, and potentially conflicting, motivations for distributed education. Even conflicting motivations can be legitimate. The challenge to institutional leaders is to sort out the motivations and rationales. The institutional motivation(s) driving distributed learning often fall into one of four broad categories: Expand access. Most states need to expand access to meet the education and training needs of state residents and businesses, as well as to provide education to underserved populations.

Many institutions are expecting more college students than their facilities can accommodate in the next decade. Some colleges and universities hope to leverage the scalability of distributed learning to avoid their existing bricks-and-mortar capacity constraints.

The quest for lifelong learning has increased the demand for higher education across all age groups. Many institutions hope to generate new revenue from distance education by targeting emerging segments such as international education or working adults. Serve as catalyst for institutional transformation. Institutions are being challenged to adapt rapidly in a more competitive environment.

Many are using information technology (IT) as the impetus to rethink content and pedagogy. Others are finding it the best tool for addressing information age learning styles. Whether focusing on the learning environment, student services, or even back-office operations, IT and distributed learning are being used as catalysts to stimulate institutional transformation. In fact, most institutions are motivated by more than one of these goals. However, it is doubtful that any institution will be able to meet all four goals with a single model of distributed education. The organisational structure, governance, programmatic emphasis, and/or financial model required may be different, depending on the strategic goal.

The intended audience for distributed education can be segmented into numerous categories, ranging from traditional students seeking additional flexibility to "recreational learners" engaged in expanding their personal knowledge. Segment definitions may depend on factors such as the goals of the learner, the individual's maturity level, and who makes the purchasing decision. The following is a sample set of learner segments:

i) *Corporate learners* work for corporations and are seeking education to maintain or upgrade their skills. The purchasing decision is made by the employing corporation and not by the individual acting alone.

ii) *Professional enhancement learners* are seeking to advance their careers or shift careers. They are working adults who make the educational purchasing decision on their own.

iii) *Degree-completion adult learners* are working to complete a degree at an older age. They frequently are working adults who must balance work and family needs with their educational goals.

iv) *College experience learners* are preparing for life. This segment includes many of the 18-to 24-year-old residential college students for whom the coming of age process is almost as important as academic achievement.

v) *Pre-college learners* are interested in doing baccalaureate-level work prior to the completion of high school. This segment may be interested in getting a jump start on college.

vi) *Remediation and test preparation learners* are focused on learning as a prerequisite to an examination or enrolment in another programme.

vii) *Recreational learners* are interested in education for its own sake. They enjoy learning and view additional education as a hobby or as a source of personal enjoyment.

Many of these "competitors" represent multi-institutional partnerships that allow a company to leverage content from educational providers who have expertise in serving specific segments.

These characteristics drive specific distributed education components such as courses/curricula, pedagogy, or marketing. The types of programmes that are likely to be successful with K -12 learners are distinct from those for corporate learners. Services may vary, as well. Test preparation learners may value tutoring services; recreational learners are less likely to do so. The type of instructional support required by faculty members also will vary depending upon the modality of instruction appropriate for the intended audience.

In the case of actual distance education, how the institution markets its offerings will vary. Selling a distance education programme to a multinational corporation with thousands of learners differs from marketing remedial courses to individual learners. Other factors may vary as well, such as the strength of a particular institution's image and the capital required to be successful in a specific segment.

GROWTH OF DISTANCE EDUCATION

Before initiating a distance education programme, an institution must consider whether it is in a strong competitive position relative to other higher education institutions or to e-learning start-ups. Among some US colleges and universities that have developed aggressive distance learning programmes, the reported growth rates (from 1999 -2000 to 2000 -2001) range from 200 per cent (Pennsylvania State University's World Campus) to over 1,000 per cent (University of Maryland's University College). While the success of these institutions should be applauded, it would be unwise to assume that these growth rates can be emulated without considerable time, investment, expertise, and development of sound strategies.

Many successful distance education programmes are based on years of experimentation with pedagogy and delivery systems. Establishing technical infrastructure and support programmes may require millions of dollars and take years to develop. Investments can exceed $1 million per course. Despite such concerns, optimism continues to permeate the market. Those in US higher education have not only come to believe that the distance education market is large, growing, and profitable, but that the appeal of a US degree in the international market is great. The sheer numbers of potential worldwide learners has encouraged some to speculate that e-learning from US institutions can capture a portion of the ever-increasing global audience.

Governance and organisation choices can have a major impact on funding strategies, as well. Some issues extend beyond the dollars themselves and relate to controlling fund allocation. If the *modus operandi* of the campus is to distribute funds to individual departments, it may be difficult for a cohesive e-learning programme to develop across the institution. Holding funds at the institution or system level may make it possible to mount a major initiative, but the process could be at odds with a decentralised culture.

Attracting and motivating a new breed of entrepreneurial faculty is likely to be an important challenge, as well. Some faculty may be willing to trade security for greater economic opportunities and pay-offs. Although new models for faculty recruitment and retention may be required, such approaches will be difficult, if not impossible, within the confines of traditional faculty governance and the existing employment rules in higher education. Perhaps the most challenging talent issue involves finding the necessary instructional support personnel.

Selection of an organisation and governance model that works for distributed education may not align with the existing culture of the institution. In some instances, distributed education may represent a logical extension of the historic mission. In others, online learning appears to be anathema to the ideal of close, personal relationships between students and faculty.

Distance education poses serious challenges to the alignment of these programmes with existing academic, financial, and technology plans. The governance issues are even more daunting. Across the United States, colleges and universities have taken different approaches to establishing distance education organisations. A number of universities have created units that are extensions of the current college or university organisation. These entities generally are located within the central administrative unit and tend to be funded through foundation or university monies. Colleges and universities using this approach include the University of Illinois, University of California-Berkeley, UCLA, the University of Texas, and the State University of New York (SUNY).

Several universities have established distance education programmes in not-for-profit organisations that are separate from the university. These entities are essentially new businesses with a mission and culture distinct from the traditional university. In an effort to improve organisational responsiveness and attract capital, a growing number of traditional institutions, both public and private, are creating for-profit spin-offs. .

More than a dozen states have launched virtual universities in an effort to address statewide policy issues such as work-force development. Aggregating content from state higher education institutions, virtual universities market courses to learners by developing and maintaining a single e-learning portal and course catalogue. In some states, learners can even register for courses through the virtual university portal. States with virtual universities include South Dakota, Tennessee, Minnesota, Michigan, Kentucky, Florida, Georgia, and Arizona.

An important role of governance is to identify those who are decision makers. Creating a matrix of responsibilities and agreeing on who makes what decisions speeds the decision-making process and reduces the divisiveness of issues ranging from programme planning to technology delivery. Although the right mix of responsibilities will vary from campus to campus, the following groups may be appropriate decision makers for the issues listed below. Although many distributed education discussions seem focused on the technology, most of the issues and those responsible represent the traditional academic groups. Distributed education is fundamentally an academic issue, not a technological one. Although IT may be the stimulus or change agent, the essential matters are complex and will be the purview of academics.

In a growing number of cases, a separate distance education organisation is established to provide marketing and services as a complement to the traditional academic enterprise. Because distributed learning is often thought of as being driven by technology and technologists, it is important that we not confuse academic prerogatives with marketing or technology functions. Drawing clear distinctions between academic and non-academic activities helps. An organisational or governance structure that will help ensure that distance learning is well-integrated with the rest of the institution.

Partnerships can provide higher education institutions the services they require and can allow them to manage the risk inherent in this fast-paced environment. These services may range from online admissions to textbook sales to career services. In the past year, over a hundred e-learning firms entered the education space. New ventures are constantly surfacing and existing ones are merging, being bought out, or quietly disappearing. The churn in this market is staggering. Monitoring these alternative providers is challenging; knowing with whom to partner is an even more daunting task. Collaboration with other entities also can help educational institutions round out their distributed education programmes. It is not just with whom the institution has a relationship, but the nature of that relationship, that is important. Although the term "partnership" is used often, many relationships between suppliers and educational institutions focus on obtaining the lowest cost for goods or services.

Partnerships are a way for organisations to share risk and leverage each other's expertise. Many internet start-ups are being provided with content through partnerships with educational institutions. In these cases, the structure, marketing, and new business models may come from the start-ups and the content from stable, highly reputable academic institutions.

Partnerships may form between a higher education institution and a vendor, or among academic institutions. By entering into partnerships or consortia, educational institutions can leverage their collective market size and strength, reducing risk and sharing resources. There are many examples of consortia, one of the largest being the Electronic Campus of the Southern Regional Education Board (SREB). The concept behind the Electronic Campus is to use the "connectedness" of SREB and the region's colleges and universities to establish a regional marketplace, which reduces barriers to learning, increases access, and encourages the sharing of resources.

Today, more than 260 colleges and universities are involved with the Electronic Campus. More than 3,000 courses are offered across 100-plus degree programmes. Other consortia focus on specific disciplines, a particular set of institutions, or a geographical area. The Associated Colleges of the South has, for example, formed a consortium to offer a comprehensive classics major via the internet to students in residence on its member campuses.

In US, the National Education Association (NEA) poll of instructors who teach distance learning courses, three-quarters were positive about distance learning. One common reason cited was that technology can extend educational opportunities to students who cannot take courses in a traditional, onsite setting. The most significant finding was that quality and access are central considerations that dictate how faculty members feel about teaching and learning, regardless of whether the forum is a traditional classroom or an online environment. Faculty surveyed believed web-based courses do a better job of giving students access to information, helping them master the subject, and addressing a variety of learning styles. However, they believed traditional courses do a better job of strengthening group problem-solving skills, verbal skills, and oral presentation abilities. Measures of learning -and of quality -are elusive and often controversial in higher education. For example, attempts to measure the value that has been added by a course or a degree programme typically are received with skepticism.

The quality of the student body is considered a prime determinant of the quality of education a student receives. However, there are few answers for questions such as whether this cohort effect is stronger or weaker in a distributed learning environment. Yet, in all fairness, there are few studies that measure the effectiveness of textbooks and lectures as an educational delivery system. Providing adequate academic and student services to distance learners is a critical quality issue. The needs of students enrolled in distance learning programmes carry implications for existing library, academic advising, career counselling, financial aid, registration, and other operations.

A multitude of policy issues associated with distributed education exists -ownership of intellectual property, conflict of interest, workload, accessibility, and appropriate use, to name a few -ranging from department-based policies to national ones. Of many policy issues, intellectual property has drawn the most attention. Intellectual property issues associated with distributed education may involve patent, copyright, and software infringement; for some institutions, their trademark, multimedia, and video-taping policies may be affected as well.

The American Association of University Professors (AAUP) recommends that the copyright of materials produced by faculty should belong to them, except in specific instances, such as when it is a work for hire. Certain circumstances, such as when faculty use technical and/or design experts employed by the institution, may affect faculty ownership of intellectual property.

Some institutions are developing conflict of commitment and conflict of interest policies that may transcend intellectual property policy issues. An assortment of faculty policies associated with distance education. These include policies related to workload, compensation, and support. In 1999, an AAUP committee proposed that policies associated with distance education state that the faculty role in distance education courses should be the same as in traditional classes, with the faculty retaining their usual responsibilities for choosing and presenting material. The Americans with Disabilities Act (ADA) guidelines must be adhered to for distance education courses. Specific guidelines are available — for example, not using graphics that cannot be seen by those who are visually challenged or substituting text for sound to accommodate those who are deaf or hard of hearing. Most material is now being designed to comply with ADA guidelines. However, no one knows what the costs might be of modifying the thousands of instructional applications and hundreds of thousands of web pages already in existence.

Issues of privacy protection and internet security are worrisome for those offering distributed education courses. The practice of some for-profit companies to track student interests through "cookies" illustrates one stimulus for unease. "Cookies" allow web managers to develop a profile of a user's internet activities; this information can then become the basis for customised advertising solicitations. Privacy concerns now have expanded to many previously innocuous areas such as what students purchase or what books they check out of the library. With the advent of online admissions, registration and payment systems, privacy and security have taken on additional significance. As a result, many institutions encrypt data while in transit to protect privacy and the confidentiality and integrity of data.

In US, the National Education Association has developed guidelines for security and privacy policies, designed to protect both an institution's records and individual students. In fact, all institutions should adopt privacy policies that include an Acceptable Use Policy for computing resources, as well as "rights and responsibilities" statements that define accountability and responsibility practices for both providers and consumers of computing resources.

Policy issues go well beyond the campus to include state regulations and regional accreditation. For example, an institution that is considering offering distance education courses in another state or country must determine whether it needs approval from accrediting organisations or higher education boards in the areas they are targeting. Accrediting bodies are considering alternative guidelines to accommodate distance learning institutions. Already some for-profit online programmes have received accreditation. Distributed learning requires a significant up-front investment in technology. Without robust networks, scalable applications, and adequate user support, an institution might be well-advised not to begin.

There are numerous barriers to distributed education. Many stem from faculty concerns; others are artifacts of an organisational and financial structure that was designed in a former era. It is a challenge to know which barriers derive from resistance to change and should be set aside, as opposed to those that represent serious concerns requiring thoughtful deliberation. Some barriers will need to be addressed whether or not the institution moves forward with distributed education.

A major barrier to the widespread use of web-based education is the absence of articulation policies within and among states. Broad articulation agreements are rare and their absence creates a high barrier to expanded student participation. Concerns about reduction of revenue or loss of academic quality control often inhibit the adoption of such agreements. For distributed education to attain its full potential, states and institutions will need to remove policy barriers to the free exchange of credits; this includes both credit acceptance and tuition policy.

Distributed education can be an expensive proposition. Although institutions are creating digital infrastructures, significant investment is required to establish successful and scalable distributed education programmes. When campus resources are already stretched, being able to finance what may seem to be a secondary enterprise is problematic. Beyond base funding, how the costs and revenues of distributed education programmes are divided is a topic of significant debate.

Distributed learning organisations often seek to develop an entrepreneurial culture as well as to attract technical talent.

At some institutions, salaries and benefits are lower than in local private sector jobs. Compounding the compensation issue is a tendency for salary scales to be based on seniority, while some of the most talented technology staff may be under 30. With many companies offering stock options and hiring bonuses, educational institutions are at an even greater disadvantage than in previous years.

The greatest obstacle to creating a complex and comprehensive set of distributed learning offerings lies in meeting the information needs of students in an electronic medium. While many campuses have defined initial approaches to offering courses over the internet, few, if any, have defined a scalable and viable strategy for making information resources available to these distant learners.

Particularly for state-supported institutions, political barriers to distributed education can arise. In some cases, resistance to an alternative form of learning develops. In other cases, governors, legislators, or other influencers may impose solutions on academic institutions. New funds for e-learning programmes are often times accompanied by demands for accountability.

Distributed learning can be a highly emotional topic for both supporters and critics. As a result, the process by which these discussions are introduced to various groups must be crafted thoughtfully. In many respects, the buy-in process appears to be a "pay now or pay later" approach. Institutions can engage in discussion and buy-in on the front end of announcing a distributed learning initiative or they can announce a programme and spend the next several months dealing with the resistance generated by not involving the appropriate groups.

Distributed learning challenges our institutions not only to look at new ways of doing what we have always done, but also to look at doing new things. Students with an Information-Age mindset expect education to emphasise the learning process more than a canon of knowledge. They want to be part of learning communities, rejecting the broadcast paradigm of television.

One of the fundamental challenges with distributed learning may be a matter of values. Today's higher education leaders have a particular definition of education and a set of values that derive from our experiences in the 1950s, '60s, and '70s. We are now dealing with the first generation of students who have never known life without PCs or the internet.

One of the first challenges facing institutional leaders is how to find the time to understand distributed learning in sufficient detail to lead their institutions. Although the president or chancellor need not be an expert on the subject, it will be important to have enough background -and time for reflection -to be comfortable with the subject and associated issues.

Distance education can be a polarising issue, the challenge - maintaining balance is very real. Consistency and communication likely will evolve as leadership challenges for distributed education. For example, it is atypical for all groups to have the same definition much less expectation of distributed learning. Institutional leaders will find that consistency of message and repeated communication can help. Cultural change is one of the most significant challenges that institutional leaders will face. It is important that institutional leaders raise troublesome issues to the national level, as well. Some of the challenges associated with distance education may require regional or national action. The collective action of higher education leaders can focus attention on these challenges and move distributed education forward.

NEED OF INSTITUTIONAL LEADERSHIP

As we emerge from a decade marked by broad and deep changes in academe many resulting from the rapid development of networked information technology (IT) the future toward which technology is propelling us may appear hazy. The challenge to institutional leadership remains the same today as it always has been: to become informed about the issues and challenges at hand and to chart a path to the future, not by following existing paths, but by inventing our own.

Transformational change through distributed learning can occur only when institutional leaders articulate a clear, bold vision, demonstrate a broad understanding and acceptance of that view, apply a focused use of resources, and encourage widespread collaboration throughout the institution. True transformation occurs when change is so pervasive that it redefines individuals, institutions, or processes, and when the result of this change yields such significant benefits that the individuals, institutions, or processes do not voluntarily revert to the old ways.

The web supports both synchronous and asynchronous delivery, permitting information access and communication whenever convenient. It integrates multiple internet protocols, including e-mail, file transfer, and hypermedia, as well as multiple information formats including text, graphics, images, video, and sound. Inherently interactive, the web not only allows the user to select content and navigation paths. It supports online communities, allowing individuals from diverse locations to interact in a common information space. Most colleges and universities host numerous institutional web sites, and many are implementing web portals to enhance service delivery and communication with key constituencies. Clearly, the web has become a force that is dramatically changing many areas of college and university life.

Today's distributed learning programmes — namely, those that serve both on-and off- campus students, involve technology-based delivery systems, and require sophisticated faculty and course development support — require skills not commonly found within the typical extension unit, academic department, or IT organisation. Assembling the breadth of expertise needed to develop and deliver high-quality distributed learning programmes often requires creating new organisational structures. However, a modified relationship between campus organisations that encompass programme development and instructional technology is another way to develop and deliver high-quality distributed learning programmes.

Distributed learning is now a leadership issue because instructional applications of technology are no longer the province of a few faculty pioneers. Faculty in all disciplines are using the web to enhance their courses. Without institutional leadership and systemic support, such efforts may vary widely in design, quality, cost, and effectiveness, perhaps resulting in questionable or, at the least, highly varying -educational experiences for students. In order to make technology work for all students and faculty, the president must lead the campus in developing a systematic, comprehensive technology agenda to achieve institutional goals for student learning, productivity, and cost effectiveness.

Distributed learning requires significant institutional commitments that it must carefully align with the institution's strategic plan, as well as its announced goals and directions. Following are the different institutional commitments:

i) *Perceived competition*: The rapid adoption of distance education by traditional institutions, as well as the proliferation of commercial and corporate e-learning companies, may appear threatening. Unlike brick-and-mortar campuses, virtual universities do not observe boundaries or defined service areas. Institutions whose service areas or programmes are threatened may choose to mount a distributed learning initiative as a defensive strategy. Even students at primarily residential institutions may turn to an institution offering classes that recognise the learning and technology preferences of today's students, rather than attend an institution that clings to more traditional forms of faculty-student engagement such as the large lecture hall.

ii) *Revenue*: The demand for education is global. The University of Phoenix and others have demonstrated that instruction can be profitably delivered to geographically diverse audiences. Institutions may look to distance education with the goal of developing a lucrative national or international market for their programmes; however, increased revenue is far from guaranteed. The recent closures of several major distributed learning initiatives underscore the immaturity of the e-learning market and the risks that await the commercial online ventures of traditional institutions.

iii) *Faculty or student interest*: Faculty may wish to use the web and other technologies in their on-campus courses, either because of their own interests or because their students have encouraged them to do so. Faculty initiative is laudable, but such ventures may struggle to achieve success if they lack institutional support, standards, and infrastructure.

iv) *Everyone else is doing it*: Faculty and staff at a particular institution may believe that theirs is the only college or university not providing its students and alumni with distance education opportunities. Oblinger and Kidwell note that "higher education appears to be on the verge of getting caught up in a herd effect, with institutions all moving in the direction of developing online courses."

The asynchronous nature of distributed learning is highly suited to the lifestyles of busy students, because it enables them to participate in class activities at convenient times. Changes in the workplace require most adults to continuously add or update skills throughout their working lives. Technology also can help institutions improve efficiency and productivity, which may in turn allow them to serve more students.

Students who are challenged by physical, visual, or hearing disabilities may find the web, with its hyperlink navigation and rich multimedia content, frustrating and sometimes inaccessible. Likewise, some students may not be able to afford computer and internet access. Institutional leaders, therefore, must carefully avoid denying online educational opportunities to those who most need them.

Researchers at the University of Central Florida (UCF) have observed, during six years of analysis, that students enrolled in mixed-mode distributed education courses consistently obtain grades of A,B, or C at a rate of up to 6 per cent higher than that of students in comparable face-to-face or fully online courses. With UCF's growing enrolments, this improvement in student success is significant. Virginia Tech has shown similar enhancements in access and quality through its Math Emporium. Preliminary assessment data suggest that the Math Emporium is indeed helping improve student learning.

Although few institutions have chosen distributed learning solely to reduce instructional delivery costs, institutions can achieve significant cost reductions. The Pew Grant Programme in Course Redesign has funded 30 projects designed to maintain or increase quality while reducing costs. Early results from this programme suggest that institutions can yield cost savings as high as 86 per cent (the average is 41 per cent) through carefully designing and restructuring the resources required to provide high-quality learning environments. Of course, such cost savings are not immediate. Typically, an institution must make a significant upfront investment in hardware, software, and specialised technical personnel to make a large-scale distributed learning programme work. The president and other senior leaders must determine whether these investments are worthwhile, evaluating the investments not only in terms of eventual cost savings but, more importantly, also in terms of the institution's mission and the likelihood that distributed learning will improve student learning.

Distributed learning initiatives require a change in leadership role and a different leadership style. Leaders who desire such transformational changes in their institutions need to be more internally engaged in administration and more active in their leadership style. Leaders will need to take several specific steps to ensure a successful transition to distributed learning. Be willing to use heir influence and power with many different constituencies to move he agenda forward.

Presidential power and influence are limited, and appropriately so, but they are real. Presidents can exert a tremendous amount of influence. If they do so properly, that influence can help the institution make a difference in the application of information technologies in ways that advance academic institutions' core missions. Understand he implications of technology and be willing to engage in technology-related strategies and decisions. Senior institutional leaders must imagine their own new worlds of ideas and energy, learn to recognise the power of technology, and discover how to harness it to help move the institution forward.

Institutional leaders must be prepared to recognise and pursue such opportunities when they arise. Understand hat institutional leaders can make change "safe." The application of technology, by its nature, is disruptive. It changes the *status quo,* replaces the familiar with the unfamiliar, and requires us to change the ways we think and work. Institutional leaders can make change "safe" by knowing the negative effects of technology,ensuring that they are not imposed on the institution, and giving faculty and staff adequate opportunities to learn.

Distributed learning challenges many of the basic assumptions that faculty hold about teaching and learning. Success requires rethinking how to best present and learn content, as well as which faculty and student roles best contribute to student success. A high-quality online course is much more than a web page with a syllabus and lecture notes. The prior experience at many institutions suggests that faculty can best make this transformation when leaders provide them with well-designed faculty development opportunities. Because of the time commitments required, faculty members may need release time or additional compensation. But an investment in high-quality faculty development can yield a high return because faculty who achieve online success often become motivated and enabled to improve their other courses as well.

Faculty are accustomed to being solely responsible for the content and delivery of their courses, yet the preparation and delivery of online courses will most likely involve a team, including instructional designers, programmers, and digital media specialists. Faculty development is one of the most important factors in achieving successful outcomes and satisfied faculty. Institutional leaders must recognise the need for high-quality faculty development opportunities and provide the appropriate support personnel to accomplish this function.

To achieve quality and consistency in their online courses, faculty will need the assistance of instructional technology and IT practitioners. An institution will need to assemble a team of instructional designers, digital media specialists, programmers, and software engineers to provide faculty members with the level of support they require to achieve success.

For those who wish to take greater responsibility for developing or maintaining their online courses, this unit will help to develop the course, then train faculty, staff, or student assistants to maintain the course thereafter. Few institutions are likely to possess the required breadth and depth of expertise within existing campus units, and they must therefore bring about the required organisational realignments or create this capacity by hiring the necessary talent.

Distributed learning is a multifaceted and complex activity. Consequently, existing campus support units are not likely to be able to respond immediately with systemic support, as opposed to the more traditional boutique-style, one-on-one support model that favours faculty innovators but does little to encourage or support mainstream faculty who are late adopters of technology. IT organisations may know little about learning theory or instructional models, and teaching and learning centres are not likely to have the necessary depth of technical talent. Neither unit may employ the necessary instructional designers or digital media specialists or know how to shift from boutique-style tool training to systemic support.

A new organisational model is emerging within many of the institutions that are pursuing large-scale distributed learning initiatives. This new model combines the best of traditional IT units with an instructional technology perspective, resulting in a fusion of the two ITs. Among the defining characteristics of these new distributed learning support organisations are the central prominence of instructional designers, the use of support teams for faculty and course development, and the use of instructional systems design methodologies. Again, institutional leadership must recognise and respond to this need.

Student access requires network bandwidth and modem pools or internet service provider connections. These facilities must be well managed and maintained to achieve a high degree of reliability. Although much of the required infrastructure may already be in place, distributed learning imposes unique demands that institutional leaders must understand. Often, institutions must implement special operational procedures to address the requirements of distributed learning, especially regarding system performance, scalability and availability.

Online learners who are seldom or never physically present on campus need the same access to networked library resources and services as on-campus students. An extensive array of electronic library resources, especially full-text resources coupled with electronic library services, will meet the needs of distance learners and enhance information access for on-campus students and faculty, the institution is obligated to ensure that any online course provides adequate online access to resources required for course participation. In addition to accessing electronic information resources, distributed learning students also need electronic access to services such as registration, advising, financial aid, and the bookstore.

Other needs include course-specific support, guidance in navigating the course management system, proper configuration of their computer to access the campus network, or resolution of ISP issues. And because many online students participate in their courses late at night or on weekends, their needs conflict with traditional service hours. As a result, these students often turn to their instructors with a wide range of support needs to which the faculty member may have neither the time nor expertise to respond.

Support services for online students are a critical success factor for distributed learning programmes and also an emerging accreditation requirement for such programmes. This critical need for support means that the institution must first recognise the need, then plan accordingly and invest resources in providing such services online. This process can appear complex because, potentially, institutional leaders may need to make the full range of student support services accessible to online students. However, the trend toward providing online access to student services is well established at most institutions and, once in place, such services benefit all students, including those enrolled in online courses.

The challenges for institutional leaders are to understand the potential of distributed learning, connect that potential to institutional goals, implement appropriate organisational structures and policies, and enable the institution to harness the potential of distributed learning to achieve success. Use of the web in teaching and learning is inevitable. The question is not whether it will happen, but how, why, and with what outcomes. Like any powerful tool, technology and the web can be used strategically or haphazardly.

In the hands of visionary leaders, distributed learning can become a force for institutional improvement and transformation. The true challenge for current and future campus leaders lies in making critical connections between technological possibilities and institutional priorities and using their vision and influence to chart a successful course. The degree of success that institutional leaders will achieve in meeting this challenge will profoundly influence the future of higher education in our country.

REFERENCES

American Council on Education, "Assessing the Quality of Online Courses Remains a Challenge, Educators Agree," *The Chronicle of Higher Education*, A59, Feb. 18, 2000.

Barone, A., and Paul R., Hanger, "Technology-enhanced Teaching and Learning: Learning Supporting the Transformation on Your Campus", *EDUCASE Leadership Strategies Series*, Jossey-Bass, 2001.

Bates, A.W., *Managing Technological Change: Strategies for University and College Leaders,* San Francisco: Jossey Bass, 2000.

Bartolic, S., and A.W. Bates., "Investing in Online Learning: Potential Benefits and Limitations," *Canadian Journal of Communication,* 24, 349–366, 1999.

Christensen, C.M., *The Innovator's Dilemma: When New Tech-nologies Cause Great Firms to Fail,* Boston: Harvard Business School Press, 1997.

Eaton, J.S., "Maintaining the Delicat Balance: Distance Learning, Higher Education Accreditation and the Politics of Self-regulation, *Distributed Education Series*: No.2. Washington DC: American Council on Education and EDUCAUSE, 2001.

Hawkins, B.L., "Distributed learning and institutional restructuring", *EDUCOM Review* 34 (4),12 –15,42 –44, 1999.

Huang, J., *Distance Education: A Key Strategy for Lifelong Learning in Chinese Taipei*, Taipei: Department of Research and Development, National Open University, 1997.

John. J. Hitt, Joel L. Hartman, "Distributed Learning: New Challenges and Opportunities for Institutional Leadership", Americal Council on Eductaion Center for Policy Analysis, EDUCASE, 2002.

Johnston, David et al., "The e-learning evolution in colleges and universities: A Pan-Canadian Challenge," Ottawa: Industry Canada, 2001.

Kenniston, K., and D. Kumar, *Bridging the Digital Divide: Lesson from India,* India: National Institute of Advanced Sciences, Indian Institute of Science, 2001.

Kerry, Bob et al., "The Power of the Internet for Learning: Moving from Promise to Practice," Report of the Web-Based Education Commission to the President of the United States. Jessup, MD: U.S. Department of Education, 2000.

Larchmont, NY:Mary Ann Liebert, Inc. "National Education Association, "Quality on he line:Benchmarks for success in Internet-based distance education", Washington, DC: National Education Association, April 2000.

Oblinger, D., Barone,C.A., Hawkins, B.L., "Distributed Education and its challenges: An overview", *Distributed Education Series:*No.1, Washington, DC: *American Council on Education and EDUCAUSE*, 2001.

Oblinger, D., Kidwell, J., "Distance learning:Are we being realistic"? *EDUCAUSE Review* 35 (3):30 –34,36,38 –39, May/June 2000.

Parrish, Debra M., and Alexander Wills Parrish, *Developing a* Distance Education Policy for 21st Century Learning, Division of Government Public Affairs, American Council for Education, 2000.

Rai, Amar Nath, *Distance Education: Open Learning vs. Virtual University Concepts*, Authorspress, New Delhi, 2001.

Rowley, D.J., H.D. Lujan, and M. Dolence, *Strategic Choices for the Academy,* San Francisco: Jossey Bass, 1998.

Rumble, G., *The Costs and Economics of Open and Distance Learning,* London: Kogan Page, 1997.

8

Learning to Live in a Virtual World

Learning, as we have traditionally defined it, needs no longer be located within particular or specialised institutions. Learning now becomes an activity of problem solving applied to every aspect of daily life. The conjuncture of computers, networks, lifelong learning and a vast array of new tools for human interaction variously described through the tropes of the virtual and the cyberspatial, means that teachers will have to reinvent themselves. Virtual spaces generate hybrid environments for the interaction of people and computers. As we negotiate new relationships with these emerging technologies, we are defining new spaces for learning. At the dawn of the 21st century, we have to build the first stages of an extraordinary infrastructure which will enable us to communicate across time and space, using all media, in ways that many would have thought impossible just a few years ago.

Today, we are more and more capable of solving problems that seemed intractable. We are researching the very basis of life itself and unveiling the cartography of the genetic codes that determine our biological make-up. We have gained insights into the way the brain works and insights into our cultural, social, spiritual and economic connections to the environment. In all of these activities, individuals and communities have worked hard to facilitate change. There has been a genuine effort to create and sustain the institutions that are necessary to bear witness to and communicate the vast array of knowledge we now have available to us. This effort has extended in so many varied directions and has involved so many different constituencies, that even those with the most dystopic visions would have to agree that a fundamental re-orientation of the values of Western society has been underway for some time.

The educational system has undergone a massive shift. A core element of what education was always about has remained untouched in the midst of these upheavals. We have ceased to recognise how profoundly embedded that corr is, to the point that the changes being envisioned in the 21st century may not respond to that very history nor recognise what this history has made possible and what it has prevented. It is not within the scope of this presentation to examine the historical legacy of education in the 21st century.

Both Socrates and Freud talked different times about radical impossibility of teaching. A recognition of the impossibility of teaching, enables and encourages the development of new and innovative approaches to pedagogy and learning. The contradiction is that learning can never be reduced to the way information and ideas are structured for communication. The core confusion is between the authority of the teacher and the authorship that goes into various educational discourses and the manner in which those discourses are exchanged among learners and teachers. At the root of the claim about the impossibility of teaching is the idea that learning never progresses along a "simple one-way road from ignorance to knowledge." In addition, teachers cannot fully anticipate the outcome of the processes of communication and interaction with their students unless the learning process is framed by a set of very narrow concerns.

The balance between where students have come from and where they are headed is rarely linear and is often not clear. There is a legitimate desire on the part of teachers to structure ideas and values, and knowledge and content for the purposes of presentation and discussion. What must be recognised is the role of "desire" in communication and teaching, as well as the gap between what teachers know and how well they have come to grips with what they don't know. This profoundly affects the teacher's capacity to create a site of learning for students. The same problems and potential solutions apply to learners.

Learning is a part of everything we do as human beings. We have developed models of human thinking and models of mind that could best be described as functionalist and reductive in orientation. These models narrow the potential for learning and particularise the processes that make learning possible. "Functionalism assumes that psychology can be adequately described in terms of the 'functional organisation of the brain'—much in the way that software determines the performance of computer hardware." This reductive confusion of brain and mind has gathered strength in the last half of the 20th century and has been applied to the learning experience. Learning and communications are as intertwined as vision and thought, but more often than not, mechanical models of mind eliminate the complexity that is the ground upon which knowledge can be acquired. The problems here are not in the availability of information, but in the means used to communicate data, ideas, points of view, and so on.

The presentation of ideas from teacher to student is not inherently wrong or misguided. The irony is that students in a classroom develop this wonderful phantasmagoria of emotions, experiences, thoughts, daydreams and projections to guide them. This plethora of experiences may not always be visible to teachers, who may be so focused on the content of the communication, that they do not recognise the complex internal world of their students.

Vast amounts of money are being pumped into skills development with little substantive reflection on the differences between skills and learning. The assumption is that they are fundamentally the same. The further assumption is that without a set of generic skills students will not be able to function in the modern world. The irony is that most students now arrive in school with a vast body of knowledge and find that it is not really applicable to their experience in the classroom. For example, although television has been around for close to fifty years, we still react to its presence in an antagonistic fashion. Yet, students learn a great deal from their experiences of viewing. The incorporation of those experiences would alter many of the presumptions that we have about curriculum development. The ease with which our culture has internalised the metaphor of the computer as a thinking machine is perhaps best expressed by the notion that computers have memory. The anthropomorphic conferral of so much power to the computer has had an impact on the ways in which we think about learning. It also reflects an historical heritage that links learning to information.

The move from information to understanding, let alone from information to knowledge, is very complex. One should keep in mind that the metaphors of memory in use here, influence the way information will be structured for the purposes of comprehension and communication. We have to be very careful about the assumptions that go into the creation of information, both for the classroom and for networked forms of education. In some respects, as the memory of a computer fills up, it takes on more and more of the characteristics of the user. The hard disk becomes a compendium of work, writing, software and general information that reflects the orientation and selectivity of the human behind the computer. The personalisation of computers means that they are not simply tools. The pragmatic use of computers puts them, more and more, into the category of companions. This phenomena alone contributes to a modelling activity that links the thinking human with the thinking machine.

The idea that we can connect to any part of the world through our computers is as important as the fact that we are involved with networks on an everyday basis. Networks constitute the new social morphology of our societies, and the diffusion of networking logic substantially modifies the operation and outcomes in processes of production, experience, power and culture. These are very general claims, but the point is that even accounting for the specifics of gender, class and ethnicity as well as the particularities of national identity, our culture is 'thinking' about connectivity as if we have uncovered a new model of mind. The impulse to describe a 'networking logic' is part of an evolutionary paradigm destined to locate human thought in functional terms. A functionalist approach envisages thinking and hence the brain itself, as a series of algorithms. The brain becomes an information- processing machine that uses mathematical sequencing to solve problems and responds to a set of instructions that are embedded in our neuronal structure.

The initial metaphorical strength of the computer-human connection takes on a literal character. Deep Blue, the computer that defeated Garry Kasparov in a chess series, is now talked about in almost reverential terms, even though the programmers who designed its software are quite skeptical about many of the cultural claims that have been made for Deep Blue's intelligence. Murray Campbell who helped to develop Deep Blue suggests that, although the computer plays chess better than most humans, "excellent chess play also requires imagination, intuition, ingenuity, and the passion to conquer." Crucially, Deep Blue is "unable to appreciate its own moves." This lack of self-awareness is fundamental to the difference between computers and humans.

From a pedagogical point of view, a perfect teaching and learning system based on computer-mediated technology, the system would have to be sensitive to the profound differences between students. It would have to be capable of distinguishing among many varieties of human responses in diverse and sometimes unpredictable circumstances. It would have to understand how human beings are able to make jumps in logic and are able to explore their own thinking through imagination and daydream. The system would have to contain enough variations to be able to respond to questions that had never been programmed into it. Its internal architecture would have to grow with the students it taught or informed. In other words, it too would have to be capable of learning.

The computer would have to be erudite enough to anticipate the direction students take when they discover new ways of understanding familiar issues. It would have to be capable of comprehending ambiguous statements that might contain the kernel of an important thought, without jumping to the conclusion that the students have not understood the work they have been assigned. It would have to incorporate a general understanding of the importance of evaluation and self-assessment in the learning process. It would have to be able to understand the subtleties of reasoning that often guide the thinking process into unanticipated realms of thought. It would have to be inventive and yet not too innovative for fear of leaving its students behind. It would have to recognise patterns of student emotion that often hinder clarity of thought and efforts at problem solving. It would also have to distinguish between the truth and the not so true. It would have to respond to ambiguity by recognising the relationship between memory and language.

Not everything we say is informed by what we consciously know. In some senses, the computer would have to emulate the role of the teacher in a classroom in order to generate some sense of dialogue and conversation. It might be the case that the computer will have to enter into arguments about existence and the meaning of life in order to find some common ground with students who are asking foundational questions about these very notions.

Even the most utopian models of computer-human interaction hesitate when it comes to self-awareness. The simple symmetry of machine and human does not seem to work when the most basic questions are asked about knowledge. The extraordinary proliferation of sources of information and contact across the web and through e-mail are potential sites of learning. The construction and growth of the internet is one of the great achievements of the 20th century. It is also the case, that from research activities right through to electronic commerce, the web is opening up new horizons, as well as making it possible for human beings to interact and communicate in fresh and unpredictable ways. It is perhaps too early to assess what we are learning and how the experience will change our culture and ourselves. The problem is, that even if we qualify human-computer interaction, the growth of information sources seems to suggest that the link to the educational process is natural, if not inevitable. What worries here is that the technologies we are using to connect learners may constrain, if not overwhelm, the fragile cultural faith that we have in the experiential base of learning. We may thus end up creating training environments for narrow-based skills, oriented towards goals that can be quickly attained, rather than contribute to the growth of genuine learning environments.

The new networks of instruction we are creating will foreground the richness of human knowledge and eventually bring that complexity into a fresh and exciting context. An overwhelmingly pragmatic attitude has taken root in our culture with respect to learning. It is simultaneously holding onto some of the most conservative traditions in education, while proposing revolutionary solutions that will allow for a growing segment of the population to gain access to more and more information. This is why terms like 'educational provider' or 'delivery' appear over and over again in the literature. It is as if learning is about receiving, as if information is about delivery.

Access means nothing if there isn't a foundation upon which the information can be transformed into knowledge, and it means very little to gain access to an archive if one has no connection to, or understanding of, history. It is here that the concept of a networked connection has overwhelmed and perhaps obscured our ability to explore what connections actually mean. The conventional classroom is a living laboratory of the contradictions, potential, and unpredictability of connections.

The 'impossibility' of teaching is situated in a fear of fragmentation and breakdown, in other words, the flux and flow of contradictions that may have no immediate solution. Teaching, as much as learning is about the struggle to keep these issues in the foreground, and to keep the conflict between all of these factors rebounding against each other in a productive manner. The people who are building technology into education and learning, will have to heed these lessons.

Learning is a crucial dimension of the human existence. It dispositions us to interact constructively with change. Constructive interaction is not the same as 'reaction to change' or 'adaptation to change.' The latter notions are based on the assumption that change is a given, the former one envisions human beings as part of the changing environment, i.e. as actors who engage in intelligent behaviour as they see things change around them, aware that by doing so they, too, produce change themselves. Such conscious, intelligent behaviour, based on what is sometimes called 'deep understanding', is the result of true learning. The degree to which we will be able to interact constructively with change, i.e. the extent to which we will be able to develop our capacity to learn and to learn continuously, will be a major determinant of our chances to survive on the planet.

Both the schooling tradition and many of the alternative pathways to learning that complement it, such as much of the distance education tradition, still treat knowledge as a commodity, as something that can be passed around, that represents value in monetary terms, and that has an existence independent of the relationship between the beholder and her or his world. Currently emerging notions of the knowledge society tend to reinforce such perceptions.

One of the greatest challenges therefore is to move beyond the paradigm that defines learning simply as the acquisition and accumulation of knowledge. We must come to grips with, and be constantly cognizant of, the dimension of development, growth or process of knowledge in which uncertainty prevails, while moving towards attaining deeper understanding.

A second major challenge relates to the dialogical nature of learning and therefore its essentially social nature. This aspect finds clear expression in the notion of learning to live together, one of the four pillars — perhaps the most important one — on which, according to the 1996 report to UNESCO of the International Commission on Education for the Twenty-first Century, learning throughout life should build. This important and overriding dimension of any successful learning experience has long gone unnoticed. Due to the dominance of the traditional schooling paradigm, learning was usually seen as something that is — and should be — done alone, a view that is perhaps most strongly expressed in how learning gains are being assessed.

The third major challenge has to do with the nature of knowledge itself. Societal processes of dealing with a vastly growing body of knowledge — growing both in extent and complexity— have, over the centuries, led to increased specialisation. A tendency has thus emerged to deal with the complexity of the world by breaking it down into parts that, when dealt with in isolation, could be comprehended. This process has greatly contributed to the advancement of science. However, it has also led to a view of the world, and thus to ways of dealing with it, that are no longer able to account for its complexity. This is becoming problematic as many of the issues the world has to deal with now have, in a very fundamental way, to do with the phenomena of exploding change and rapidly increasing complexity referred to earlier. Whence the need to overcome the shortcomings of the disciplinary structure of knowledge, moving beyond also multidisciplinarity and interdisciplinarity, to start seeing things in a transdisciplinary perspective.

Learning communities of different kinds and at different levels of organisational complexity function within it. They use its resources, interact with each other and with the environment at large, each of them being a potential resource for all other learning entities — whether learning individuals or collectives of individuals — that constitute the environment. A reconceptualisation of the learning environment must recognise the multiplicity of learning spaces. Such spaces can be defined in physical terms, but they are equally expressed in terms of the interactions among people via such media as the internet and they also have an important time dimension, a-synchronicity becoming an increasingly important feature of many learning experiences and the communities that generate them.

BARRIERS TO DISTANCE LEARNING

Distance education has been in existence for at least 100 years, the medium has changed from pencil and paper correspondence courses to real-time internet courses. But regardless of the medium, distance courses have common characteristics and, likewise, have similar problems. It examines the different types of distance education and its significance as a learning method. Student demographics are presented and their relevance to distance learning barriers established. Lastly, the nature of student, faculty, organisation, and course curriculum and their respective impact on distance learning are explored.

In distance learning students and teachers will find themselves playing different roles than is the norm in traditional education. The teacher is no longer the sole source of knowledge but instead becomes a facilitator to support student learning, while the student actively participates in what and how knowledge is imparted. More than any other teaching method, distance learning requires a collaborative effort between student and teacher, unbounded by the traditional limits of time, space, and single-instructor effort.

Technology has also changed the face of education. Advances in telecommunications technology has opened up the possibility of personal and group interaction in distance education. Both computer and audio conferencing permit the introduction of class discussions without the group meeting face to face. Phone calls and electronic mail replaces personal office visits.

The distance learner can now have almost the same instructional contact and interaction as the student on campus.

But remote access education does not need to eliminate all the benefits of human contact. In fact, the proliferation of the modem, teleconferencing, and the web provide a rich expanse of both information and contacts that were previously unavailable. Albeit two dimensional, these media lend themselves to pure ideas and thought processes. This purity lends itself to isolation of both the cognitive and affective domains — an additional benefit of this communication medium.

Changes in technology have accelerated the growth of distance learning. The improved access and availability of electronic technology has enabled more adult students to participate in the learning process. Students who enrol in distance learning courses do so for convenience. They are either time-bound due to work or travel schedules or location-bound due to geographic or family responsibilities. Distance learning is student-centered learning; thus knowing the characteristics and demographics of the distance learners helps us understand the potential barriers to leaning.

Although students' characteristics and needs may not guarantee success in a distance education course or programme, it is easy to defend these factors as contributing to success. Additionally, knowledge about student characteristics and motivators help us understand who is likely to participate in distance education and, conversely, why others choose not to participate. Student motivation has a powerful affect on attrition and completion rates, regardless of institutional setting. Motivators for adult distance students are often different from those of traditional students.

The educational background of distance students ranges from less than high school to completion of a university degree. However, 20 per cent of US tele-course students had at least an associate degree. It is plausible that these students have and edge over new students because they already have study habits necessary to be successful in any academic setting. It is not surprising that researchers have found that students who had prior experience with non-traditional education were more likely to persist than those with exclusively conventional experience.

In addition to prior educational level and prior experience level, personal factors and academic information help us to understand what motivates, and therefore, what potential barriers exist, in educating the distance student. Older students appear to have higher course completion rates. This makes sense in that older students probably have greater coping skills in dealing with the problems of distance learning. Interestingly, housewives tended to drop out less than the general distance learner population. Conversely, the course dropout rate of those who listed manual trades as an occupation was 50 per cent higher than the overall rate. Putting student demographics together, one can see adult distance learners are a diverse population; however, in general one can say the adult distance learner is typically employed full time, and has personal commitments that compound his efforts in furthering his education.

Problems and barriers encountered by the student fall into several distinct categories; costs and motivators, feedback and teacher contact, student support and services, alienation and isolation, lack of experience, and training. More so than traditional students, distance learners are more likely to have insecurities about learning. These insecurities are founded in personal and school related issues such as financial costs of study, disruption of family life, perceived irrelevance of their studies and lack of support from employers.

These barriers can be mitigated through technological methods such as e-mail. Computer conferencing and electronic mail can be integrated into the delivery of the course to provide the missing interactivity. Because both are essentially asynchronous, they continue to leave the student in charge of setting his or her own work times — a critical success factor for the distance student. It is important that the student receive prompt feedback in any institutional setting, particularly in distance learning where the learner is impaired by the lack of casual contact with the teacher and other students. This is especially important for those students who live outside metropolitan areas. They may not have access to reliable telecommunications, computers, and postal mail. The frustrations resulting from problems with communication between student and academic institution are factors of which distance education planners should be well aware.

The distance students is the lack of support and services such as providing tutors, academic planners and schedulers, and technical assistance. The isolation that results from the distance learning process can complicate the learning process for adult students. Support for distance learners should not be overlooked when planning distance programmes. Students need tutors and academic planners to help them complete courses on time and to act as a support system when stress becomes a problem.

Student services are a significant part of the budgeted costs of the programme. Success in attracting, serving, and retaining students will hinge more on excellent student support services than on any technology issues. Technology costs and considerations can be a source of budgeting problems; however, student support for distance learners should take precedence.

The "distance" aspect of distance learning takes away much of the social interactions that would be present in traditional learning environments. This problem must be mitigated by institutions providing a sense of personal involvement between the student and the institution. One way to help solve this problem is through the use of tutors that communicate with students either electronically or by phone. Students believe that having a good tutor is vitally important in helping them get the most out of a course and achieve a credit.

Geographical isolation has been identified as one of the major problems for distance students. In addition to the practical problems of contacting academic and administrative staff, obtaining study materials and borrowing library books, distance students suffer from the disadvantage of being unable to interact with other students and are often denied the perception that they belong to a scholarly community. This may lead to feelings of inadequacy and insecurity, and a lack of confidence in their own abilities.

If distance learning institutions are serious about providing equity of educational opportunity to all, then careful consideration must be given to the special needs of students undertaking distance education for the first time. Of particular importance is the design of study materials for distance students. Study materials must take into account the significant proportion of students who enrol with little or no experience of distance study. These students are at risk of dropping out unless they develop study survival skills as rapidly as possible.

Many adult students are not well versed in the uses of technology such as computers and the internet. Using electronic medium in distance learning can inadvertently exclude students who lack computer or writing skills. These skills are required if computer technology is used. Students will typically be offered volumes of electronic-based information. Using this information will be a problem for some nontechnical students. They must be taught how to manage, not only their study time, but the materials presented as well. If students are undertaking distance learning courses that require knowledge of computers, then the students must be taught, at a minimum, the fundamentals of operating the system of choice of the distance-taught course. If distance learning is to be successful, technical barriers must be made a non-issue.

Faculty experience problems such as lack of staff training in course development and technology, lack of support for distance learning in general, and inadequate faculty selection for distance learning courses. Sometimes the coursework for traditional and distance students is the same. Often it is not. There can be a lot of up front effort in designing distance learning material. This can impose a burden on teachers who already have material for traditional classrooms.

Computers, video equipment, communications software, and the like, present challenges and frustrations. Faculty must know how to the use these technologies if they are to teach distance courses. Training students and staff, particularly in troubleshooting problems, is imperative to success in technical distance learning. Perhaps the biggest problem for distance programmes is the lack of support by the faculty. The endorsement by department faculty is viewed as a critical instructional element in any distance education programme. More than any other participant, faculty roles must change the most in administering distance learning programmes. This can be difficult adjustment for some teachers. They must change teaching styles to that of a mentor, tutor, and facilitator. They must meet the needs of distance students without face-to-face contact.

Since the majority of distance learners are adults, teachers may need to change their teaching style. This may be challenging for teachers who are used to teaching with 18 to 22-year-olds. Faculty is responsible for changing their course content to accommodate diverse student needs and expectations. So long as college faculty feels there is a burden associated the distance education programme currently in place, there will be little support for expanding distance education opportunities.

Teachers may lack the basic skills or hardware to fully participate in distance education. The advent of computers, telecommunications, and the web provides an unprecedented opportunity for faculty and students to learn in a cooperative environment. It is interesting to note, however, that students respond to this changing environment more adeptly than teachers do.

Organisational problems, especially infrastructure and technology problems, also present challenges. Faculties who teach distance education courses need organisational and administrative support from the institution. Funding should be provided to create an administrative unit that is to be responsible for managing the programme. Institutional leaders must be committed to distance programmes. Technology considerations are self-evident but are the most easily solved. Technology problems include; financing new technology, telecommunications, hardware issues, course production and technology, and internet problems.

When technology is used, the costs increase substantially for both the student and the institution. Universities must consider the initial costs as well as the continuing costs of installing, maintaining, using, and upgrading technology to support distance services. Institutions must plan to have competent computer staff to support internet use. These staff must then be kept up-to-date on the newest, fastest, cheapest technology available; therefore, ongoing staff training costs must be considered. The student must also incur technology costs. If the internet is used, then the student must have access to a computer, modem, and associated software.

Additionally, telephone charges to the internet service provider will be incurred. For many institutions; however, technology pays for itself in terms of allowing more students to participate, thus increasing tuition funding. This sounds good on paper but technology must not be abused to save money. Regardless of cost issues, distance education should be instituted to advance the cause of education for the institution, not as a sole effort to save money.

Distance education via simultaneous two-way audiovisual interaction systems such as video teleconferencing, brings an additional set of issues to be considered by the instructor and effective models for this delivery system need to be identified. Some students, particularly those without home computers with modems could have difficulty communicating with the university or teacher. Lack of adequate hardware and the subsequent cost barrier of obtaining equipment could place undue hardship on some remote students.

Learning institutions must develop distance learning course material or pay a hefty price to order materials from distributors. For some institutions, the investment in production technology may be worth the cost; however, a significant investment is necessary for production facilities, equipment, and personnel to produce video-tapes. Using the internet instead can overcome some of this problem but it poses additional difficulties in insuring all students have adequate access to the internet. The internet is proving to be an effective delivery medium that enables communication of knowledge at the student's convenience. It has the potential, in fact, to change the nature of distance learning.

Some fear the existing world wide telecommunications network is ill equipped to handle the rapid expansion of the internet. Relying solely on the internet for courseware and communications transmission is risky. In addition, using the internet can degrade of the quality of interactions between and among staff and students. Due to the perceived anonymity provided by the internet, abusive behaviour could become a problem; however, these problems can be mediated with proper care and regulation. The newest of the technological challenges lies in complying with government regulations.

Distance learning institutions must be aware of, and plan for, regulatory issues if the internet is used for conveying course content. Certainly not all distance courses use the internet. Other technologies present ergonomical problems. For distance programmes that implement video teleconferencing techniques, the physical environment and equipment set up is important. Because a classroom is often a noisy place, sensitive microphone equipment and non-sound absorbing rooms can seriously diminish the sound quality. Likewise, inadequate lighting and improper camera placement can diminish the video quality.

Distance courses are inferior to traditional courses. Careful attention must be paid to the quality of the material presented in distance courses. Curriculums and assessment materials must be developed that equal that of the traditional classroom if distance courses are to receive the respect they deserve.

Maintain the same course content, learning objectives, standards, and credits for all sections, regardless of method of delivery. Assessing student performance is a problem area in distance learning. It is a commonly held belief that distance students perform more poorly in assessment than do internal students because of the additional pressures and burdens of distance study.

MANAGING DISTANCE LEARNING ENVIRONMENT

Over the next few years most university staff enjoy learning, but the methods of learning they mastered (from face-to-face discussions to solitary burrowing through the stacks of a library) may not be as comfortably available to our students in our joint future. As our society moves from universal secondary education to universal tertiary education we will increasingly be subject to pressures designed to influence us to make the University experience more accessible, allowing busy people to fit it in to their working day when they see fit. We will lessen the disruption to students' lives by reducing the need for them to travel to the central University site in order to engage with the University experience. We will do this in part by providing learning interactions through a variety of electronic communications.

On the visual level the differing characteristics of the media require quite different formatting of textual material. On the organisational level, breaking the lock-step of classroom sessions and mass concurrent teaching will require much greater flexibility on the part of the bureaucracy, as exemplified in the negative by the current insistence of many institutions on students' personal attendance for re-enrolment. The loss of face-to-face behavioural, gestural and tonal cues may give rise to many misunderstandings and will require particular attention in our educational designs.

Many teachers have to imitate existing familiar teaching situations and strategies when delivering instruction via new technologies, and the problems this approach causes in the successful adoption of the new technologies. Besides raising the need for staff development in the use of new teaching media, two of the 'missing' components in conventional distance education are student/instructor interaction and class collaboration. Retaining the immediacy of these learning interactions will not be accidental. Learning from a well-made Open Learning package may be like having a good human coach or tutor, but the skills involved in preparing that package are quite different from those required to deliver a useful lecture.

Beyond these issues, however, many operational difficulties arise in our use of such educational communication technologies, as we have experienced in the adoption of earlier technologies in face-to-face teaching. The use of video-projection from a computer to replace the use of static overheads does not dispose of the need to prepare a certain amount of static overhead material as a backstop in case the video-projection system fails. For differing reasons, this doubled preparation will be repeated as we introduce more flexible methods into our teaching. Both the face-to-face or audio-taped lecture and the web page need to be prepared if we are to provide increased flexibility rather than merely a substitution of delivery media.

While in an ideal university there would be sufficient support staff to relieve the lecturer of the technological aspects of this task, experience suggests that the present dearth of such support staff will continue, a lack both in absolute numbers and specifically of those who are sensitive to and have some allegiance to the needs of teaching as opposed to the needs of machines. In the short term many electronic lectures will be created, driven by the pressures of time and lack of support and justified as being at least partial steps along the way to providing more flexible learning conditions.

Learning activities that lack social interaction usually fail to evoke emotional involvement from learners and thus deny the learners engagement with the culture of the "community of practice". Most classroom learning activities involve knowledge which is abstract and out of context, is unsituated. Problem-based learning approaches tend to reduce these effects and well-made multimedia interactives can restore some context to the learning, but teaching that interposes current communication technology between the learner and the teacher risks engaging the student with the wrong "community of practice". The technologically-aware lecturer needs to be sensitive to the danger of having students apprenticed to technology rather than their chosen discipline.

Mass teaching has reduced this contact and the use of educational technology can sometimes lead to further depersonalisation. Teachers seek to ameliorate this depersonalisation by, for example, trying to make the mass lecture a two-way communication: standing at the front of the theatre while showing slides: setting aside times when they are available for personal discussions in their office. The increased use of technology dictated by our move to greater flexibility needs to be leavened where possible by increased interactions between student, teacher and learning community.

Current affordable network tools supporting remote learners allow e-mail, file transfer, computer conferencing and web browsing, but these various tools demand a serious learning effort from their users, not only from the students as learners but also from their lecturers as administrators. This extra learning effort adds an additional barrier between learner and teacher, between learner and learning. The use of a computer in the message-passing stream can be considered an impediment to learning for many students.

In addition, the lead-time and response-time in student-teacher interactions are lengthened. With paper and chalkboard, these times are quite small. Involving a bureaucracy in assignment reception and registration can add weeks to the interaction process. Using electronic communications that require reprocessing and involve an educational technician may also slow the process enormously unless the lecturer takes action to minimise delays, preferably by retaining as much control as possible.

Just as the growth of desktop publishing has benefited semiprofessional authors by passing control over the appearance of a work from the printer back to the author and reducing the overall production time, web publishing and course management tools need to be put into the hands of teachers to retain as much immediacy as possible in student-teacher interactions.

Where learning material is essentially static and designed to be read and copied by students, it can be stored on a university's web server computer and maintained by emailing updates to Computing Centre staff directly or by file transfer using tools such as Fetch. If, however, you want to retain the more personal elements of teaching that many staff find rewarding, you may be interested in communicating on an individual level with your off-campus students, receiving and managing student responses, assignments and enquiries online, promoting class-wide discussion of a topic or even adjusting course material for individual student differences.

Web Educational Support Tools (WEST) is a system developed at University College Dublin which makes it easier to manage the creation and delivery of learning materials over the web. The ease with which this system can be set up and maintained puts it well within the technical ability of the majority of university computer users. Once the server is running, all lecturer tasks can in fact be carried out from any computer on the network. If the current interest in using the web to increase the flexibility of course offerings is maintained, personal web servers backed by management systems like WEST could proliferate on lecturers' desktops, just as presentation software has become a standard part of the lecturer's toolkit. Just as HTML and its associated tools offer "multimedia for the rest of us", desktop educational support tools may add real value to the "ubiquitous servers" in educational institutions.

The system presents a simple consistent interface making heavy use of buttons and forms, as shown in the Figures below, thus avoiding the need for staff and students to master a variety of different interfaces to achieve the mix of messaging most appropriate to flexible learning. The WEST system provides facilities for individual registration and controlled access by students who are part of a class studying some course; it allows the allocation of learning materials as web pages to students or to the whole class; it provides one-to-one messaging between student and tutor and between students.

Students each have access through their Home Page to their own coursework page, which is a linked table of contents for the course they are working on. Students can send messages to their tutor and submit assignments. They can also send messages to specific students or to the entire class through the open-to-everyone discussion list, where they can read what other students have written about a course discussion topic.

Tutors can receive messages and assignments from students, reply, mark and return assignments or have them automatically marked and returned. They can make announcements to the whole class or address individual students. Any of the variety of messages can include HTML code and thus include hypertext references to other resources on the internet.

The WEST system is used in the USA, Canada and Ireland for courses varying from a resource of information and research on Chemistry to delivery and management of course material for a multi-disciplinary Open Learning course on the Famine in Ireland. WEST does not keep track of student accesses, nor of how far a student has progressed. These are important features for staff administering courses for remote students, whose flagging motivation may require restorative action unnecessary for on-campus students. These features have been requested for a future version. Additionally the need for students to be able to display non-textual material for discussion and to annotate course materials has not yet been addressed within WEST, thought the personal server solution described above does permit the first of these. Because of these missing features, teachers may feel the need to add further web utilities to their armoury. This will unfortunately reduce the integrity of the system for the sake of improving its functions.

Many teachers will need to learn new ways of teaching as flexible teaching and learning become an expected part of our course design and delivery. The design of material for learning at a distance is not a trivial task, but it will be made easier if the hurdles of Educational Technology can be lowered. Hopefully tools such as WEST will be improved without losing their ease of use and will allow teachers to incorporate a variety of message streams into their course material, to build in interactions that involve their students.

REFERENCES

Anzalone, S., (ed.), *Multichannel learning: Connecting all to education,* Washington, D.C.: Education Development Center, 1995.

Bacsich, P., Submissions to the *Virtual University Strategy Forum, TeleTeaching 96*, vu-strategy@opennet.net.au, quoted by Crock, 1996.

Bouton, D., "Learning to Learn", *New Horizons for Learning Newsletter*, XIII(2), Winter, 1992.

Chapman, D., "The death of distance education; Long live distributive learning", In: Learning Without Frontiers portfolio on *Technology and learning* (electronic version), 1998.

Gardner, H., *Frames of the Mind: The Theory of Multiple Intelligences,* New York: Basic Books, 1983.

Goldberg, M. W., "CALOS: First results from an experiment in computer-aided learning for operating systems", *SIGCSE Bulletin 29*, 1, March 1997.

Kay, D., "Bandwagons considered harmful", *SIGCSE Bulletin* 28, 4 December 1996.

Pearson, P. D., Iran-Nejad, A., *Review of research in education,* Washington, DC: American Educational Research Association, 1998.

Perraton, H., (ed.) *Distance education: An economic and educational assessment of its potential for Africa,* Washington, D.C.: World Bank, 1986.

Reich, R., *The work of nations: Preparing ourselves for 21st century capitalism*, London, UK: Simon and Schuster, 1991.

Stasko, J. T., "Using student-built algorithm animations as learning aids", *SIGCSE Bulletin* 29, 1, March 1997.

Sternberg, R. J., Detterman, D. K. (eds.), *What is intelligence? Contemporary viewpoints on its nature and definition,* Norwood, New Jersey: Ablex, 1986.

______________, Wagner, R. K., (eds.), *Practical intelligence: Nature and origin of competence in the everyday world,* New York, NY: Cambridge University Press, 1986.

Young, J. R., "Rethinking the role of the professor in an age of high-tech tools", In *The chronicle of higher education,* 1997.

Bibliography

Allen, M., "Don't be a troll! Using the Internet for successful higher education", *Paper presented at Queensland University of Technology*, Brisbane, Australia, January, 2000.

American Council on Education, "Assessing the Quality of Online Courses Remains a Challenge, Educators Agree," *The Chronicle of Higher Education*, A59, Feb. 18, 2000.

American Council on Education, *Developing a Distance Education Policy for 21st Century Learning,* Washington, D.C.: American Council on Education, 2000.

Anzalone, S., (ed.), *Multichannel learning: Connecting all to education,* Washington, D.C.: Education Development Center, 1995.

Bacsich, P., Submissions to the *Virtual University Strategy Forum, TeleTeaching 96*, vu-strategy@opennet.net.au, quoted by Crock, 1996.

Bandura, A., *Social learning theory*, Englewood Cliffs, NJ: Prentice Hall, 1977.

Barker, K., "Consumer-Based Quality Guidelines for Learning Technologies and Distance Education." *FuturEd,* February 2001.

Barone, A., and Paul R., Hanger, "Technology-enhanced Teaching and Learning: Learning Supporting the Transformation on Your Campus", *EDUCASE Leadership Strategies Series*, Jossey-Bass, 2001.

Bartolic, S., and A.W. Bates., "Investing in Online Learning: Potential Benefits and Limitations," *Canadian Journal of Communication,* 24, 349–366, 1999.

Bates, A.W., *Managing Technological Change: Strategies for University and College Leaders,* San Francisco: Jossey Bass, 2000.

Belawati, T., "Increasing Student Persistence in Indonesian Post-Secondary Distance Education", *Distance Education* 19 (1) 81–108, 1998.

Besser, H. and S Donahue., "Introduction and Overview: Perspectives on Distance Independent Education", *Journal of the American Society for Information Science* 47(11) 801–804, 1996.

Bester, G., "Guidelines for Structuring and Managing Multi-purpose Community Learning Centres," *Unpublished Master's Thesis*, 2001.

Botkin, J., et al., *No Limits to Learning: Bridging the Human Gap*, Club of Rome, Oxford: Pergamon Press, 1979.

Bouton, D., "Learning to Learn", *New Horizons for Learning Newsletter*, XIII(2), Winter, 1992.

Brown, K., "The Role of Internal and External Factors in The Discontinuation of Off-Campus Students", *Distance Education* 17 (1), 44–71, 1996.

Burnett, R., "Intervention during the first meeting of the Learning Without Frontiers Advisory Task Force held at UNESCO Headquarters, Paris, France on 25 and 26 November 1996", Reported in United Nations Educational, Scientific and Cultural Organization (UNESCO), 1996.

______________, "Networks of knowledge/networks of learning", *UNESCO Learning Without Frontiers (LWF) Advisory Task Force Meeting, held at UNESCO*, Paris, 25-26, November 1996.

Butterfield, S, et. al., "External Quality Assurance for the Virtual Institution", *AAU series on Quality* Number 4, Wellington: New Zealand Universities Academic Audit Unit, 1999.

Candy, P., "How People Learn to Learn", in: R. Smith (ed.), *Learning to Learn Across the Lifespan*, San Francisco: Jossey-Bass, 1990.

Carr, S., "Two More Universities Start Diploma-Granting Virtual High Schools," *The Chronicle of Higher Education*, Dec. 10, 1999.

Chapman, D., "The death of distance education; Long live distributive learning", In: Learning Without Frontiers portfolio on *Technology and learning* (electronic version), 1998.

Christensen, C.M., *The Innovator's Dilemma: When New Tech-nologies Cause Great Firms to Fail,* Boston: Harvard Business School Press, 1997.

Collins, A., "Cognitive apprenticeship and instructional technology", In L. Idol and B. F. Jones (eds.), *Educational Values and Cognitive Instruction: Implications for Reform*, Hillsdale, NJ: Erlbaum, 1991.

DAE, Association for Development of African Education, Formulating education policy: Lessons and experiences from sub-Saharan Africa. Six case studies and reflections from the DAE biennial meeting held in Tours, France, in October 1995. Paris, France: Association for the Development of African Education, c/o UNESCO (IIEP), 1996.

Darkwa, O., and F., Mazibuko, "Creating Virtual Learning Communities in Africa: Challenges and Prospects", *First Monday* 5, no. 5, 2000.

Delors, Jacques, *Learning: The Treasure Within*, UNESCO Commission for the 21st Century, Paris: UNESCO, 1996.

Dewey, J., *Democracy and Education: An Introduction to The Philosophy of Education,* New York: Free Press, 1997.

Dhanarajan, G., "On-Line Learning — A Social Good or Another Social Divide?" *Keynote address presented at the International Conference on Learning and Teaching Online*, South China National University, Guangzhou, China, January 2001.

Dirr, Peter, J., "Distance and Virtual Learning in the United States." In *The Development of Virtual Educa-tion: A Global Perspective.* Vancouver: The Commonwealth of Learning, 1999.

Eaton, J.S., "Maintaining the Delicat Balance: Distance Learning, Higher Education Accreditation and the Politics of Self-regulation, *Distributed Education Series*: No.2. Washington DC: American Council on Education and EDUCAUSE, 2001.

Erhmann, Stephen, C., *Ivory Tower, Silicon Basement: Transforming the College*, Washington D.C.: The Learning Technologies Group, 2000.

Farrell, Glen M., (ed.), *The Development of Virtual Education: A Global Perspective*, Vancouver: The Commonwealth of Learning, 1999.

_______________, *The Changing Faces of Virtual Education*, Commonwealth of Learning, Vancouver, Canada, 2001.

Galagan, Patricia A., "The E-Learning Revolution," *Training & Development Magazine,* December, 2000.

Gardner, H., *Frames of the Mind: The Theory of Multiple Intelligences*, New York: Basic Books, 1993.

_______________, *The Unschooled Mind*, New York, Basic Books, 1991.

Garrison, D.R., "An analysis and evaluation of audio teleconferencing to facilitate education at a distance", *The American Journal of Distance Education*, 4(3), 16-23, 1990.

Goldberg, M. W., "CALOS: First results from an experiment in computer-aided learning for operating systems", *SIGCSE Bulletin* 29, 1, March 1997.

Goodson, Carol., "A Continuing Challenge for Librarians: Meeting the Needs of Distance Education Students", *MC Journal: The Journal of Academic Media Librarianship* 4.1, Summer 1996.

Greeno, J. G., Collins, A.M., Resnick, L. B., "Cognition and learning", In D. C. Berliner, R. Calfee (eds.), *Handbook of Educational Psychology*, New York, NY: Simon and Schuster MacMillan, 1996.

Hawkins, B.L., "Distributed learning and institutional restructuring", *EDUCOM Review* 34 (4),12 –15,42 –44, 1999.

Heller-Ross, Holly, "Librarian and Faculty Partnerships for Distance Education", *MC Journal: The Journal of Academic Media Librarianship,* 4.1, Summer 1996.

Horton, W., "How we communicate", *Paper presented at the meeting of the Rocky Mountain Chapter of the Society for Technical Communication*, Denver, CO, June, 1994.

Huang, J.,*Distance Education: A Key Strategy for Lifelong Learning in Chinese Taipe*i, Taipei: Department of Research and Development, National Open University, 1997.

Huang, J.,*Distance Education: A Key Strategy for Lifelong Learning in Chinese Taipe*i, Taipei: Department of Research and Development, National Open University, 1997.

Hutton, L., "Distance Education: Players and Changes," *The Advising Quarterly* Summer, 1999.

International Commission on Education for the Twenty-first Century, UNESCO, *Learning: The treasure within,* Paris, France: UNESCO, 1996.

Jagannathan, Neela, "Library and Information Services for Distance Learners", *Resource sharing and Information Networks,* 11.1-2 159-170, 1996.

John. J. Hitt, Joel L. Hartman, "Distributed Learning: New Challenges and Opportunities for Institutional Leadership", Americal Council on Eductaion Center for Policy Analysis, EDUCASE, 2002.

Johnston, David et al., *The e-learning evolution in colleges and universities: A Pan-Canadian Challenge*, Ottawa: Industry Canada, 2001.

Jonassen, D. H., Mayes, T, and McAleese, R., "A manifesto for a constructivist approach to technology in higher education", In T. Duffy, J. Lowyck, and D. H. Jonassen, *Designing environments for constructive learning*, Berlin, Germany: Springer Verlag, 1993.

Kascus, Marie A, "Library Support to Distant Students as a Library Education and Continuing Education Issue", *Journal of Education for Library and Information Science* 35, 344-347, Fall 1994.

Kay, D., "Bandwagons considered harmful", *SIGCSE Bulletin* 28, 4 December 1996.

Keegan, D., *The Foundations of Distance Education*, London: Croom Helm, 1986.

Kenniston, K. and D. Kumar., *Bridging the Digital Divide: Lesson from India*, India: National Institute of Advanced Sciences, Indian Institute of Science, 2001.

Kenniston, K., and D. Kumar, *Bridging the Digital Divide: Lesson from India,* India: National Institute of Advanced Sciences, Indian Institute of Science, 2001.

Kerry, Bob et al., "The Power of the Internet for Learning: Moving from Promise to Practice", Report of the Web-Based Education Commission to the President of the United States, Jessup, MD: U.S. Department of Education, 2000.

Kerry, Bob et al., "The Power of the Internet for Learning: Moving from Promise to Practice," Report of the Web-Based Education Commission to the President of the United States. Jessup, MD: U.S. Department of Education, 2000.

Land, S., M. Hannafin, "A conceptual framework for the development of theories in action with open-ended learning environments", *Educational Technology Research and Development*, 44 (3), 1996.

Larchmont, NY:Mary Ann Liebert, Inc. "National Education Association, "Quality on he line: Benchmarks for success in Internet-based distance education", Washington, DC: National Education Association, April 2000.

Longworth, Norman, "Creating and Building Learning Communities", *European Lifelong Learning Initiative*, Eus, France, 1996.

Millbank, G., "Writing multimedia training with integrated simulation", *Paper presented at the Writers' Retreat on Interactive Technology and Equipment*, Vancouver, BC: The University of British Columbia Continuing Studies, 1994.

Moe, M., and H., Blodget, *The Knowledge Web*, New York: Merrill Lynch, 2000.

Moore, G. M. and Kearsley, G., *Distance education: A systems view*, Belmont, CA: Wadsworth Publishing Company, 1996.

Naik, J.P., *Equality, Quality, Quantity: The Elusive Triangle in Indian Education*, New Delhi: Allied Publishers, 1975.

Oblinger, D., Barone,C.A., Hawkins, B.L., "Distributed Education and its challenges: An overview", *Distributed Education Series:*No.1, Washington, DC: *American Council on Education and EDUCAUSE*, 2001.

____________ Kidwell, J., "Distance learning:Are we being realistic"? *EDUCAUSE Review* 35 (3):30 –34,36,38 –39, May/June 2000.

OECD Report, "New Technology and Its Impact on Educational Buildings," Paris: Organization for Economic Co-operation and Development, 1994.

Orr, Debbie, Trish Andrews, Margaret Appleton, "The Creation and Delivery of a Residential School Program for Geographically Dispersed Students", *MC Journal: The Journal of Academic Media Librarianship* 4.1, Summer 1996.

Parrish, Debra M., and Alexander Wills Parrish, *Developing a* Distance Education Policy for 21st Century Learning, Division of Government Public Affairs, American Council for Education, 2000.

Pea, R.A., "Seeing what we build together: Distributed multimedia learning environments for transformative communications", *Journal of the Learning Sciences*, 3(3), 285-299, 1994.

Pearson, P. D., Iran-Nejad, A., *Review of research in education,* Washington, DC: American Educational Research Association, 1998.

Perkins, David, *Smart Schools: Better Thinking and Learning for Every Child*, New York, The Free Press, 1992.

Perraton, H. (ed.), *Distance education: An economic and educational assessment of its potential for Africa*, Washington, DC: World Bank, 1986.

Perrin, D. G., "The new knowledge society and higher education", *Paper presented at the International Conference on Reinventing Higher education*, Bangkok, Thailand, July 1996.

Porter, David (ed.), New directions in distance learning: Interim report, March, 1994, available: David Porter, Manager, Schools Curriculum Programs, 4355 Mathissi Place, Burnaby, BC., Canada.

____________ , *Learning in a Wired World: Moving Beyond the Course as the Unit of Learning*, Vancouver: Open Learning Agency, 2000.

Postman, N., *The End of Education: Redefining the Value of Schools*, New York: Alfred A. Knopf, 1986.

Pournelle, J., "An Educational Trip", *Byte*, 197-210, July, 1994.

Prawat, R. and Floden, R.E., "Philosophical perspectives on constructivist views of learning", *Educational Psychology*, 29(1), 37-48, 1994.

Psacharopolous, G., "Why educational policies fail", *World Bank Discussion Paper*, Washington, DC: The World Bank, 1990.

Rai, Amar Nath, *Distance Education: Open Learning vs. Virtual University Concepts*, Authorspress, New Delhi, 2001.

Reich, R., *The work of nations: Preparing ourselves for 21st century capitalism*, London, UK: Simon and Schuster, 1991.

Report on Copyright and Digital Distance Education, US Copyright Office, May, 1999.

Rose, E., "An Evaluation of Online Distance Education Course Databases," *DEOSNEWS 10*, no. 11, 2000.

Rowley, D.J., H.D. Lujan, and M. Dolence, *Strategic Choices for the Academy,* San Francisco: Jossey Bass, 1998.

Rumble, G., *The Costs and Economics of Open and Distance Learning*, London: Kogan Page, 1997.

Scardamalia, M., Bereiter, C., "Computer support for knowledge-building communities", *Journal of the Learning Sciences*, 3(3), 265-283, 1994.

Schlosser, C.A., and Anderson, M.L., "Distance education: review of the literature", *Association for Educational Communications and Technology*, Washington, DC, 1994.

Sherry, L., "Issues in Distance Learning", *International Journal of Educational Telecommunications*, 1 (4), 337-365, 1996.

______________, Morse, R.A. , "An assessment of training needs in the use of distance education for instruction", *International Journal of Telecommunications*, 1(1), 5-22, 1995.

Shneiderman, B., "Designing the user interface", *Reading*, MA: Addison-Wesley, 1992.

Simon, H.A., Interview, *OMNI Magazine*, 16(9), 71-89, 1994.

Smith, P., and C.L., Dillon, "Comparing Distance Learning and Classroom Learning: Conceptual Considerations", *The American Journal of Distance Education* 13, no. 2, 1999.

Smith, R., "E-learning — it's the new rage in distributive training, but is there a downside?" *E-learning Magazine,* October, 2000.

Sponder, B., "Distance education in rural Alaska: An overview of teaching and learning practices in audioconference courses", *University of Alaska Monograph Series in Distance Education,* No. 1., Fairbanks, Alaska: Alaska University, Center for Cross-Cultural Studies, 1990.

Stasko, J. T., "Using student-built algorithm animations as learning aids", *SIGCSE Bulletin* 29, 1, March 1997.

Sternberg, R. J., Detterman, D. K. (eds.), *What is intelligence? Contemporary viewpoints on its nature and definition,* Norwood, New Jersey: Ablex, 1986.

______________, Wagner, R. K., (eds.), *Practical intelligence: Nature and origin of competence in the everyday world,* New York, NY: Cambridge University Press, 1986.

Talab, R.S., Newhouse, B., "Self-efficacy, performance variables and distance learning facilitator technology adoption: Support for the teacher needs hierarchy", *In Proceedings of Selected Research and Development Presentations at the convention of the AECT*, Research and Theory Division, New Orleans, January, 1993.

Tapsall, S. and Yoni Ryan, "Virtual Education Institutions in Australia: Between the Idea and Reality", In *The Development of Virtual Education: A Global Perspective,* Vancouver: The Commonwealth of Learning, 1999.

Taylor, James C., "Distance Education: The Fifth Generation", *Paper presented at the 19th ICDE World Conference on Learning and Distance Education*, Vienna, June 20-24, 1999.

UNESCO, *Higher Education in the Twenty-First Century: Vision and Action*, World Conference on Higher Education in the Twenty-First Century, 1998.

Unwin, L., Bolton, N. and Stephens, K., *The Role of the Library in Distance Learning*, Final Report, London: British Library, 1997.

Visser J. and M. Jain, "Towards Open Learning Communities: Recontextualizing Teachers and Learners", *Learning Without Frontiers Unit*, UN, 1996.

White, M.A., "Information and imagery education", In M.A. White (ed.), *What curriculum for the information age*?, Hillsdale, NJ: Lawrence Erlbaum Associates, Inc., 1987.

Willis, B., "Instructional development for distance education", *ERIC Document Reproduction Service* No. ED 351 007, 1992.

Wilson, Alane, "Library Connection: Education From a Distance", *PNLA Quarterly* 59, Winter/Spring, 1995.

Young, J. R., "Rethinking the role of the professor in an age of high-tech tools", In *The chronicle of higher education,* 1997.

Index